The World
Aerospace Industry

THE ROYAL UNITED SERVICES INSTITUTE
for Defence Studies

Founded in 1831 by the Duke of Wellington, the RUSI is the senior Institute of its kind in the world, setting defence and international security affairs in their wider political, economic and technological contexts.

An independent centre free of political ties, the RUSI is dedicated to the study, analysis and debate of issues affecting defence, the military sciences and regional and international security. Tested before a world-wide critical and professional membership, which includes the armed services, government, industry and commerce, the media, academics, and all those interested in or involved with international security, the work of the Institute is practical and forward looking. The RUSI strives to develop and promote objective and fresh thinking on the complex issues dominating the current and future security environment.

The World Aerospace Industry
Collaboration and Competition

Keith Hayward

Duckworth & RUSI

First published in 1994 in association with the RUSI by
Gerald Duckworth & Co. Ltd.
The Old Piano Factory
48 Hoxton Square, London, N1 6PB
Tel: 071 729 5986
Fax: 071 729 0015

A catalogue record for this book is
available from the British Library.

ISBN 0 7156 26027

Typeset by RUSI
Printed and bound in Great Britain by
Biddles Ltd, Guildford and King's Lynn

Contents

To the memory of Arthur Hayward

Preface

The aerospace industry has always existed in an environment characterised by uncertainty and dynamic change. But no one could have expected the extent to which the security needs which had fuelled demand since the 1950s would change, and change so rapidly in the late 1980s and 1990s. Like many other industries linked to defence, aerospace has seen its traditional markets shrink and has had to come to terms with new demands and new requirements. But even before the end of the Cold War era, there were pressures for large scale industrial change forcing nationally-based firms increasingly to look to international collaboration. This book will examine these changes and their consequences for the major aerospace companies. In particular, it will focus on the necessary adjustments those companies are having to make as well as the impact on the relationship with their state sponsors.

The Chinese curse bids us to live in interesting times, and for the academic, such conditions generate interesting problems. For those working in the industry, the consequences of such times all too often relate to survival and the risk of unemployment. No one can take joy from that, even if the industry's crisis may be a symptom of a safer world for others. We can, however, all appreciate the value of safe and reliable civil aircraft and the routine contributions to the modern world of space-based communications. Unquestionably, the corporate and government responses to this changed world confirm, to my mind, the continuing fascination of aerospace as a complex politico-industrial problem. Once again, I can only thank those who are having to contend with these difficult times on a daily basis and who, nevertheless, could still discuss their industry with an outsider. There are many from government and industry in the US, Britain, France and Germany who have helped in my researches; I hope that I have done justice to their contributions. I am again grateful to Mr Lawrence Corbett for applying his proof-reading skills to my grammar and presentation. I would also like to thank the Director and staff of the Royal United Services Institute for their support and encouragement. In particular, I owe much to the care and attention taken by Professor Ron Smith in advising on the project and reading the final manuscript, especially his reminder to consider China in my conclusions. However, all of the errors of fact and interpretation are mine.

Keith Hayward
Staffordshire University

Abbreviations

A/STOVL	Advanced Short Take-off and Landing
AECMA	European Aerospace Industry Association
AI	Airbus Industrie
AIAA	Aerospace Industries Association of America
ASST	Advanced Supersonic Transport
ATA	Advanced Tactical Aircraft
ATC	Air Traffic Control
ATF	Advanced Tactical Fighter
BA	British Airways
BAe	British Aerospace
CAD/ CAM	Computer Aided Design/Manufacturing
DASA	Deutsche Aerospace
DIB	Defence Industrial Base
DoD	Department of Defense (USA)
EC	European Community
ECU	European Currency Unit
EFA	European Fighter Aircraft
MoD	Ministry of Defence (UK)
ESA	European Space Agency
FY	Fiscal Year
GATT	General Agreement on Tariffs and Trade
GD	General Dynamics
GE	General Electric
GIE	Groupement d'Intérêts Economiques
GM	General Motors
GPA	Guiness Peat Aviation
GPS	Global Positioning System
IATA	International Air Transport Association
ICAO	International Civil Aviation Organisation
IEPG	Independent European Programme Group
IHI	Ishikawajima Heavy Industries
KHI	Kawasaki Heavy Industries
MDC	McDonnell Douglas Corporation
MHI	Mitsubishi Heavy Industries
MITI	Ministry of International Trade and Industry (Japan)
NASA	National Aeronautics and Space Agency (US)
NASP	National Aerospace Plane

NATO	North Atlantic Treaty Organisation
OTA	Office of Technology Assessment
P&W	Pratt and Whitney
RO	Royal Ordnance
SDI	Strategic Defense Initiative
SDIO	Strategic Defense Initiative Office
SST	Supersonic Transport
TAC	Taiwan Aircraft Company
TQM	Total Quality Management
UTC	United Technologies
WEU	Western European Union

1

An Industry in Transition

The aviation industry is a product of the twentieth century. Although the science and practice of aeronautics emerged earlier, heavier-than-air flight dates from 1903 and aviation's 'industrial' era began with the First World War. In the years which followed, aviation became a *strategic* industry, vital to national security and an integral part of a technology-based economy. As the century nears its end, however, the aerospace[1] industry is in trouble. Traditional markets in the defence sector have shrunk dramatically and lines of moth-balled airliners in the Mojave desert point to problems (even if temporary) elsewhere in the industry. Throughout the world, aerospace companies are rationalising and shedding labour. The US aerospace industry lost 106,000 jobs in 1991; employment in the French industry fell by two per cent to 118,000; and in the UK the total was less than 150,000, down from 194,000 in 1989. According to several estimates, during the late 1980s and early 1990s there was a thirty per cent over-capacity in the industry and rationalisation could halve the number of aerospace firms in the United States alone by the Year 2000.[2]

The main reason for this crisis was clear and immediate: the closing of the Cold War era signalled a rapid de-mobilisation of large parts of western and ex-Soviet armed forces and, with this, came an apparent end to the arms race dynamic which fuelled much of world aerospace development and output since the late 1940s. In some respects, this may have been a belated arrival of a more 'normal' security environment, but it blasted a hole in the comforting cycle of national defence needs which had underpinned much of the industry's activity over the last fifty years. Other recessionary effects in the late 1980s undermined civil sales, and doubt clouded the more optimistic assumptions of future air traffic

1

growth and the ability of airline customers to buy new equipment. On the other hand, the world still needs the aerospace industry. In both its civil and military roles, nations and individuals have come to rely on aerospace and the services it provides. National defence requires adequate air power; international business and mass tourism could not function without civil aviation and space-based telecommunications. Some of these functions may be of questionable benefit for mankind, but aerospace is an integral element of the modern age and will retain a central position in advanced industrial systems.

But to serve these recognisable and continuing needs, internationally the aerospace industry faces a future which will be marked by considerable upheaval and change. The inflated demands of defence spawned by the Cold War will not return; national budgets will not sustain ambitious programmes to explore space; and there is only room for a relatively small number of civil producers. Some possible directions of that change are already discernible. Cost and market limitations have long forced many national aerospace firms and their state sponsors to seek partners abroad. The steady internationalisation of development and production has already changed the shape of the world aerospace industry. More companies in more countries have become to a large degree industrially interdependent in aerospace. The further development of this already complex network of global linkage represents one obvious pathway to the future.

Countering this generally positive picture of global industrial cooperation is an alternative scenario of ever fiercer competition and regional rivalry fuelled by politically-driven concerns for protection and 'beggar-my-neighbour' subsidy policies. Despite attempts by GATT to regulate the extent of state subsidy in the civil sector, aerospace has emerged as one of the key trade battlegrounds of the late 20th Century.[3] There is a danger that, as conditions become tougher for the major players - predominantly located in the US and Western Europe - the temptation to seek national (or bloc) solutions to industrial and technological problems will affect the global aerospace network. This fear would, of course, be exacerbated by the emergence of independent aerospace forces in the Far East (led by Japan).

The general view presented by this book is that the latter scenario is still preventable, but all too likely. We are already seeing the appearance of aerospace industrial blocs in the US and Western Europe. At the moment, they are perhaps best pictured as loose clusters of regionally-based firms with several and strong inter-regional linkages. But as market conditions worsen, as they surely will over the final years of this century, the temptation may increase (either on the part of corporate or political leadership) to consolidate those clusters into more formidable, competing regional groupings. This would be to the long term benefit of neither the world aerospace industry nor the consumer of aerospace-based goods and services. But first, a few basic questions.

Why do states want an aerospace industry?

Despite the current problems affecting aerospace, there appears to be no shortage of ambitious newcomers; nations and their governments throughout the world are seeking to build-up or to acquire aerospace capabilities. Given the high costs of aerospace development and the problematic economics at the best of times of both military and civil production, these ambitions might seem perverse. There is a magic and romanticism surrounding aircraft and their operation which might help superficially to explain this phenomenon. But this is a weak reed on which to sustain billions of dollars of investment often extending over several decades. There are other, more rational, reasons for possessing an aerospace capability. Large profits can be earned from successful programmes; this always remains a tempting though often illusory objective for governments and aerospace firms alike. However, an unqualified market justification for investing in aerospace would be, for many national industries, hard to sustain. Economic facts are starkest in the civil aerospace sector. Of the 26 large commercial aircraft launched since the early 1950s, seven failed to exceed sales of 120 units and only four or five have been profitable (although several of the current generation may achieve profitability over the next decade). According to a 1984 report from First Boston Corp, jet airliner programmes launched to that date had accumulated total losses of $40 billion on total sales of $180 billion.[4]

As we move towards the Millenium, the blunt truth is that given current market conditions, there is an over-capacity in most sectors of aerospace. There are some monopoly products, such as the Boeing 747, for which prices may reflect real costs; similarly, substantial returns can still be earned from sub-contracting and from supplying equipment to the main players; but in many cases, a commercial justification for aerospace investment must be supplemented by reference to 'externalities' such as employment, balance of payments effects, generalised notions of economic development generated by a technology intensive, high-value added industrial activity and, of course, national defence.[5] Governments clearly support national aerospace industries for reasons associated with policies aimed at obtaining wider economic, industrial and technological goals as well as for less definable national interests.   As a 1977 French Parliamentary report asserted, 'more than in any other sphere of activity, aerospace is a test of strength between states in which each participant deploys his technical and political forces'.[6] Investment in aerospace has formed part of regional policies in the UK, Germany, France and Italy. Japan and Korea, amongst others, have cited aerospace as a force for the upgrading of their industrial base and the Brazilian and Indonesian governments regard aerospace as a vehicle for furthering industrial modernisation.

Such externalities are hard, if not impossible, to quantify. The most problematic is the impact aerospace has on the general level of a nation's or region's economic development. This rationale undoubtedly has a wide appeal to many governments; it is an argument continually stressed by national trade-associations seeking to justify continued support for the industry.   In 1991, the US Aerospace Industries Association opened a major review of the prospects for the 1990s with the bald statement that 'the US aerospace industry is one of the fundamental sources of America's economic strength and world leadership'.[7] In the case of the US, aerospace was one of the few remaining areas of manufacturing which could deliver a trade surplus and for the UK alone, cumulative data for the 1980s showed a positive balance of trade worth over £10 billion.[8]

None of these externalities have been shown unequivocally to generate a net benefit to national (or regional) economies. Investment in aerospace (especially as part of the defence sector) has often been the focus of critical attention for 'squeezing-out' resources which could have been more profitably deployed elsewhere.   Nevertheless, the perceived benefits of strategic investment in aerospace as 'high technology' are still powerful political arguments deployed in favour of acquiring and maintaining an aerospace industry. As one European Community (EC) report from the 1970s put it:

> the aeronautical industry of the Community is a key sector of the European industrial base. Aviation makes a vital contribution to the civil life and commerce of the Community and aircraft and helicopters are indispensable elements of the military forces which contribute to the defence needs of Europe. The activities of the industry involve the continued advance of knowledge and technique over a wide range of high technologies, a process which yields important spin-off benefits to other sections of industry...[9]

These sentiments were reaffirmed by a later EC report which underlined aerospace's position at 'the leading edge of technology' and, as such, had a special significance for European economic growth.[10]

The Gulf War of 1991 provided a dramatic illustration of air power and of the value of access to high-technology airborne weapons and support systems. It confirmed that the most compelling 'externality' justifying the possession of some independent industrial capability is still the contribution aerospace makes to national security. Despite the end of the Cold War, military threats remain and many states still feel it necessary to retain some form of autonomous, or largely autonomous, defence industrial capability. There is certainly no shortage of possible dangers outside the old theatre of confrontation. Other nations perceive a similar range of defined and ill-defined threats and would prefer not to rely entirely on the political goodwill of outside suppliers for such a potent family of weapons.

Yet here lies the paradox of the modern aerospace industry. The most convincing rationale for possession relates to national defence and, perhaps, the economic consequences of allowing foreigners to control access to, or to fix the price of such strategic goods (which would in this context include commercial transports and other aerospace-dependent services such as access to space). However, the costs and risks of developing increasingly sophisticated and expensive aerospace products, or of trying to enter the industry has forced national industries to work internationally - national firms linked by an increasingly complex web of development and production coalitions.

What is the aerospace industry?

During the 1950s, the aircraft industry was transmuted into an aerospace industry. Hitherto, one could make a simple distinction between aircraft (the basic airframe) and the engines which powered them and other discrete items of equipment which made them work such as undercarriages and hydraulic systems. There were broad categories of aircraft, civil and military, within which size and specific function would serve further to differentiate types. In terms of technology, most aircraft depended on similar developments in aeronautical and mechanical science; indeed, during the 1920s and early 1930s, civil aviation tended to drive the pace of overall aircraft development. During World War Two, the advent of electronic systems, especially radar in all its forms, added another dimension to the aircraft industry. But again, this equipment could usually be considered independently of the airframe.

Signs of fundamental change could nevertheless be discerned. The advent of missiles and guided weapons presaged a different type of product with a much greater integral dependence on electronics. The post-war development of more complex bombers and fighters, with an increasing array of attack and defensive equipment reinforced this tendency. By the mid 1950s, the term 'weapons system' - denoting a need to design and to develop a complete technology package - was common parlance. The final stage in the transformation of aircraft to aerospace industry came with the arrival of space programmes and increasingly complex missiles. In the course of this change, the basic airframe and engine companies were joined (in some senses, challenged) by specialist electronics and equipment firms. At the same time, while all aerospace sectors would have some common basic research and technological needs (in aerodynamics, materials, systems architecture etc), the specific requirements of civil and military, space and conventional aircraft, began to diverge. Although there are still core areas of common interest, such as materials, systems architecture and aerodynamics, the demands of civil aviation tend to stress reliability and cost-efficiency rather than the outright performance and special characteristics such as 'stealth' demanded of the modern combat aircraft.[11]

In functional terms, the industry can be described in terms of a pyramid structure. At the top are a few fully capable[12] prime contractors, or systems integrators[13] - usually, though not exclusively, airframe manufacturers; an equally small group of engine makers; a larger group of discrete systems and equipment firms; and a huge 'comet's tail' of medium and small suppliers and sub contractors. Within the civil sector, the top of the pyramid is even more narrowly drawn, with only five or six firms or consortia (including the former USSR) capable of developing airliners over 100 seats in capacity. There is a close connection between the health of the prime contractors and the supplier chain. Although many equipment and sub contractor firms trade successfully in a world market, their success, and their technological competence, is often dependent on access to indigenous airframe activity or major collaborative programmes. This is explained partly by R&D funding which may come from government sources and partly by the need to be involved in systems design and development processes.

As we will consider in more detail in Chapter Two, geographically, the global aerospace industry is equally concentrated. The industry is dominated by the US, Western Europe and the area covered by the former USSR (largely the Russian Republic). In terms of global trade in aerospace products, the ex-Soviet industry drops out of the picture - although it does remain a major arms trader. There are important aerospace centres and individual firms of note outside this select band, and one of the key dynamics is the rate of growth outside the traditional aerospace core regions. Of the traditional leaders, even after a period of declining market share, the US remains the largest single national player with over 60 per cent of the 'free-world' market in 1990. By comparison, Western Europe as a whole commanded about one-third of the total.[14]

What are its operating characteristics?

The economics of aerospace favour large industrial units which can capture economies of scale and, increasingly, economies of scope.[15] The 'tyranny' of the learning curve of development, with its huge initial costs to be defrayed through production, gives an overwhelming advantage to companies assured of long production runs and/or support from national governments. The need for large capital sums to launch projects and the importance of accumulated design, development and production expertise in several, individually complex technologies, ensures that aerospace can have very high (and rising) entry costs (see Table 1.1). Market size and the commensurately large industrial and technologically comprehensive units that emerged to meet this demand, largely explains US dominance of the industry since 1941.

Aircraft Development Costs

Aircraft	In-service date	Development costs ($m)	Development costs (1991 $m)	Development costs per seat (1991 $m)
DC-3	1936	0.3	3	0.1
DC-6	1947	14	90	1.7
DC-8	1959	112	600	3.75
747	1970	1,200	3,300	7.3
777 (estimate)	1995	5,000	4,300	14.0

Table 1.1   (Source: NASA)

Although the top layer of the industry pyramid is dominated by a small number of very large firms, the industry sustains a large diversity of specialist suppliers; some of whom may be parts of larger, diversified companies, but many others may be relatively small, independent niche manufacturers. But in general, the structure of the industry world-wide has tended towards monopoly or at best a limited oligopoly. Although governments may have been prepared to pay a premium for nationally-produced defence equipment, budgetary pressures have led to the adoption of international collaboration in military aerospace as a routine procurement strategy. Similar economic incentives have stimulated collaborative programmes in the civil sector where again launch costs of even small airliners have outgrown the capacity of individual companies and national markets safely to sustain. In others cases, even where products are developed nationally, the absence of a full range of technological capabilities have required overseas purchases of components and sub-systems. Internationalisation has been further encouraged by the search for new sources of capital, lower cost production centres and by the demands for offset and technological transfer by foreign governments as a price for market access.

The result has been the formation of an international network of industrial linkages, some based on simple subcontract relationships, others on risk-sharing partnerships, and, at the highest level, comprehensive design and development consortia, several of which have accumulated over twenty years of collaborative experience. The main focus of this collaborative activity is within the European region, but collaborative agreements link European, US, South American and Far Eastern partners.

However, the main competitive dynamics underpinning much of the industry's activities are based on the protection or development of a national or regional capability. This is undoubtedly true of European national and EC-level where the main objective of collaboration is to maintain an industrial and technological base capable of matching and competing with the US. The failure of individual European national industries to overcome the largely structural advantages of the US triggered the drive to collaborate in the early 1960s; the search for regional autonomy in civil and military aerospace has continued to shape overall policy towards the sector. A further incentive for regional cooperation is that aerospace represents one of the few clear areas of competitive advantage which Europe has *vis á vis* Japan.

To date, therefore, collaboration in Europe and elsewhere has been centred on national companies, either privately-owned or nationalised enterprises. The pattern has been one of negotiation and international agreement on specific projects with development and work sharing subject in general terms to the principle of *le juste retour*. However, the pattern of collaboration is changing, with the emergence of transnational subsidiaries and the prospect of autonomous trans-national enterprises emerging from long term consortia such as Airbus Industrie. In some cases, primarily in the systems sector, partnership agreements are emerging in advance of specific national or regional requirements.

What is the aerospace technology base?

The importance of maintaining a national (and by implication) regional capability in aerospace is further underlined by the high value-added nature of aerospace production and by the broader technological benefits believed to accrue from aerospace activities. However, while aerospace is undoubtedly a high-technology industry, it cannot generally be classed as a source of 'enabling technologies'. Aerospace is better seen as a major user - often the first user - of advances in other areas, particularly in electronics and materials. This role should not be underestimated; the operational requirements of military systems and commercial aircraft have tended to drive all of its component technologies to the edge of the state-of-the-art. By the same token, aerospace firms and national (i.e government sponsored) research establishments have promoted original R&D in key areas such as materials for use in aircraft structures and engine components. Finally, exacting technological requirements have also led to pioneering work in the use of of complex computer-aided design technology, testing and modelling.[16]

In recent years, however, aerospace has benefited from 'spin-on' generated by the general stream of innovation in areas such as information technology and advanced integrated circuitry often driven by a more generalised commercial, consumer-orientated demand. The industry is, for example, likely to benefit from wider developments in process technology and the increased flexibility and productivity enhancement that this may engender. In general, as the industry becomes more cost sensitive and development costs, especially for military products, have to be amortised on the basis of shorter production runs, improvements in process technology and their applications to aerospace will be a key dynamic in shaping the future of the industry. The adoption of 'lean production' and other design and manufacturing concepts developed in other manufacturing sectors could have a profound effect on the aerospace sector, destroying in the process many of the myths which have appeared since 1945 that making aeroplanes is 'different' from any other manufacturing industry and some how immune to normal commercial disciplines.[17]

Aerospace's particular technological importance lies in its ability to integrate these discrete technologies at a high level of complexity and, therefore, deliver a very high value end product. In this respect, systems integration skills lie at the heart of national capabilities and underpin national and regional policy towards the industry.   These have traditionally been the prerogative of the airframe designer and manufacturer - the 'platform' makers. However, as we have noted above, their monopoly has been challenged by the increasingly central role of electronics and software engineering and has provided opportunities for specialists in these areas to assume a leading role in systems integration.

In the final analysis, aerospace is a 'project-led' industry. That is to say that commitments to specific tasks provide a focus for activity over a long period. The conception of an aircraft (or engine) to its replacement, including upgrades can extend over three decades.[18]   While the industry will undertake (of its own volition or under government tutelage) research projects and build technology demonstrators, the primary aim is to achieve a smooth and consistent cadence of design, development and production with new projects overlapping to avoid any hiatus in scale manufacturing.   In the future, particularly for military aircraft, this ideal pattern may have to change, with fewer new 'platforms' introduced over more extended time periods. These products will also demand more sophisticated electronics and software packages with airframes designed to anticipate from the outset 'up-grading' potential and new sub-systems opportunities.

Who buys aerospace products and why is technological innovation so important?

Aerospace products have a dynamic relationship with their markets.[19]   A better, more efficient airliner will cut operational costs; technological performance in the military often provides a critical 'edge' in combat. Customer requirements, either the armed forces or civil airlines,   structure demand, but the aircraft manufacturer, through the adoption of new technology or design characteristics, can   influence   the timing and direction of replacement. For example, the introduction of jet engined airliners in the 1950s forced a rapid and early replacement of a whole generation of piston-engined and even turbo-prop aircraft. Customer competition, either commercially driven or the consequence of a regional or global arms race, has encouraged rapid rates of obsolescence and investment by the manufacturers in new design concepts and associated R&D.   In turn, anticipation of new products has fuelled competition, particularly in the military sector. Customers also play a direct and interactive role in shaping the aerospace products. In the case of military designs, there may be a difficult trade-off to be made between a national requirement, the needs of any collaborating partner and those of a wider global market. Again, one of the key elements shaping the future will be the extent to which the end of the Cold War will slow down the rate of aerospace technological innovation.

The civil market is technologically more stable, although as in the case of the jet engine, a major discontinuity is always possible. The main question here is the pattern and structural characteristics of future demand. Historically, sales of civil aerospace goods have been highly volatile and cyclical. The convergence of several additional factors, including premature retirement of inefficient and noisy aircraft, combined with a steady increase in the predicted growth of air travel, have led to projections of high levels of growth in demand for civil aircraft and engines. However, the airline industry has become much more sensitive to the expense of technological innovation and airlines now have to be convinced that the higher price of new technology is justified by long term savings in operational costs. Technology alone no longer drives the market - even military customers are looking at life-cycle costs and reliability rather than outright performance before they buy - but aerospace remains a technologically sensitive industry which rapidly loses its competitiveness without continual investment in basic and applied research.

Subsequent chapters follow a simple structure: Chapter Two provides a general introduction to the major industrial players and Chapter Three an examination of the key role played by the state in funding aerospace activities: two market-related chapters follow, detailing the changing patterns of demand for first military and then civil and space products (this also includes an examination of the impact of procurement practices and new financial forces in the civil aerospace business); Chapters Six and Seven focus on the structural developments, both national and international, affecting the industry. The Concluding Chapter returns to the theme of change and its likely impact on the industry over the next decade.

2

The World Aerospace Industry

Introduction

The core of the world aerospace industry comprises the United States and Europe, with 17 of the top thirty aerospace firms and commanding 60 per cent of the world market for aircraft, engines and major systems (see Tables 2.1 and 2.2). There are other individual national industries of note, including those of less developed countries such as Brazil and Indonesia. Several companies in these countries have impressive design and development capabilities and a strong individual presence in niche markets. Many states, including Japan, have ambitions to become major supporting players, if not independent actors. Most national aerospace industries are keyed into a global network of sub contracting and collaborative partnerships. The aerospace industries of the ex-Soviet Union (mainly concentrated in the Russian and Ukrainian Republics) remain an important part of the world aerospace industry. Their defence equipment still acts as a bench mark against which western designs are calibrated and the prospect of a flood of cheaply-priced military aircraft could have a serious impact on the global defence market. On the other hand, the aerospace companies of the ex-Soviet Union need western help in up-grading their civil aircraft which will provide opportunities for collaboration with the US and Western Europe. Equally, the ex-Soviet Union's space technology and vast experience of space operations, could provide the basis for joint ventures with Japan and the European space industry. But for the present, the aerospace industry of the former USSR remains something of a peripheral actor in the world aerospace industry, although we shall be considering some aspects of the Russian and Ukrainian aerospace industries in later chapters. [1]

World Market Shares (1991)

USA	60%
Europe	30%
Canada	3%
Japan	3%
Others	4%

Table 2.1   Source: AECMA 1992

The World Aerospace Top 30 Companies (1992)

Company	Country	Sales (Aero) $ m	Sales $m	Personnel
Boeing	USA	29,562	30,184	142,000
McDonnell Douglas	USA	17,020	17,373	87,377
United Technologies	USA	10,923	21,641	178,000
Martin Marietta*	USA	10,759	15,954	56,000
British Aerospace	UK	9,630	17,507	108,500
Aerospatiale	France	9,449	9,874	46,110
DASA	Germany	9,052	11,064	81,872
Lockheed*	USA	8,883	10,100	71,700
GM/Hughes	USA	7,558	12,297	90,000
General Electric	USA	7,368	40,141	268,000
Raytheon	USA	6,230	9,058	63,900
Rockwell	USA	5,869	10,910	78,685
General Dyn*	USA	5,714	13,472	29,600
Northrop	USA	5,457	5,550	33,600
Thomson CSF	France	5,412	6,462	42,357
Allied Signal	USA	4,937	12,042	89,300
GEC	UK	4,882	16,556	104,995
Snecma	France	4,315	4,315	26,374

Rolls-Royce	UK	3,760	6,250	55,000
Alenia	Italy	3,723	n/a	29,471
MHI	Japan	3,662	22,025	n/a
Textron	USA	3,642	8,347	54,000
Dassault	France	3,098	3,098	13,592
Loral	USA	3,098	3,335	24,500
Grumman	USA	2,951	3,492	21,200
TRW	USA	2,933	8,311	64,100
Westinghouse	USA	2,874	8,447	109,050
Alcatel	France	2,570	30,550	203,000
Fokker*	Holland	2,201	2,323	12,363
Bombardier	Canada	2,147	3,631	34, 316

* Data prior to merger or sale

Table 2.2   Data: *Flight* - OC&C *Flight*   4 August 1993

The United States

Since the end of the Second World War, the world aerospace industry has been dominated by the United States. Between 1980 and 1990 the total value of US aerospace deliveries was three times that of the European industry. This dominance was not necessarily founded on an overwhelming technical lead over European industry, but stemmed more from the productive power of US companies and the leverage afforded by a large integrated home market. In the post war period, others would sometimes introduce major innovations ahead of American companies - most notably Britain's use of jet engines in civil airliners - but the technological confrontation with the Soviet Union, backed by the resources of a Superpower, stimulated US technological development across the board. Since the 1960s, some of this dominance has been eroded by a resurgent Europe and by other international competitors. Nevertheless, the US still has the largest and most technologically capable aerospace industry in the world, with a total turnover nearly three times that of the European Community and employing over twice as many people.

The scale and importance of aerospace in the US economy in general, and in US manufacturing in particular, is marked. In 1990, US aerospace sales (including aircraft [military, civil, general aviation and guided weapons], space systems and associated electronics and equipment) totalled $131 billion, representing over two per cent of US GNP. With export sales of $39 billion, and a positive balance of trade worth $27 billion, the aerospace sector was responsible for over nine per cent of the nation's total export earnings.   The significance of civil exports was particularly noteworthy, accounting for over three quarters of US aerospace overseas sales.   As the Aerospace Industries Association of America (AIAA) observed, this performance offset 'to some degree a massive national trade deficit and underlines the importance to the US economy of high value, high technology exports.'[2]

The aerospace and associated electronics industry is the single most important element in the US defence industrial base (DIB).   Of the top five US defence contractors, four are predominantly aerospace or aerospace-related companies.   Roughly half of the US defence procurement budget (over $100 billion annually during the 1980s) was allocated to aircraft, with a further 25 per cent spent on missiles and electronics.[3]   Over half of the industry's total sales are to the US government (either the Department of Defence [DoD] or to NASA).   Aerospace was responsible for 73 per cent of US R&D, just under half of which was funded by the Federal Government (again mainly under DoD contract).   (See table 2.3).

Despite the apparent health conveyed by these data, the US aerospace industry was under pressure throughout the late 1980s. In part, this was due to fiercer international competition, especially in the civil sector.   In 1970, the US had 80 per cent of the world aerospace market, but by 1975 this had dropped to 66 per cent.   US firms then benefited from the Carter-Reagan defence build-up of the late 1970s and early 1980s. As a result, by 1984, US market share had climbed back to 69 per cent,   but by 1988, it had again sunk to 60 per cent.[4]

Many US firms have argued that during this period they were increasingly disadvantaged by competition from state-subsidised foreign companies.   This was especially so in the case of civil aircraft, where a 90 per cent market share in the 1960s dropped to sixty per cent in the late 1980s, with the blame firmly fixed on the investment made by European governments in the Airbus.   There were, however, other factors to explain the slip in US market shares. The relative decline in the US's international competitive position in military markets was also due to the priority afforded to the domestic market.   Buoyant domestic market conditions during the 1980s caused many firms to lose their competitive edge in world markets. Other export opportunities, especially in the Middle East, were constrained by Congressional or governmental restrictions on arms sales and technology transfer.   Easy profits from this period also served to mask structural deficiencies in the US aerospace sector stemming from substantial over-capacity and poor management.   Many US defence products had become too costlyand/or technologically over-sophisticated for wider sales.

US Aerospace Firms - Defence Dependence 1990

Company	% defence dependence
Northrop	90%
Martin Marietta	87%
General Dyn.	86%
MDC	63%
Grumman	64%
Raytheon	55%
Rockwell	26%
UTC	22%
Boeing	21%
GE	17%

(Table 2.3)   Source: *Defense News*

More significantly, however, during the early 1990s, the US aerospace industry began to feel the effects of pressure to cut domestic defence expenditure - problems which were exacerbated by a period of reform in the procurement process which left many firms in a very weak financial position.[5]

Although the US industry began more widely to embrace 'internationalised' forms of production, American companies and the US Armed Forces found it difficult to accept the need for full and open collaboration in the development of major weapons systems which had become the norm in much of the rest of the world aerospace industry. This may have lost US companies several opportunities to participate and to shape major international programmes.[6] US firms also lost out in international production following decisions by foreign firms to exclude, or to 'design-out' US equipment from domestic and international programmes, which were prompted by US government restrictions on third party sales and technology transfer.

Nevertheless, the extent of the US 'decline' should not be overestimated nor obscured by special interest pleading. American firms still have an overwhelming presence in virtually all of the main aerospace markets. The US aerospace industry remains *the* global industrial and technological powerhouse. While others have achieved parity with the US in some areas (perhaps even a lead), no other industry has the range of capability nor the extent of productive capacity possessed collectively by US firms.

The US Aerospace Industry - A Brief Outline

In the early 1990s, the US aerospace industry comprised seven aircraft prime contractors - Boeing, Lockheed, Northrop, McDonnell Douglas (MDC), General Dynamics (GD), Grumman and Rockwell International. Of these, Boeing and MDC were two of the world's major civil aircraft producers. In addition, there were two dedicated helicopter design centres, Sikorsky and Bell, and two manufacturers of large civil and advanced military aero-engines, General Electric and Pratt and Whitney (P&W). In addition, there were several large missile and electronics systems integrators such as Westinghouse, Hughes, Raytheon and Martin Marietta. Beneath this top layer was a multitude of equipment and component suppliers, as well as large specialist subcontractors such as Textron-Lycoming.

This simple picture belied a more complex reality. Most of the US primes were, and still are, parts of defence/aerospace or general manufacturing conglomerates. Boeing, for example, has missile, space and electronics interests as well as its airliner and military aircraft activities. Rockwell International is a diversified multinational engineering company with military aircraft, missile, spacecraft and civil and military avionics capabilities. Until 1992, GD's defence business ranged from fighter aircraft, through cruise missiles to nuclear submarines and electronics. MDC currently produces fighters, heavy transports, missiles and helicopters and has an active space division. Grumman builds fighters, space vehicles and major command, control and surveillance systems such as J-STARS. Lockheed has developed specialist aircraft including the F-117 Stealth bomber, is a major military space contractor and has built SLBMs for the US Navy. Northrop was responsible for the B-2 bomber and other important 'black' missile programmes. In addition to producing aero-engines, GE, one of the US's largest industrial groups has an extensive defence/aerospace electronics business. P&W is part of UTC which owns Sikorsky and has other high technology interests. Hughes, one of the worlds' major satellite and radar systems manufacturers, is a subsidiary of General Motors. Textron owns Bell helicopters and the Lycoming small engine company. Finally, many of the primes also sub contract to other US companies - Northrop, for example, builds 747 fuselage sections for Boeing, which in turn, manufactures parts of the B-2 bomber for Northrop. Since the 1980s, the links between firms have become even more complicated due to 'teaming' on major military projects such as the F-22.[7]

As will be examined in greater detail below, the downturn in defence requirements and the financial problems stemming from the procurement reforms of the late 1980s, created major difficulties for the US aerospace industry. During the early 1990s, every defence/aerospace company announced successive rounds of job cuts, and most expressed a determination to reduce their dependence on defence activities. A majority began to look for diversification in parallel sectors or outside the aerospace business. Some, such as Boeing, MDC, the engine companies and most of the dual-technology avionics companies, were already positioned to benefit from the long term expansion of the civil airliner market. On the other hand, others, such as Lockheed, looked for salvation by concentrating on their defence/aerospace business cores.[8] As a result of these pressures, by the early 1990s an extensive contraction in the overall size of the US aerospace industry was under way with some hitherto key players leaving, or poised to leave the industry. For example, in 1992, GD sold both its missile and its tactical fighter divisions to Martin Marrieta and to Lockheed respectively. This was one of the most spectacular changes in the structure of the US aerospace industry, but there were many others throughout the US industry supply chain, and few expected it to be the last.

Rationalisation in the US aerospace industry

The upheaval of the 1990s is likely to be one of the most significant periods of change in the US aerospace industry, but it has experienced other bouts of rapid structural change. This was inevitable given the broad oscillations between 'boom and bust' in the major aerospace markets. For instance, several firms were unable to make the transition to peace in 1945 or to adapt to the new technological demands of the post-1945 era. The Korean and Vietnam Wars precipitated other periods of rapid expansion and equally fierce contraction. Curtiss-Wright, a major manufacturer since the early days of the US aircraft industry, failed to meet the challenge of the jet age, and disappeared in 1950. Republic dropped out in the early 1960s after failing to win the TFX (F-111) contract. Others, such as Fairchild, lost prime contractor status but nevertheless became successful sub-contractors. A number survived near-misses: Lockheed, Northrop and Douglas all faced financial crises in the 1960s which took them to the edge of bankruptcy.[9]

Merger activity after 1945 was steady but not spectacular. The 1954 union of Convair and Electric Boat which created the defence conglomerate General Dynamics, McDonnell's acquisition of Douglas in 1966 and the creation of North American Rockwell (now Rockwell International) in 1969 were the most significant changes in the structure of the US aerospace industry up to the 1980s.[10] Amalgamations and take-overs were also restricted by the application of US anti-trust law, as well as by the reluctance of some 'founding fathers' to give up control of 'their' companies.[11] But more important, the general buoyancy and expansion of the US market, combined with American dominance of world aerospace markets for most of the post-war period, clearly removed much of the pressure which drove European rationalisation during the 1950s and 1960s. Similarly, the early development (in the 1930s) of conglomerate aerospace companies such as UTC and Boeing, as well as the larger size of US firms generally, helped to maintain structural stability. The strong oligopolistic tendencies in the US market were also reinforced by design specialisation, often encouraged by US military customers and bolstered by intra-firm sub contracting.[12]

Nevertheless, US government officials frequently observed that there were too many firms in the US industry and that some mergers might be desirable. Such advice usually came during periods of recession - after the Second World War and again in the early 1970s.[13] In the past, these suggestions went largely unheeded and recovery put an end to speculation about 'relegation and rationalisation'. In general, however, the US government saw no reason to encourage rationalisation nor to emulate European governments in guiding the formation of larger units. Indeed, the predominant reaction of US governments was to oppose mergers on anti-trust grounds. This position was especially strong during the 1930s when several aircraft-airline and auto-aircraft combinations were broken-up. In 1969, the US Justice Department forced Rockwell to sell its general aviation business when it bought North American. McDonnell's acquisition of Douglas was allowed because the former had no competing civil aerospace interests and Douglas only had a small amount of defence business.[14]

As we have already noted, during the 1980s and 1990s, broader changes in the aerospace market, combined with the consequences of half a decade of domestic problems, began to threaten the structural stability of the US aerospace industry. Although initially, most of the pressure to rationalise was felt by the second and third tier suppliers rather than the prime contractors, the loss of key contracts in 'winner-take-all' contests and rising levels of debt during this period took several firms to the edge of relegation. From the mid 1980s, the effects of a more stringent domestic environment forced many US supplier firms to leave the defence business and threatened to undermine several of the primes.

A consequence of these problems was a growing concern that many firms, driven by financial constraints and unfavourable contract terms with the DoD, were reducing their private commitment to R&D, and that, as a result, the US aerospace industry generally would begin to lose its technological edge. Several US industrialists called for leadership from the centre:

...the problem with the defence business is not who's going to lead
but who's going to starve. Instead of feeding the strong and letting
the weak die, the Pentagon's policy is to let them all starve - let the
law of the jungle apply, but don't let the losers die.[15]

As the US Congress Office of Technology Assessment (OTA) reported,
the US needed a long term strategy for R&D and budgetary
allocations to promising technologies and prototypes if it wanted a
defence industry in the twenty-first century to be comprised of
more than 'a collection of lucky survivors'.[16]

Once again, US government officials warned of the need for, and
likelihood of rationalisation.[17] But the US government was still
reluctant to guide or to structure the rationalisation process. If
rationalisation was to occur, it should follow the lead of market
forces. As Donald Atwood, the Pentagon's acquisition under-
secretary in the early 1990s, put it 'the DoD does not have a
defence industrial policy' and intervention would only be considered
in 'very unique cases in order to preserve key technological or
manufacturing capabilities'.[18] The government encouraged some
degree of domestic 'teaming' in high value defence and strategic
research programmes. But this was not envisaged as a means of
anticipating the creation of stronger groups; indeed, several
analysts argued that 'teaming' simply postponed rather than
facilitated rationalisation and was designed to protect independent
design and production centres.[19] The current crisis in the US
industry might yet lead to a fundamental change in relations between
the industry and the US government. The state has always played an
influential but indirect role in the development and operation of the
US aerospace industry, but the new conditions may require the
adoption of a more overtly interventionist strategy in order to
protect US industrial preeminence.

The Clinton Administration has begun to heed the call for
affirmative action on the part of the US government to protect the
US DIB and US civil aerospace programmes through an increase in
its commitment to basic R&D.[20] Yet paradoxically, the 'hands-off'
policy adopted by the US government seems to have forced the US
aerospace industry to respond faster and more effectively to the post
Cold War environment. It may have caused individual companies
much pain and it may have led to the loss of some capability. But at
least the US industry may be on the road to a more stable and
coherent structure whereas the Europeans, for all their government
intervention, are still grappling with the problem.

The harsher and the more competitive business environment of
the last decade may also have alerted US companies to the importance
of international collaboration. US firms have had a long tradition of
international sub contracting and international co-production - for

example, the International F-16 programme linked GD with the Benelux and Norway in the early 1970s. Similarly, the costs of developing civil aircraft since the early 1970s led both Boeing and MDC to look for risk-sharing partners in Europe and Asia.   By the same token, P&W and especially GE are long standing members of international consortia and have a wide range of foreign partners/subcontractors.   MDC and BAe have worked for several decades on joint programmes such as the AV-8/Harrier and T-45 trainer.   In general, however, the adoption of collaborative strategies by the US has been, and remains problematic: in order to sell abroad, US firms have had to accept offset agreements and work-sharing packages, but they have been reluctant to accept the compromises over design and management leadership which are often necessary in the more complex collaborative programmes. The US Armed Services and Congress have also found internationalisation hard to accept and the uncertainties of US government funding and the absence of clear government support for a US partner have often created difficulties for prospective partners.[21] As US defence spending continues to fall, some of this reluctance may begin to disappear.   Commercial pressures have already forced the civil sector into accepting   internationalisation of development and production (albeit usually on US terms). But it is unlikely that the US industry will need to adopt international collaboration on the scale accepted as routine by Europeans and by aspirant aerospace nations.

The European aerospace industry

Aerospace is one of the success stories of European high technology. Europeans helped to pioneer the development of aviation and have been responsible for many of the key innovations in aerospace. The Second World War destroyed or badly weakened European national capabilities and post-war competition exposed the structural limitations of small national industries and markets. Nevertheless, European governments wanted national independence in key military technologies and were prepared on strategic grounds to underwrite their domestic aircraft industries.   Aerospace was also regarded as a necessary element in a modern industrial economy and was often supported as part of broader industry and technology policies.   In all cases, however, national policies have tended to converge on collaborative solutions. Although European countries individually produced several advanced military aircraft and a few commercially successful airliners, national industries - even after rationalisation - could not compete with the productive power of the US aerospace industry. Although there were several exceptions, cooperation between European companies has become the only effective means of challenging US dominance. An independent aerospace capability now has key role in European industrial and ttechnological development and is closely associated with concepts of European security and political autonomy.[22]

Despite the fact that European companies have been cooperating systematically for the better part of four decades, the structure and operation of European aerospace is still largely based on national units. Each is still affected by differing national perspectives, interests and government policies; patterns of ownership vary from state enterprise to private corporation; and there are considerable differences in size and technical competence. However, the idea of a 'European' aerospace industry is a valid concept - the more so as trans-national consortia and subsidiaries emerge as a permanent feature of the European industrial landscape.

The consolidated turnover of the European aerospace industry in 1990 was over ECU 30 billion - about three per cent of total EC industrial production.[23]   Aerospace employed around 500,000 - just over one per cent of European industrial employment. A little more than half of the total turnover was in aircraft and missiles; aero-engines and equipment accounted for about 43 per cent; and space a touch over five per cent. The bulk (60 per cent) of European aerospace activity was directed at military markets, although this was a substantial reduction on the average for the 1980s. With the contraction in defence spending and the success of several civil projects, this has been falling steadily. Like US firms, European companies, especially those in the aero-engine sector, have also taken positive decisions to increase civil and non-aerospace work in order to compensate for the decline in military sales.

Over the last decade, the European aerospace industry has been responsible for over 13 per cent of EC industrial R&D. More than half of the funding for this activity has come from public sources, but the proportion of state-supported R&D has fallen from 75 per cent in 1975 to 58 per cent in 1988. This has been largely a result of lower spending on defence and, over the longer term, ever smaller defence budgets will continue to depress spending on European aerospace R&D. The fall in defence commitments has been offset to some extent by the availability of state funding for European civil programmes, and increased spending on space research, either nationally or channelled through the European Space Agency (ESA). However, the 1992 GATT agreement to limit civil airliner subsidies and growing problems with funding for high-profile space programmes might also have a negative effect on European aerospace research.[24]

The European Aerospace Industry - an outline

Although a majority of the European Community member states have some aerospace interests, the 'European' aerospace industry is largely the business of four countries - the United Kingdom, France, Germany, and Italy. A fifth important European aerospace player, Sweden, is applying for EC membership. The UK and France are responsible for 33.5 per cent and 31 per cent of EC aerospace turnover; German aerospace, although one of the fastest growing industries in the EC, is still some distance behind at 24 per cent and Italy is in fourth place with 8.6 per cent of EC output. Holland, Belgium and Spain each account for one per cent of the total (Holland's relatively lowly position belies its technical capabilities in the small to medium-sized airliner sector). In terms of the overall EC economy, the industry accounted for 1.04 per cent of the Community's 1987 GDP - a substantial increase on the 1972 level of 0.6 per cent.[25] In turn, aerospace production (here defined sectorally in terms of airframes, aero-engines and major subsystems) is concentrated in a small number of nationally-owned companies.

The current structure of the European aerospace industry is the product of a steady process of rationalisation and consolidation which has been underway at a national level since the mid 1950s and which is now beginning to assume a trans-national dimension. The main pressure forcing the pace of this process was the need to match the scale of American firms and the market opportunities afforded to US industry. European governments played a major role in the restructuring process, either directly through public ownership and central direction, or indirectly through their role as a national industry's main customer and source of development capital. In recent years, although European governments have continued to play a part in the rationalisation process, much of the latest round of national and international consolidation has been driven by the commercial interests of European aerospace firms.

The main European airframe companies are British Aerospace (BAe), Shorts-Bombardier (UK), Aerospatiale, Dassault (France), Deutsche Aerospace-DASA (Germany), Fokker (Holland), Alenia (Italy), CASA (Spain) and Saab (Sweden). All of these have some systems integration or substantial independent design capability, but only BAe, Aerospatiale, Dassault and Saab are indisputably in the first rank of aerospace companies. All four are capable of designing and managing complex civil programmes and the most technically demanding of advanced combat aircraft. Fokker has a strong design and development capability in the small to medium civil aircraft sector. Deutsche Aerospace (DASA) and Alenia have some design capability, but are best defined as major collaborative partners. However, DASA has ambitions, and, as part of the Daimler group, the backing to seek a more influential role within European aerospace.   Its acquisition of Fokker in 1992-3 further strengthened its claim to front rank status in the European industry. European helicopter development is centred on Eurocopter (a jointly-owned subsidiary of DASA and Aerospatiale), Westland (UK) and Agusta (Italy).

BAe, Shorts (part of the Canadian Bombardier group), Aerospatiale and DASA, along with Matra and ESD (France), are major centres for European tactical guided weapons design and development. Matra, ESD (the electronics arm of Dassault), DASA and Aerospatiale are the main focus for European space programmes, with Alenia playing a strong supporting role. Largely because of government neglect, British industry has had a relatively minor part in the development of major European space projects, although BAe and GEC have produced a range of scientific and military satellites.

The engine sector is even more narrowly drawn. Only Rolls-Royce (UK) has the capability of designing and developing independently both advanced military and large civil aero-engines. Rolls-Royce has also developed engines in collaboration with European and US firms. Snecma (France) has a comparable standing in military engines, but its civil operation has been based on a long-standing collaboration with GE of the US. MTU (part of DASA) has been wholly dependent on cooperative agreements with Rolls, Snecma and both American companies. As part of DASA, MTU has ambition to become a major partner in international aero-engine programmes. To this end, it signed a comprehensive Memorandum of Understanding (MoU) with P&W in 1991. Volvo Flygmotor (Sweden), Fiat (Italy) and BMW (Germany) are also largely dependent upon partnerships with other European or US firms.

The European equipment industry is more diffuse, although its development has seen a similar pattern of national consolidation and European cooperation. The main European companies are GEC, Smiths, Dowty (UK), Sextant, (Aerospatiale-Thomson-CSF), Electronique Serge Dassault (ESD) (France) and the Deutsche Aerospace subsidiary, TST. In general terms, the British and the French industries are the most comprehensive, with the British still having the edge in terms of turnover and overall technical competence and a stronger independent presence in the US aerospace market. Although the German equipment industry grew as a result of collaborative programmes, it has tended to suffer from the absence of national programmes to support an independent design capacity.[26]   Italian companies have acquired a useful niche capability, again largely as a result of joint programmes. Several of the electronics firms, such as GEC and Thomson, are also involved in guided weapons and space programmes.

Many of the European equipment companies (particularly in the avionics and electronics sectors) are part of larger, diversified conglomerates. GEC and Thomson, for example, have interests in other areas of defence electronics, and consumer and general industrial electrical equipment. The sector is further complicated by the presence of prime contractors like BAe which also have extensive electronics capabilities. The European equipment sector also contains a number of foreign-owned (largely US) firms such as Texas Instruments, Raytheon (Cossor (UK)) and Litton (Littef (Germany)).[27] Generally, the equipment industry has been the focus of some of the more significant cross-border acquisitions within Europe; Thomson, for example, is now the fourth-placed UK defence/aerospace electronics company.

There have been important differences in the ownership of the major European aerospace industries (see Table 2.4). For most of the post war era, the British and German industries have been privately-owned, whereas French aerospace has been dominated by nationalised companies.[28] In 1993, the newly elected conservative government announced its intention to privatise French aerospace companies, but even so, the French state will retain a large degree of control over the industry. The Spanish industry remains publicly-owned while the Italian government decided in 1992 to selloff the state controlled aircraft companies. The Dutch government acquired a 31.8 per cent share of Fokker as part of a rescue operation in 1987, but has since seen Fokker become part of DASA. As will be considered in more detail in chapter three, public ownership has not necessarily increased governmental control over individual companies. But in general, public ownership in France may have helped to encourage the development of a more coherent, long term national strategy for aerospace compared to Germany and, especially, Britain. On the other hand, the Italian industry has been hampered by political intervention; in particular, the major political parties have used their control over the state holding companies as part of their patronage system and often blocked much-needed rationalisation; even cooperation between individual companies was sometimes vetoed.

In recent years, the European aerospace industry has seen the appearance of diversified industrial conglomerates. British Aerospace diversified into munitions, construction, automobiles and telecommunications. The German aerospace industry has been largely unified under the Daimler-DASA umbrella: a unique concentration in Europe of airframes, engines and systems activities

Ownership of major European aerospace companies

Aerospatiale	State-owned *
Agusta	State holding company *
Alenia	State holding company *
BAe	Private
CASA	State holding company + 40% MBB
Dassault-Electronique	Private
Dassault Aviation	Private/state owned (46%)
DASA	Subsidiary of Daimler
Fokker	Private subsidiary of DASA, state
participation (31%)	
GEC	Private
Lucas	Private
Matra	Private/state owned (15%)
Rolls-Royce	Private
Saab	Private
Sextant	Subsidiary Thomson-Aerospatiale (state 45%)
Shorts	Subsidiary of Bombardier Canada
Siemens	Private
Smiths	Private
Snecma	State owned *
Thomson-CSF	Private/state owned (40%)
Turbomeca	Private

* As at December 1992

Table 2.4

The emergence of large conglomerates such as BAe, Daimler-DASA, Thomson and GEC has begun to change the face of European aerospace, both strengthening national positions and opening up new avenues for cooperation. Daimler's control over German aerospace was, for example, an important factor in its increased assertiveness in European aerospace affairs. By the same token, BAe, Daimler, GEC and Thomson, have a wide range of industrial linkages with other European, US and Japanese firms.[29] From one perspective, a large, diversified company may be better placed to cope with increased competitive pressure in defence procurement and require less public support for aerospace programmes generally. From another, the defence of such vital national industrial and technological assets may become even more imperative for European governments, a trans-national basis.[30]   However, the difference in scale and resources available to the US industry is still marked: although BAe, Aerospatiale, Daimler-DASA have achieved a 'corporate mass' equal to if not greater than most US aerospace firms, Europe only has six of the world's twenty largest aerospace companies. More generally, the average size ratio between US and European prime contractors was still 3:1.[31]

In terms of world aerospace trade, the European industry has narrowed the balance of defence trade with the US and has made a deep inroad into the commercial aircraft and space markets once virtually monopolised by American firms. Although there are several examples of successful national programmes, most of this improvement has been the product of a collaborative effort which has extended over more than thirty years. Most of Europe's leading programmes - Airbus, Tornado, Ariane, several helicopters and a raft of guided weapons—are joint ventures (see Table 2.5). As a result, the links between European firms form a rich and complex tapestry including several sophisticated consortia such as Airbus Industrie, Panavia/Eurofighter, Eurocopter and Euromissile. A number of these have formed, or could in the future form, the basis for fully-fledged trans-national companies. Independently, several European companies have established jointly-owned subsidiaries such as Matra-Espace.

For most European companies, international collaboration has become a routine response to commercial and industrial problems. This has not prevented competition between European firms and there is still potential for bruising conflicts between individual national and corporate interests. Nor is cooperation necessarily with other Europeans: the civil aero-engine sector, particularly the French, has tended to look to the US for partners; BAe has several key joint ventures with MDC; Alenia is linked with MDC, Boeing and Embraer of Brazil; and even CASA has an independent partnership with the Indonesian company IPTN. In many cases, European firms have acquired a global manufacturing presence, especially in the US. By the same token, several US firms have entered the European market through subsidiaries and acquisitions (see Table 2.6).   Finally, there are important independent programmes such as the French Rafale and the Rolls-Royce RB-211 civil aero-engine family.   But the primary axis of European industrial development has been within the 'home' region and this is likely to remain the most important focus for future industrial development. The main question seems to be the extent to which this will be based on the development of more integrated European companies.[32]

Selected European aerospace collaborative projects

Project participants	Type	Main
Airbus Industrie	civil airliner	Fr, G, UK, Sp
Adour	military engine	UK, Fr
Arianespace	satellite launcher	Fr, G, It
ATR	civil airliner	Fr, It
AV-8/Harrier	military aircraft	UK, US
Columbus	space station	G, Fr, It
EH101	helicopter	B, It
Euromissile	missile system	Fr, G
Eurocopter	helicopter	Fr, G
Eurofighter	military aircraft	UK, G, It, Sp
Eurojet	military engine	UK, G, It, Sp
Eurosam	missile system	Fr, It
Goshawk	military aircraft	UK, US
Hermes	space vehicle	Fr, G, It
NH90	helicopter	Ne, It, G
Panavia	military aircraft	UK, G, It
Turbo Union	military engine	UK, G, It

Aero-engine collaboration

Engine	Company
Trent	RR, BMW, Hispano, IHI, KHI
Tay	RR, BMW, Alfa, Volvo
RB211-524	RR, IHI, KHI
GE90	GE, Snecma, Fiat, IHI
CF6-80E1	GE, MTU, Snecma, Volvo
CFM56	GE, Snecma
PW4000 series	P&W, Fiat, MTU, KHI
PW2000	P&W, MTU, Fiat, Volvo
V2500	P&W, RR, MTU, Fiat, IHI
BR700	RR, BMW
M123	GE, Snecma

Table 2.5

The second tier

Outside the two core regions of the US and Western Europe, there is an increasing number of other smaller aerospace manufacturing centres.[33] Some, such as Canada are long established; others should be seen as new entrants. For convenience sake, we have called these the second tier of aerospace producing nations.[34] The extent of the aerospace activity in the second tier countries varies, as do their individual ambitions to expand the scale and the scope of their aerospace industries. But the gap between these countries and the industries of the US and European core is marked. Of the second tier, only Canada and Japan have firms in in the world's fifty largest aerospace companies and each has in total, around three per cent of the world market. In 1989, the Japanese aerospace industry employed 28,000 people, production was only five per cent of the US and total sales were less than half those of the British aerospace industry.[35] Although Japanese and Korean aerospace firms are parts of larger, sometimes very large, conglomerates, such as Mitsubishi and Daewoo, these subsidiaries are small compared with US or European aircraft companies. Several members of the second tier countries such as Canada, Brazil, China and Indonesia have developed low budget civil and military products for both Third World and western markets. Development of second tier aerospace has usually been facilitated by association with established European and US companies. This has often stemmed from offset requirements.[36] However, many second tier companies, especially those in Asia, are capable of matching - sometimes surpassing - American and European levels of productivity. As such, they have become 'partners of choice' for western firms looking to lower the cost of production and to gain access to new sources of development capital.

Some European-based Aerospace TNEs

Company	Holdings in
Aerospatiale	G, US
Agusta	US
Alenia	US
BAe	G, Ne, US
DASA	Fr, Sp
Dassault Av.	Be
Dowty	Ca, Aust
Fokker	Bel
GEC	Fr, It, US, Aust
Lucas	Fr, G, Sp, US

Matra	UK, G, Sp, US
Siemens	UK
Snecma	Bel, Nor
Smiths	US
Thomson-CSF	UK, Ne, G, Bel, US

US-based TNEs in Europe

Allied-Signal	UK, Ge, Fr, Sp, Sw, Ire
General Dynamics	Turk
General Electric	Ge, Fr
GM-Hughes	UK, Ge, Sp
Honeywell	UK, Ge
Litton	Ge, Fr, It
Lockheed	UK
Raytheon	UK
Rockwell	UK, Ge, Fr
Textron	UK, Ge
UTC	Ge, Sp, Ne

Table 2.6

Canada is a good example of an established second tier country whose industry has focused on niche markets and international sub contracting. Following the cancellation of the Avro Arrow advanced fighter in the early 1960s, its industry was forced to abandon any pretence of becoming a major independent player. But Canadian firms have developed a successful range of small 'feederliner' and executive aircraft. The Canadian firm of Bombardier-Canadair, through its acquisition of Shorts, has also achieved a foothold in the European civil and military industry. Several US firms, including Boeing, MDC and P&W, have Canadian subsidiaries - and have benefited from Provincial and Federal aid. P&W Canada, for example, is the world's largest producer of small turboprop and fanjet engines. Two thirds of Canadian aerospace sales are in North America. Other Canadian companies, including Bombardier and Dowty (Canada), subcontract to Airbus Industrie. The Canadian space industry is similarly well regarded, having developed the manipulator arm for the Shuttle and currently as a member of the International Space Station team.[37]

Canada's main problem has been to ensure that its industry does not simply become an off-shore manufacturing arm of US and European companies. For example, Canadian firms, especially those owned by US companies, were directly affected by the aerospace recession south of the border. The maintaince of an independent presence in world markets was, for example, the central issue in determining the future of de Havilland, one of the two main Canadian aircraft design centres. Sold to Boeing in 1986, the US company initially marketed De Havilland's range of small aircraft along with its family of large airliners. In the event, Boeing was unable to effect the improvement in productivity which it felt was necessary to achieve commercial viability. Boeing also found it difficult to come to terms with the small airliner market inhabited by de Havilland.   In 1991, Boeing initially sold de Havilland to the ATR partnership of Aerospatiale and Alenia. The Canadian government, fearing that the Europeans only wanted a production base for their range of small airliners within the North American market, intervened to seek assurances that de Havilland's design and development capabilities would be maintained. In the event, the sale was vetoed on competition grounds by the EC Commission. A controlling interest in de Havilland was acquired by Bombardier for $54.6 million, backed by a Federal and Provincial aid package worth some $400 million.[38] In the longer term, however, Canadian aerospace will face increasing competition from other members of the second tier. In these circumstances, its location inside the putative North American Free Trade Area and its close relationship with the US industry may be its main line of defence.

A number of the newer entrants have aspirations to become significant actors in the aerospace business. Their motives are a familiar mix of security and economic interests. Important regional powers such as Indonesia, India and China want an indigenous defence industrial base, as well as viewing aerospace as a means of encouraging overall economic development. The more developed states in the region, pre-eminently Japan, but also South Korea and the other 'Little Dragons', regard aerospace as a high value-added technology which will help to sustain existing industrial growth rates into the next century. Taiwan, for example, has a government fund of over $100 billion to facilitate the upgrading of national industrial capabilities through investment in high-technology sectors such as aerospace.[39] The South Korean government has also positioned aerospace in the forefront of a national industry and technology policy.[40]

In most cases, the main route into the aerospace industry has been through licence-production, risk-sharing sub contracting and, increasingly, full scope collaboration with US or European firms. The Japanese have a long term relationship with Boeing and were founder members of the International Aero Engine consortium. Taiwan tried to accelerate its entry into the big league of civil aerospace manufacturing by joining MDC's MD11 and proposed

MD12 programme, but in the event found a more modest deal buying into BAe's Regional Jets a more acceptable and less risky venture.[41] For many second tier nations, participation in international programmes remains the limits of their ambitions. But the combination of security and industrial goals underlies the efforts being made by several countries in the second tier to develop indigenous advanced fighter aircraft and small civil aircraft. For Korea, the threat comes from its unpredictable northern cousin; Taiwan is largely isolated from the world arms market by Chinese pressure; and Israel has traditionally looked to its own resources to meet some of its core defence needs. For these countries, the possession of some degree of operational as well as strategic independence in defence industrial matters has been of considerable importance. But most also had economic and industrial interests in developing indigenous aerospace programmes, if only to reduce the balance of payments costs of defence. But more important, the acquisition of more advanced systems integration and programme management skills would increase the value of indigenous aerospace production and would serve as a platform for encouraging other ancillary technologies. Most of these programmes have been based on US or European technology - both the Japanese FSX and the Korean Fighter Project (KFP) are derived from the F-16. Development of the KFP, for example was described as a 'cornerstone project' which the Korean government hoped would lead to a significant enhancement of Korean national capabilities.[42] The FSX and the Taiwanese IDF were also regarded as a way of broadening and deepening aerospace skills and a domestic supplier chain.

The Indonesian government has one of the most comprehensive programmes for developing a world class aerospace industry. There is a declared policy of self-sufficiency in basic defence equipment and in the longer term, hopes of creating a 'regionally dominant civil and military aircraft industry'. Again this is being accomplished through joint ventures and other links with European and US firms. The national company, IPTN, was established in the mid 1970s to fulfil offset/licensing agreements with MBB, CASA and Aerospatiale. The expansion of IPTN, which has included a full development partnership with CASA to build the CN-235 transport aircraft, has entailed $1 billion in state-aid and other privileges within the Indonesian economy. The Indonesian government has argued that this policy has created an industry with an asset base of over $1.8 billion and has created 15,000 jobs in a dynamic manufacturing sector. IPTN now has ambitions of leading a collaborative programme to develop a 130 seat regional jet. With a population of over 157 million and with a geography which demands an extensive air transport network, Indonesia undoubtedly needs a wide range of aerospace products, but whether this also requires comprehensive aerospace industry remains debatable. Its contribution to the development process is at best equivocal, and over-investment in aerospace could be diverting scarce resources and personnel from more pressing needs.[43]

Finally in Asia, the Chinese aerospace industry has the potential, and the domestic market, to become a significant player. It has a long experience of building Soviet and western products under licence since the 1950s and has developed a range of 'cheap and cheerful' military products, including the Silk Worm surface-to-surface missile which have been exported. The Chinese space programme has also produced a commercial satellite launcher, the Long March, based on a ballistic missile. But in general, the Chinese industry is backward and short of advanced technology. In order to satisfy a massive domestic need for civil aircraft China has looked to the west, mainly the US, for partners. The Chinese have established a long term relationship with MDC to build MD-80s for domestic consumption as well as supplying parts for MDC's general production. The Chinese plan to expand this capability in a major programme to upgrade the whole of its civil aerospace sector in partnership with MDC.[44]

Entering the aerospace industry entails a high risk, especially for those countries with ambitions to launch independent programmes. In many respects, the experience of the Brazilian aerospace industry provides a model and a warning for countries looking to use aerospace as a springboard to higher levels of industrial development. In the 1960s, the national aircraft company Embraer built up a basic capability through licensing and subcontract work. Protected by high tariffs, the Brazilians then went on to produce a range of light aeroplanes. Embraer's entry to wider markets came in 1970 with the launch of the 19 seat Bandeirante. This was followed by the Brasilia 'feederliner' which sold well in the US and Europe. The Tuccano military trainer won a competition to supply the British airforce with a basic trainer and a jet strike-trainer (the AMX) is under development in collaboration with the Italian firm of Alenia. However, political interference and severe national economic problems subsequently damaged Embraer's financial position. Matters were made worse by the general downturn in defence sales during the late 1980s and by the slump in both civil and military business after the Gulf War (Brazil was a major supplier of arms to Iraq). In 1991, the Brazilian government had to bail the company out with a $407 million rescue package. In the longer term, the Brazilian government intends to privatise the company in order to attract foreign equity and finance for developing new programmes.[45] But Embraer, while making significant technical progress and having some commercial success, will find it difficult to survive in a world market against bigger and more financially stable companies. In this context, much depends on the extent and determination of a national government to underpin aerospace development.

Japan, a special case?

Despite some impressive achievements, none of the above countries are likely in the short to medium term to threaten the core aerospace nations, except on the margin or in niche markets. Japan, however, is a rather different prospect. The depth of Japanese technological and industrial capacity is indisputable; aerospace (especially civil aviation and space) has been targeted by the Ministry of International Trade and Industry (MITI). MITI cited aerospace in its 1970 'Vision' along with nuclear power and information technology as a key twenty-first century technology, and the experience of other targeted industries - motor-cycles, cars and semi-conductors - stands as a warning to western aerospace companies. However, aerospace presents a different problem compared with other manufacturing industries in which the targeting strategy has worked the Japanese miracle. Over three-quarters of Japanese aerospace production is bought by the Japanese Ministry of Defence and although the Japanese defence market is large and artificially profitable, limits on military exports act as a barrier to growth.[46] Although the Japanese government has invested heavily in aerospace projects Japan still needs to increase basic aerospace R&D and to improve its research infrastructure if it is to mount a challenge to European, let alone American firms. As Mowery points out, unless the Japanese are prepared to invest heavily in this background, it will be left with a 'perpetually infantile, non-competitive industry.' [47]

The main actors in the Japanese aerospace industry are Mitsubishi, Kawasaki, Fuji and Ishikawajima-Harima, all heavy industrial conglomerates. Aerospace only represents between seven and 30 per cent of their revenues, and they have been very reluctant to assume the cost of developing aerospace technology independent of the state. The largest Japanese aerospace company, MHI, is ranked twenty-first in the world aerospace industry.[48] Most of the Heavy Industries (HIs) work together, but there is a considerable degree of specialisation. MHI has acted as prime contractor for the bulk of Japan's key aircraft programmes whereas IHI has tended to lead Japanese aero-engine development. 'Critical mass' in development has also been improved by the formation of domestic consortia to undertake major projects and to participate in international collaboration. Cooperation between firms is further enhanced by the typically Japanese pathways of informal contacts often facilitated by MITI. Similarly, the *keiretsu* structure of the

HIs facilitates good vertical linkages between related industrial and technological sectors.[49]

The Japanese aircraft industry was reborn after the Second World War through the licence production of US and some European military aircraft. In the 1960s, the Japanese government sponsored the development of an indigenous fighter, the F-5. At the same time, Japan tried independently to enter the civil aerospace market with the YS-11 feederliner, but failure to sell the aircraft outside the Japanese home market underlined the difficulties it faced as a new entrant in the aerospace industry. Japan came to accept, therefore, that the most effective and rational way of improving national capabilities and making any headway in world markets was through cooperation with US and European firms. Japanese firms working in domestic consortia encouraged and supported by the Japanese government, are linked to the US civil aerospace industry - in this instance Boeing. In the case of civil aero-engines, Japan has been a member of the International Aero-Engine consortium with Rolls-Royce and P&W. Trade and other political pressures have tended to favour links with the US, but the Japanese have in any case preferred teaming with clear market leaders as a part of a risk aversion strategy.[50]

The decision to develop the FSX advanced fighter in the early 1980s marked an important change in Japanese aerospace policy. Following several disappointing experiences (mostly over technology transfer) with US civil partners, mainly Boeing, MITI decided to encourage a more independent development strategy with stronger links between civil and military aerospace.[51] FSX may prove to be a watershed in the evolution of an independent Japanese industry, but the programme provoked considerable tension with the US, costs have risen dramatically and its direct contribution to the development of Japanese civil capabilities may have been overstated. Nevertheless, the FSX programme will unquestionably enhance Japanese industrial potential, particularly in the systems and equipment sectors.[52] In the late 1980s, the focus shifted back to cooperation; despite their earlier experiences, working with the market leader Boeing was still regarded as the most logical and less risky option.

In the longer term, the growing importance of advanced avionics in aerospace will play to Japan's existing strengths in electronics. In this respect, the FSX could provide an important 'gateway' into the world market for Japanese equipment companies. Along with commitments to space and satellite construction, the main beneficiaries of aerospace investment, and by the same token, the most dangerous threat to Western companies, will be the Japanese equipment industry. In this context, the Japanese will be working to established strengths - the 'spin-on' effect, where existing high-technology industries may find new markets for their existing skills in both product and high quality, cost-effective manufacturing processes.[53]

The Japanese are prepared to take a long term view; strategic investment in materials sciences and other basic technologies relevant to aerospace has been increased. Japan, in a joint industry-government effort, has also begun to investigate design concepts beyond the next generation of civil aircraft and space vehicles. In this context, aerospace is still seen as an integral element driving Japanese industrial growth in the next century.[54] However, the most significant change in the prospects for Japanese aerospace would follow an extension of Japanese security commitments. This could provide a base for a more extensive national defence aerospace industry. By the same token, any relaxation in the restrictions governing overseas defence sales would make a considerable difference to the viabilty and value of aerospace production. Such developments would then provide a stronger platform for an attack on world aerospace markets, raising the likelihood of serious competition for US and European companies.

Since the 1960s, Japanese aerospace has already shown an impressive rate of growth. Coming from virtually nowhere in the early 1960s, Japan now has about three per cent of the world market. In a comparable high technology sector such as computers, a 20 year government-industry partnership was able to build up a 30 per cent market share.[55] Forewarned is, of course, also forearmed. Knowledge of what Japanese firms have done in other manufacturing sectors has ensured that western companies working with Japan have carefully controlled access to key technologies. Political pressure from the US (and latterly Europe) to ease trade imbalances through buying from the established companies has also begun to limit Japan's ability to protect its 'infant' aerospace industry.

The Japanese are certainly valued partners. Part of this attraction lies in the generous funding Japanese firms can obtain from the state; but they have also acquired a high reputation for meeting schedules and delivering high quality products. Indeed, some firms have recorded productivity rates three times the US average, and, to repeat an earlier point, Japanese leadership in process technology could yet be a key to its future as a major world player.[56] Even if the idea of a Japanese national strategy directed by MITI may be overstating a more complex reality, there is evidence of a national concern to develop Japanese capabilities to a point which would increase Japan's share of high-value added work in international partnerships and win an influence over programme design and management in order to maximise opportunities for Japanese equipment companies.

In general terms, the established aerospace firms have recognised the attractions of working with the best of the second tier companies, particularly in the Far East. Productivity is very high and with an impressive build-quality. For example, MDC said that collaboration with Taiwan on the MD-12 would have saved 30 per cent of total production costs. Even the Chinese, with a less modern industry, believe that they can undercut western production by 20 per cent.[57] Government commitments to aerospace ensure that capitalisation is available and a local partner may help in sales in important regional markets. The key issue will be the extent to which these firms will gain access to critical technologies. To date, western firms have been careful to restrict transfer of central design and integration skills, but clearly the pressure will grow to transfer more technology as the price for market access and state funding. With the possible exception of Japan, however, none of the second tier aerospace nations are likely to mount more than a peripheral challenge to the US or Europe; but individual companies will clearly face an uncomfortable decade or so beating off Asian and other subcontractors and equipment suppliers.

3

The Aerospace Industry and
the State

Introduction

The importance of the relationship between between the state and the aerospace industry has already been noted: as customer, sponsor or owner, it plays a key role in shaping the context, structure and dynamics of aerospace industrial operations. Military aviation and space are, of course, the most state-oriented sectors; but the state may also play an important part in the development of commercial aircraft and equipment. The relationship varies from state to state and from period to period. In some countries, the aerospace industry can be an arm of a state-run economic and industrial system; and in others, more limited forms of public ownership may still imply a similarly direct role in financing and the selection of industrial heads. But even where the industry is privately-owned, the state's influence can be pervasive. Ownership *per se* has rarely been a useful guide to the shape of state-industry relations in aerospace. Without owning a single share in any company, the US government has considerable power to shape the health of the aerospace industry by effecting changes in procurement policy and by determining access to its defence market.[1] As one classic study of the American industry put it:

> Without the Federal government, there would simply be no aircraft industry...No aspect of the industry, including the commercial sector, could exist without the R&D funds provided by the state or the state's purchases of military equipment. It is no accident, then,

that virtually every other nation has an aircraft industry that is either heavily subsidized or indeed owned by the state. [2]

The importance of aerospace to the national defence industrial base has been consistently the strongest motive for state sponsorship. This has justified expenditure on R&D and intervention to strengthen industrial structure and it helps to explain why foreign ownership and open access to national defence aerospace markets remains a sensitive question. But even without these obvious and direct links to state power, the widely held view of aerospace as a strategic technology in its wider sense helps to explain the interest of political authorities in the industry's affairs.

On the face of it, this would appear to put aerospace in a privileged position - with ready access to state funds and protection from external competition. In practice, matters are never so straight forward. Dependence on the state for capital puts firms in a dependent and potentially vulnerable condition. Changes in policy, shifts in national priorities can all affect the livelihood of firms - and all too rapidly. State support for aerospace and, consequently, the risk of ill-judged political intervention in corporate decison-making, can be a mixed blessing for individual companies (or even entire industries). In extreme cases, such as in the Italian state-owned aerospace sector and the heavily bureaucratised structures of South American aerospace, political patronage has been a major obstacle to rationalisation and has often undermined commercial flexibility and efficiency.[3]

Government and aerospace - national experiences

The former USSR

The closest form of the relationship between state and industry was to be found in the former Soviet Union, where every aspect of development was shaped by a centralised bureaucracy.[4] Aerospace was part of an extensive military industrial complex, receiving privileged access to scarce materials and trained manpower under the direction of specific Ministries such as the Ministry of Aviation Industry and General Machine Building which was responsible for the space industry. Output was set by the state planning agency GOSPLAN, and raw materials, parts and other manufacturing resources were allocated by GOSNAB. Design and advanced development, including the construction of prototypes, was conducted by several design bureaux, for example, Tupolev, Antonov, Mikoyan (Mig) and Yakolev with basic research data supplied by state laboratories and institutions.[5] Full-scale production was undertaken by separate production factories. These were very much a legacy of Stalinist planning, and as vertically integrated complexes, they were responsible for building complete aircraft, including small components such as nuts and washers. In the case of defence hardware, the military customers maintained a close watch on quality and performance. Production levels, project launches and 'payment ' was determined by the state and the centre retained all hard currency earnings from foreign sales. Political intervention could also dictate the pattern and direction of development, especially in high profile sectors such as space.[6]

Although the system produced some technically impressive results, it contained in-built inefficiencies. The division of design and production led to duplication and scant attention to 'design to build' concepts to improve manufacturing efficiency. For example, production   of the TU-160 Blackjack bomber was carried out by 830 different organisations run by nine ministries. By having to support 'production cities', the industry was also forced to carry a high social overhead: the Ulyanovsk plant, for example, was responsible for the welfare of 160,000 people and two-thirds of its revenue was devoted to 'social spending'.[7]

The onset of *perestroika* in the late 1980s had a dramatic affect on the Soviet aerospace industry. The faltering attempts to restructure the Soviet economy included deliberate and widespread 'conversion' strategies and the defence/aerospace industry had special responsibilities to transfer its skills into the wider economy. The results were decidedly mixed; morale fell and the ease with which the specialist skills of aerospace could be converted directly to alternative uses was greatly overestimated. Following the abortive coup in 1991 and the subsequent break-up of the USSR, the pace of structural reform increased. The Ministry of Aviation Industry was dissolved and replaced by an interim federal agency to prepare the industry for decentralisation and privatisation.   The Ministry of General Machine Building responsible for missile and space systems was abolished and the armed forces moved towards a more western form of direct contracting with the manufacturers. Aviaexport, the Soviet export agency, was also wound up.[8]

The disintegration of the Soviet state added an extra dimension to the industry's problems. With the emergence of independent republics, the new governments sought to take control of 'their' aerospace industries and research institutes, often with disruptive and destabilising effects.[9] Since 1992, attempts have begun to restructure the ex-Soviet industry and to re-establish links between the various parts of the former Soviet industry. The Russian Republic has retained the largest singe element, but the Ukraine has an industry of 115,000 employees (about 10 per cent of the old Soviet industry) and Uzbekistan employs 40,000. An attempt is being made to coordinate and to integrate 22 research institutions, 95 design bureaux and 152 production plants under the aegis of a CIS-wide, private trade association, Aviaprom. Its primary task will be to prepare the industry for privatisation which will imply the creation of integrated design and production facilities along the western model linked by contract and shaped by commercial forces. The daunting nature of this task cannot be underestimated given the political chaos appearing throughout the former Soviet Union and the rate at which aerospace capabilities are decaying. Even without additional problems, the future success of the new CIS aerospace industry will depend upon gaining access to western capital and cooperation with western firms.[10]

France

The French experience is often viewed as the archetype of state intervention in a western aerospace industry. Outsiders have often envied the apparently seamless web of government-industry relations: seemingly well-planned, and actions prioritised by politicians, officials and industrialists jointly committed to the promotion of French national industrial and technological goals. Reality has not always reflected the image of consistent and un-relenting support for aerospace; although the French state has been highly supportive of all sectors of its aerospace industry, there have been differences of opinion between government and French aerospace companies and, from time to time, conflicts of interest have divided the different sectors of the industry. But to a great extent, image and reality have tended to converge in a clearly symbiotic relationship between state and industry.

The French government, as sole or dominant share-holder in the major aerospace firms, has provided investment capital which can be adjusted to meet specific demands or to cover periods of financial stress. The government has used its influence over the banking system to encourage investment in projects of national importance. The state also provides support for individual projects through national budgets for defence, civil aeronautics, space and general R&D and the French government is, of course, a major customer of French aerospace products. On occasion, French procurement policy has been shaped by the needs of French export interests, especially those of Dassault.[11] The French Ministry of Defence (MoD) is the responsible ministry for the aerospace sector; its *tutelle* or guidance function includes overall direction for civil and military activities. The MoD runs the French national R&D establishments such as ONERA. The Ministry of Transport (MoT), however, is responsible for specific civil projects, and implements the French launch aid system. The MoT oversees the civil R&D programme and provides official representation in civil collaborative programmes such as the Airbus and the ATR series of regional airliners. The MoT is also responsible for the French airline industry and a senior MoT official sits on the board of Air France. Finally, the French national space programme and its contribution to European space programmes is controlled by the state agency CNES.[12]

Most of the major French aerospace companies have been nationalised since the 1930s, and the French government has frequently intervened to improve the structural characteristic of the French aerospace industry, either publicly or privately-owned. In 1936, the founding companies of French aviation were absorbed into seven *societés nationales* - an eighth was created in 1955. French civil and military engine manufacturing has been centred on Snecma since 1946. In the late fifties the aircraft *societés nationales* were re-grouped along regional lines into Nord and Sud Aviation. Consolidation was viewed as necessary in order to facilitate expansion and to support the modernisation of the French armed forces and to fulfil French ambitions in civil aviation. These changes were accompanied by some plant closures and concentration of resources to defined regional centres. However, during the 1960s it became apparent that further rationalisation was needed to create firms of a size to match those of the UK and the US. In 1965, the French government decided to consolidate the two nationalised airframe groups, along with the rocket engine firm of SEREB, into a single company. The merger was strongly resisted by the two groups and five years of difficult negotiations were required before the formation of Aerospatiale was finally accomplished.[13]

Since 1945, there have been two important privately-owned firms in the French aircraft industry, the engine firm of Turbomeca, and Avions Marcel Dassault. Both were dominated by their founding families, and in the case of Dassault, by Marcel Dassault himself until his death in 1986. Marcel Dassault was a political associate of General de Gaulle and the company's continuing political links with the French right helped to explain its independence during the 1950s and 1960s.[14] But even Dassault could not entirely escape government intervention. In 1967, as part of the general plan to consolidate the industry, Dassault was encouraged to take over the financially weak Breguet Aviation.[15] The French government also intervened generally to encourage specialisation in the industry. Dassault became the centre of French fixed-wing combat aircraft development, while Aerospatiale was responsible for large transports, helicopters, ballistic missiles and a share of guided weapons development. Aerospatiale's defence work, which included the allocation of Dassault subcontracts, were designed to act as a corrective device when patterns of defence demand produced imbalances in capacity.[16] However, despite this attempt to ensure a rational use of resources, the French government did nothing to prevent Dassault from trying to enter the airliner market in the 1970s despite opposition from Aerospatiale.[17]

The relationship between Dassault and the French government has been particularly complex. The company was a clear beneficiary of the French military build-up in the 1960s; it was aided by French export-orientated arms sales policies and, during the 1960s, Dassault's interests shaped French policy towards collaboration. However, Dassault's position was undermined by mis-management and a financial scandal in the mid 1970s. Dassault anticipated full nationalisation by a hostile Socialist government by offering a controlling interest in the aircraft business to the government. In the event, the complex ownership structure of the Dassault group, combined with adept political footwork, left the French government with as much (or as little) control over the company after nationalisation as before. However, the death of Marcel Dassault and declining overseas military sales left the company increasingly vulnerable to government direction and the real possibility of amalgamation with Aerospatiale. In 1977, a French Parliamentary report questioned whether France could afford indefinitely two military design centres. Without advocating an outright merger, the report suggested that Dassault should regard Aerospatiale as a genuine partner in development activity.[18] From 1989, the French government pushed for much closer R&D cooperation between the two companies, including the re-assignment of personnel and regular high-level meetings to discuss research and other matters of mutual interest. Although the French government continued to support Dassault as a centre for advanced fighter aircraft, the firm's reluctance to make concessions to collaboration was increasingly at odds with government policy.[19]

In December 1992, with Dassault facing further uncertainty over its defence business, the French government began the process of merging it with Aerospatiale. The government's holdings in Dassault Aviation were transferred to the state holding company SOGEMA which owns Aerospatiale. Although Dassault has heatedly reaffirmed its autonomy, referring to the move as a 'technical change', the creation, under governmental direction, of a technical committee to explore links between the two entities may anticipate a fully-fledged union sooner rather than later.[20] Following the Socialist defeat in the 1993 elections, the right-wing government announced that, along with much of France's public sector industries, aerospace would be privatised. However, this was qualified by a promise to retain a 'golden share' over strategic industries such as aerospace. A core group of institutional shareholders would also be expected to take a long term view of their investment and respect the particular needs of the aerospace sector.

Other changes may lead to a less close relationship between the French state and aerospace. As the French aerospace industry becomes more integrated with its European neighbours, the links between the French government and the national aerospace industry may become more distant. A more commercial environment could make it harder to justify traditional *tutellage*. On the other hand, the French are still deeply wedded to the idea of national direction in the defence and aerospace industries and officials believe that a market-orientated approach in this sector is inappropriate, especially during a period of industrial crisis. Any French government will be reluctant to abandon the principle that French industry should be at least *primus inter pares* within European aerospace. It is still difficult to envisage that a French government would be prepared to tolerate the purchase of a US airliner for Air France or a foreign combat aircraft for the Air Force where there is a national alternative. French determination to seize the high ground in European joint ventures such as Airbus and European Space Agency (ESA) space programmes is likely to remain a strong feature of policy towards joint ventures. The French, perhaps more than any of their European neighbours, are still wedded to the concept of high-technology as a politico-economic activity - a philosophy which will continue to ensure a high level of support from the French state for the national aerospace industry.

The United Kingdom

Relations between the British aerospace industry and government fall somewhere between the overtly interventionist stance of France and the more hands-off role played by the US government. For most of the industry's history, the major companies have been in private hands, but the level of demand, civil aircraft development and industrial structure have all been shaped by government actions (or inaction). Intervention has usually been exercised by the state's monopsonistic control over military contracting, ministerial influence in nationalised airline purchasing and via civil launch aid policy. In some cases, financial crises, such as de Havilland in the mid 1950s and Rolls-Royce in 1971, triggered a government bail-out. In the Rolls case, nationalisation by a Conservative government underscored the largely pragmatic nature of British policy towards aerospace.[21]

The government took an active part in planning the post-war recovery of the British aircraft industry, primarily by helping to re-build the UK civil sector. However, a much needed rationalisation of over a dozen design centres was deferred partly

for security reasons.[22] Serious moves towards rationalisation date
from the mid 1950s, when defence cuts and the rising costs of R&D
in both civil and military programmes began to underline the need
for economies of scale and the need for larger industrial units.
Although the government identified 'candidates for relegation', it was
again reluctant to intervene directly in the process of
rationalisation.   Instead, the governments control over military
contracts was used to edge and nudge the industry into larger units.
The result was the formation of two airframe groups (BAC and
HSA), two engine firms (Rolls Royce and   BSE) and a single
helicopter company (Westland).   Companies which resisted the re-
grouping found it increasingly difficult to survive.   The only
exception was Shorts of Northern Ireland which was regarded as a
special case on regional grounds.[23]

Although merger (and a form of public ownership) of BAC and
HSA was recommended by the Plowden Report of 1965, and two
attempts were made to encourage further rationalisation by both
Labour and Conservative administrations, the two-group format
remained in place until the formation and nationalisation of British
Aerospace (BAe) in 1978.   The engine sector was reduced to one
major company in 1967, with the purchase of BSE by Rolls-Royce.
During this period, some semblance of competition remained, but in
practice the government shared major contracts between the two
airframe groups.   However, the collapse and bankruptcy of Rolls-
Royce in 1971 and the rising cost of civil programmes such as
Concorde exposed the ambiguities of the government's relations with
a largely privately-owned industry dependent upon the state for its
survival.

In 1974, a Labour government came to power determined to
nationalise the aircraft industry in order to improve public
accountability of publicly-funded projects and to improve the
strategic direction of industrial development. As a result, the BAC
and HSA were merged and nationalised in 1978 to form BAe.
Although BAe executives would soon welcome privatisation under the
Conservatives, they had no doubts that the creation of BAe by *force
majeur* was both desirable and a long overdue concentration of
industrial resources.   In the 1980s, the Conservatives returned
BAe, Rolls-Royce and Shorts to the private sector.

By the late 1980s, the British aircraft industry had reached a
large measure of structural stability, but during the Thatcher
administration, the effect of more competitive, value-for-money
procurement doctrines helped to stimulate further rationalisation
amongst the avionics and equipment companies.[24] The relationship
between state and industry steadily grew more distant under the
Thatcher government.   Indeed, during the late 1980s, the
government was accused of neglecting industrial R&D and adopting

other policies that were 'anti-industry' in their effect.   In particular, the aerospace industry shared a growing concern amongst UK manufacturers that the UK was falling behind its neighbours in terms of publicly-funded R&D.   The MoD studiously distanced itself from any formal responsibility for maintaining a level of domestic demand, or support for the industry as part of an explicit defence industrial base policy.[25] Industrial 'sponsorship' generally fell away during the 1980s, leaving the Department of Trade and Industry to act as a 'market' advice group to ministers and to monitor   public commitments to the Airbus and other launch-aided programmes.

Following the fall of Mrs Thatcher, and the gradual repudiation of Thatcherite industrial policies, the Conservative government began slowly to adopt a more supportive posture towards industry in general.   The aerospace industry began to hope for a more positive view of its needs.   In 1992, the DTI commissioned a National Strategic Technology Plan from an industry working party which was welcomed as a useful contribution to government R&D planning. The DTI itself began to formulate a strategy for the industry and the MoD appeared to accept some responsibility for the health of the defence industries. The House of Commons also produced a generally supportive report into the state of the national industry.[26] But the government still appeared reluctant to increase its spending on basic aerospace R&D or otherwise directly to intervene to improve market conditions.

In other respects, however, aerospace remained a privileged industry. The Ministry of Defence was still the industry's largest single customer and primary source of its R&D funding and despite its more stringent approach to contracting, the bulk of its aerospace-related purchases came from UK firms.   Even Mrs Thatcher was persuaded to grant aid for Airbus and other civil projects and British defence contractors could count on formal support from the Defence Sales Organisation, as well high level backing from the British government. Few other British industries could count themselves as fortunate - a sign again of the depth of government involvement in aerospace.

Germany

The structure of the modern German aerospace industry was in large measure the result of decisions taken in the mid 1950s by the German government to recreate a national aerospace capability. The initial stimulus was to reduce the balance of payments costs of rearmament, but other, wider interests soon gave extra impetus to both Federal and state support for aerospace development. However, German companies were too small to provide a viable base for German aerospace ambitions or, as was increasingly necessary, to play an influential role in international ventures. From the late 1950s, the Federal government encouraged rationalisation along regional lines based on domestic consortia and by 1969, twenty airframe and engine companies had been reduced to three airframe groups and a single aero-engine firm: Messerschmitt Boelkow Blohm (MBB), Dornier, the German-Dutch VFW-Fokker and Motoren und Turbinen Union (MTU).[27]

The government believed that rationalisation would reduce dependence on the state and increase German effectiveness in collaborative programmes. Rather than reducing state aid, however, commitments to programmes such as the Airbus and Tornado, while enhancing industrial capability, represented a vastly increased financial burden. Nevertheless, the German government hoped that the growth of trans-national firms patterned on the VFW-Fokker relationship would assume a larger share of the cost of aerospace. In the event, their European colleagues were less enthusiastic about an integrated approach and, by the late 1970s, with VFW-Fokker itself showing signs of strain, the Germans returned to domestic rationalisation as an answer to these problems. Even the creation in 1980 of a single large aerospace group centred on MBB failed to provide an adequate base for German aerospace development which might be large enough to finance more of its own business. In 1989, the Federal government encouraged and facilitated a take-over bid for MBB from Daimler, one of the largest manufacturing firms in Germany. Daimler had already acquired Dornier, MTU and AEG, the consumer and defence electronics firm, and was looking to expand its aerospace interests.[28] The terms offered by the German government were extremely favourable, but the fusion of much of the modern German defence industrial base in one company, Deutsche Aerospace (DASA), was highly controversial, stirring memories of the Nazi 'military-industrial-complex'. The German government also had to overrule Federal anti-trust office opposition to the merger, arguing that concentration was necessary to protect a vital industrial asset.[29]

Federal responsibility for aerospace is divided between the Economics Ministry (civil programmes and general oversight), the Ministry of Research (space and basic aeronautical R&D) and the Defence Ministry. Since 1984, a Federal Aerospace Coordinator, based in the Economics Ministry, has had the task of drawing together the various strands of German aerospace policy as well as having direct responsibility for civil and military projects. German aerospace policy has also been complicated by the role played by the various *Länder* governments. In the 1950s, the re-birth of German aerospace was shaped more by provincial competition to attract new investment, or to re-build older established firms, than by central

direction.   This left central government with the task of
rationalising the industry by encouragement and inducement. State
governments invested in 'their' industries and resisted restructuring and the transfer of work which might have threatened
regional capabilities. The unification of Germany in 1991 added
another regional complication and links between the small East
German aerospace industry and DASA have been encouraged and
funded by the Federal government.[30]

Government support for the German aerospace industry has had
its problematic moments, but for the better part of three decades
the industry has been regarded at both a national and a provincial
level as an important component of German industrial and
technological growth.   In the 1990s, budgetary constraints and
changing national priorities (including paying for re-unification)
began to put strain on the level of financial support for civil and
military programmes.[31]   With the decline in Cold War tensions,
high profile military projects, in particular the European Fighter,
were increasingly vulnerable to cuts and the threat of cancellation.
This led the industry to seek government assistance for conversion
and diversification.   Military producers also wanted some
relaxation of Germany's stringent   controls on military sales in
order to boost exports.   But despite public assurances that the
German government was still prepared to back industry's demands
for a more influential role in European civil programmes, the
German state will be poorly placed to support these ambitions with
hard cash.

Europe: general observations

State intervention in the aerospace industry has not been confined to
the major European aerospace states.   The Spanish aerospace
industry has been built-up through state aid and a mix of state and
central government shareholdings. Since a government-led bail-out
in 1987, the Dutch government has owned a third of Fokker and has
consistently supported the company with launch aid for civil
programmes and through military procurement. Political
intervention in Italy has reflected the pattern of political patronage
wielded by the two state holding companies, IRI and Efim-Finbreda,
which effectively owned most of the Italian aerospace industry from
its re-formation in the 1950s. The formation of Alenia in 1990
based on IRI's aerospace companies, although going a long way
towards improving the structural alignment, still left a number of
anomalies.[32] The political crisis of 1993 and the proposed
dismantling of the state holding companies is likely to hasten a much
needed structural reform of the aerospace sector.

Overall, the role of government in the European aerospace industry has been all-pervasive, often direct and sometimes deeply involved in the corporate decision-making of individual firms, but hardly ever absent from the industry's evolution. The effect has been to produce distinct 'national champions' which have often received special treatment from governments and support for their interests in collaborative negotiations. There is a collective dimension to European aerospace, but despite over twenty years of cooperation, national companies still look first to the support and encouragement of their own governments. Now, however, the EC is beginning to have an influence over aerospace policy. EC Competition Directives have shaped industrial decisions in respect of the ATR-De Havilland merger, and the Commission has served notice that despite Treaty of Rome limitations on interference in security issues, the defence sector will not remain immune from its oversight. The Commission has been responsible for negotiations with the US over civil aerospace subsidies. And since the mid 1980s, aerospace has been eligible for EC R&D funding, albeit in a very limited and cumbersome form.[33] In the longer term, the pressures of contracting national demand, the formation of more overtly trans-national industrial structures, further developments in the Single European Market, and especially the possibility of a common European approach to defence procurement could reduce, if not eliminate the purely national characteristics of European aerospace policy-making. This scenario contains a lot of 'what ifs' and 'maybes', and the governments of the major aerospace powers will only reluctantly allow the transfer of authority over the aerospace sector to any Pan-European body.

Japan

The importance of government support and guidance in the structure and operation of the Japanese aerospace industry has already been noted. The Ministry of International Trade and Industry (MITI) has targeted aerospace as a strategic industry which Japan should support in order to maintain the momentum of its high-technology economy into the next century.[34] MITI, and other agencies, such as the Self Defence Agency and the Ministry of Telecommunications, have funded developments in civil and military airframes, engines and space programmes. The government has protected the Japanese aerospace sector by insisting on domestic production of the bulk of its defence equipment. This has bolstered the profits of Japanese defence companies at the expense of higher costs to the Japanese defence budget and, on occasion, forced the Japanese airforce to use a second-rate indigenous product.[35] Similar protection has been afforded to the development of Japanese communications satellites.[36]

Despite the fact that Japanese aerospace firms are much smaller than their US or European counterparts, the Japanese government has not sought to encourage rationalisation. This was partly due to the conglomerate structure of the HIs which dominate the Japanese aerospace sector. But it was also due to the routine adoption of internal cooperation between Japanese firms. MITI encouraged an informal process of cooperation between the major aerospace companies which led to specialisation with defined 'leaders' in both airframe and engine activities. MITI also engineered the creation of formal domestic consortia to work on domestic and collaborative programmes. The so-called Japanese Development Corporations (JDCs) were established as non-profit, legally defined foundations with a remit to enhance the Japanese aircraft industry and to form the basis for Japanese participation in international ventures. For example, the Japanese Engine Development Corporation (JEDC) was created to coordinate Japanese work in the International Aero-Engine (IAE) programme, while the Japanese Aircraft Development Corporation (JADC) was responsible for Japanese participation in the Boeing 767 and 777. The JDCs are formally independent of government, but MITI has been able to influence its activities through funding decisions and more directly through board membership. Its influence has also been felt in the more informal mechanism of government-company consensus building typical of Japanese industry policy-making. MITI has ensured that all of the relevant HIs were involved in designated 'national programmes', regardless of who was defined as prime contractor or commercial consortium leader.[37] Working outside the 'system' can cause difficulties and tensions and participation in projects which compete with 'national' programmes is discouraged. For example, Japanese firms working on Boeing-based collaborative aircraft received full state backing, but KHI's independent subcontracts with Airbus was something of an embarrassment to Japanese aerospace officials.

The extent of Japanese long term ambitions in aerospace is still questionable: Japanese aerospace firms and MITI have differed over whether the industry should, and realistically could, achieve an independent aerospace capability. The publication of MITI's 'visions' for aerospace in 1970 and 1982, seemed to imply that independence should be the ultimate goal. Extensive commitments to space research, including the development of satellite launchers, and the protection afforded to Japanese satellite makers, underlined the level of long term investment that Japan was prepared to make in order to achieve autonomy in major space systems.[38] However, as we have noted in Chapter Two, industrialists have been deterred by the high cost and risks of aerospace, especially in civil aircraft, and have tended to deprecate MITI's more grandiose statements. Equally, the Japanese government has not always expressed a clear and coherent plan for aerospace. MITI has faced competition from other agencies with aerospace interests and increased spending on aircraft projects has encountered opposition from the Finance Ministry.[39] More critically, there been a degree of ambivalence in Japanese policy about whether the country should expand generally its national defence industrial base and military aerospace in particular. Such a step would clearly revolutionise the R&D and market base for Japanese aerospace. In the 1980s, there was a distinct shift towards the defence sector as the basis for aerospace development, a change of emphasis which led to the FSX programme.[40] But subsequent difficulties with the FSX and the end of the Cold War have again led to questioning of Japan's need for an autonomous defence industrial base and an expensive indigenous fighter aircraft.

In recent years, both MITI and Japanese industrialists have accepted that in the medium term the primary national objective should be to improve Japan's ability to participate in collaborative projects. The commercial failure of the YS-11 airliner in the 1960s underlined the need to seek international partners as a quicker and cheaper route to an aerospace capability. Nevertheless, MITI and other agencies have continued to support long term strategic investment in basic aerospace technologies - for example, in materials and hypersonics. In 1991, the Japanese government announced plans to fund an eight-year $209 million R&D programme for a hypersonic propulsion system.[41] Towards the end of 1991, the JADC appeared to be sufficiently confident of its independent skills to consider leading its own international regional airliner programme.[42]

In the short term, however, private industry remains reluctant fully to embrace the ambitions of independence that some elements of Japanese officialdom might harbour. In this respect, the advocates of an aerospace-led future have undoubtedly put aside the immediate concern for commercial return in favour of a more strategic view of economic development. Economic reality may yet constrain the extent to which Japan might threaten the established players in all aspects of aerospace, but nobody in the west can afford to be complacent about the potential of an orchestrated government-industry strategy, particularly if Japan should seek to become a regional 'power' with the defence industrial interests to match.

The United States

The Federal government has aided, and continues to support, the development of the national aerospace industry through national R&D facilities, export credits, defence procurement and a civilian space programme.[43] NASA's mission statement - frequently re-iterated by NASA officials - states that its main aim is to help maintain US leadership in aerospace technology. The US domestic defence market, although not entirely closed to outsiders, is protected by law and custom. And, as we shall discuss at length below, changes in the terms of defence procurement can have a massive impact on the profitability and even the survival of individual companies. The US government has occasionally helped to bail out companies in difficulties - notably Douglas in the mid 1960s and Lockheed in the early 1970s.   In 1991, MDC requested aid from the Department of Defense (DoD) and the deferral of penalties in order to stave-off a financial crisis and, according to the DoD's Inspector General, the Pentagon considered helping MDC to overcome cash-flow problems following difficulties with the C-17 military transport programme. However, such assistance to ailing aerospace companies has rarely gone unchallenged - the Lockheed loan was only authorised by a single vote in the US Senate; and, as one critic of the MDC plan noted, 'Secretary (of Defense) Cheney's job description does not include loan officer, nor is the Pentagon a credit union for defence contractors.'[44]

Compared to European and Japanese experience, the US government has usually adopted a 'hands off' approach to industrial restructuring and other strategic issues designed to shape the future of the domestic aerospace industry.   It has rarely singled out individual companies whose existence and independence would be essential to the national DIB. Similarly, US companies have never been defined as 'national champions' in collaborative programmes and, in general terms, the relationship between the Pentagon and US defence companies has usually been described as 'adversarial'. Finally, the development of a coherent strategy towards aerospace, and to space in particular, has been undermined by the problems faced by NASA and its obsession with problematic 'big ticket' manned space programmes.[45]

In any event, competition between companies, the vagaries of Congressional funding and the demands of sectional interests would tend to negate any centralised, government-directed approach to aerospace. US firms themselves have remained committed to the precepts of free market capitalism, at least where direct state intervention has been concerned. Even in the case of civil aerospace subsidies, where US firms have urged the government to take action against European practices, they have rarely called for comparable forms of direct aid. In this respect, the aerospace sector has reflected the prevailing 'ideology' of US government-business relations which is still distinctly uneasy with the principle of direct aid to industry.[46] On the other hand, government support for background or generic R&D was both appropriate and legitimate. As one Boeing executive put it: '... governments should support the generic, highest risk research activities which no single firm or group of firms will undertake alone because of the uncertainty of a financial return.'[47]

In recent years, however, fear of Japanese and, to a lesser extent, European industrial development and export success, led to demands for more interventionary policies in the high-technology sectors. Throughout the late 1980s and early 1990s, a plethora of Congressional, industrial and independent reports called for government action to protect key elements of the US technology base. Several of these brought into question the relevance and effectiveness of indirect support for US technological development via defence R&D and military programmes.[48] Even if most fell short of calling for direct intervention, many felt that the government should encourage a more positive climate for high-technology industries like aerospace, with measures such as the relaxation of anti-trust law in respect of domestic collaboration, the expansion of tax credits for R&D and the promotion of state-industry-academia partnerships along the lines of the EC Brite/Euram programme.[49] Underpinning all of these demands was the belief that the 'hands-off' approach to industrial development which may have served the US well enough in the past when the US market was expanding and US companies were less vulnerable to foreign competition, was no longer valid for a more competitive environment.

The arrival of President Clinton, with his promise to revitalise US high technology and to implement a more interventionist industry policy, saw a speedy commitment to increase Federal resources for commercial aeronautical research. In February 1993, the President unveiled a $16.5 billion national technology investment plan which would be directed at improving the US civil technology base. Aerospace, and civil aeronautics in particular, are to receive a substantial share of this new funding for R&TA and improvements in the national research infrastructure.[50] NASA's 1994 budget proposals contained a significant shift of priorities away from space programmes towards the aeronautical sector. Around 10 per cent of the NASA request - $1.55 billion - was allocated to aeronautics - an increase of $450 million over the 1993 figure. In particular, research in support of an advanced SST was increased by 50 per cent to $187.2 million. Spending on advanced sub-sonic technology was planned to rise from $195 million to $267 million. President Clinton was also more sympathetic towards providing Federal help for defence conversion and diversification activities. More money was pledged to NASA aeronautics research programmes and to the continuing improvement of US research infrastructure.[51]

President Clinton was also prepared to act on behalf of the aerospace industry in major sales campaigns, for example intervening with King Fahd of Saudi Arabia to encourage the purchase of either Boeing or MDC airliners for the national airline. This action, a Presidential spokesman said, 'shows that finally government and business understand that they have a partnership in the worldwide economy.'[52] In the future, therefore, the US government is unlikely to remain a distant partner in aerospace development but might adopt a more overtly interventionist policy the better to resist European and Japanese industrial pressure.[53] The new Administration has accepted the arguments that high technology and the trade in high value manufacturing products cannot be left entirely to a free market.

Government and civil aerospace

The support afforded civil programmes constitutes a special case of government involvement in aerospace. Commercial aircraft have rarely been profitable and without state-aid, few firms outside the US would have been able to stay in the business or have had any realistic chance of entering it. The avowed aims of such support have been the importance of maintaining counter-cyclical civil business in a predominantly military industry, employment, technology generation, balance of payments advantages and prestige. In recent years, the fear of a US oligopoly on airliner prices has also been cited as a reason for aiding civil programmes.[54] On the other hand, state-aid can distort the market by significantly reducing the risk faced by companies in launching civil projects. Government support - or the belief that *in extremis* a company will be bailed out if it gets into financial difficulties - may encourage the acceptance of a level of risk which no commercially-driven firm would accept.[55]

Government support for civil aerospace development

Direct support policies for civil aerospace development vary from state to state, but the general principles are much the same: the government provides launch capital for non-recurring development costs which is repaid from levies or royalties on the sale of aircraft or engines. A few states, such as France, may also extend launch aid to the development of other major systems and components. The terms of repayment will differ, but generally they will be more generous than the cost of raising capital from commercial sources. Some governments may help with production financing and other aspects of recurring costs, usually by guaranteeing loans. Most, including the US, have export financing systems which help to support foreign sales. As we have noted above, state-owned firms may also receive equity infusions to help pay for civil programmes and, in some cases, debts may be 'forgiven'.

Immediately after the Second World War, both the British and French governments adopted policies aimed at re-establishing a civil capability. Prototypes were built under government contract and national airlines were compelled, or put under strong pressure, to 'fly the flag'. The results were mixed. Britain developed the first jet and turboprop airliners. France launched the first economic medium-haul jet airliner. But with few exceptions, commercial success largely eluded both countries. This was due partly to design failings, accidents and, according to the French, deliberate obstructionism in the US market. Together, the French and British built the Concorde SST which cost over $6 billion and were sold in tiny numbers to the two national airlines. Germany and Japan also funded small civil airliners in the 1960s, also with little commercial success.[56]

In the UK, current launch aid policy requires firms to carry a substantial part of the development risk. In recent years, government assistance has been limited to no more than 60 per cent of non-recurring costs and, since the late 1970s, levies have been paid by UK companies for work done at state research facilities in support of specific civil projects. Forced purchases (or even strong encouragement to 'fly the flag') by British airlines ceased in the 1970s. Launch aid is generally repaid from a levy on sales, although in the case of aid to BAe for the Airbus A320, repayment terms were more stringent and had to be re-paid from corporate profits. The French government provided up to 90 per cent of the development costs of some Airbus types and initial costs of the CFM-56 engine, although subsequent models received less. The French government has also provided credits and capital equity to support civil production. The German government has funded civil aircraft through budgetary allocations and has guaranteed loans to cover production costs. In the case of Airbus, most of the latter were written-off when MBB was bought by Daimler. Daimler also negotiated an exchange rate guarantee to cover part of its dollar risk up to 1999. Finally, Fokker has had access to a 'rolling' fund for civil development, to be repaid with interest through royalties on sales.[57]

The Japanese government has supported civil programmes with a mixture of research funding and launch aid since 1952. For example, MITI provided 54 per cent of the funding for the YS-11, and provided launch aid to cover half of the cost of the Japanese contribution to the 767. The specific formulae governing aid have varied over the years, but since 1986, the Japanese Development Bank has lent up to 50 per cent of the cost of aircraft projects to industry with the interest rates directly subsidised by MITI to be reclaimed through royalties on sales. Up to the mid 1990s royalties had only been paid on the 767 investment, returning about 66 per cent of the original loan. These loans are not guaranteed, but if this system ran into severe difficulty it is unlikely that MITI would force Japanese firms to repay the loan in full.[58]

The US position on direct government aid for civil programmes stands in stark contrast to practice throughout much of the rest of the aerospace community. In the US, support for commercial aircraft has been provided primarily through spin-offs from other programmes rather than 'directly or with the intent of improving competitiveness'.[59] In the 1960s and 1970s, the US was able to dismiss the European habit of supporting commercially unsuccessful civil programmes as a costly aberration.[60] However, US attitudes have changed thanks to the success of the European Airbus and the threat it posed to the US domination of large civil airliner markets. The Europeans have not contested that fact that they provide direct aid for civil development in general and for the Airbus in particular. However, they have argued that this has only balanced the indirect help afforded to US civil manufacturers. This has included the technical links between US civil and military programmes, the general level of defence spending and specific NASA programmes which have helped US civil aerospace.

Although European companies have had a similar cushion from defence spending, US spending has, of course, been far larger in total and not spread across several countries. US military requirements and R&D have also favoured the development of large airframes and high power aero-engines, all of which have provided substantial assistance to the commercial sector. The scale of US defence activity, and the cash-flow it generated, was of considerable benefit to US civil development.[61] A steady source of income, even if at a relatively low level of profitability improved the credit rating of US aerospace companies in the commercial money markets. For example, MDC's ability to ride out a series of unprofitable civil programmes was considerably helped by two decades of uninterrupted success as a defence contractor. A timely order for a military version of the DC-10, the KC-10, also enabled MDC to keep its civil production line open and to facilitate the development of a more advanced derivative, the MD-11 - help which saved MDC 75 per cent of the cost of developing the MD-11.[62] Other benefits, either direct or generic, have stemmed from work performed under

DARPA contract and other DoD-funded research activity such as MANTECH, a \$2 billion programme investigating advanced manufacturing technologies.[63]

In recent years, the value of defence-related R&D as a basis for civil programmes has tended to diminish. The linkages between defence and civil aerospace technology have become increasingly difficult to pinpoint. Although they are still important, particularly in the engine sector and in some areas of aircraft equipment, there has been a steady divergence between the demands of civil and military aerospace technology. Moreover, in some areas - mainly in electronics - civil technology leads the military sector and consequently civil and military aircraft tend to derive greater benefit from the general stream of technological innovation than from dedicated military R&D programmes.[64] Equally significant, in the mid 1980s, the US defence business generally became decidedly less attractive. Defence contractors had to spend large sums of their own money on major defence contracts and the rate of return from defence programmes shrank markedly.[65] The DoD's insistence on a separation between civil and military activities, exacerbated by the increased use of highly classified, 'black' programmes, has also reduced the direct spin-off value of military work.[66]

Whatever the difficulties associated with DoD contracts, NASA research contracts have aided, and continue to assist the development of US civil programmes. Work on fundamental aerodynamics, high fuel efficient aero-engines and carbon-fibre structures has been supported by NASA contract. NASA facilities are heavily used by the commercial aircraft companies. As a result, US spending on basic aerospace R&D has not only been higher (just under \$1 billion in 1991) but crucially, more unified than comparable work funded by European governments in their national R&D programmes. NASA's research facilities are also more extensive and elaborate than any single European national or Japanese centre.[67] While NASA-funded research is in the public domain and has been accessible for all users, including foreigners, the publication of crucial findings can be delayed for a commercially significant period. Moreover, the US contractor obtains the 'hands-on' experience vital in translating research findings into commercial products. Finally, the US civil manufacturers have received substantial relief through the US tax system.[68] As Mowery and Rosenberg add, 'in this way, the federal programmes operate in a fashion that closely resembles the cooperative programmes in the Japanese economy'.[69] Finally, there have been instances of 'direct' public support for US civil programmes - even if not from the US government. MDC sought aid from US states hoping to be chosen for the site of a new MD-12 production facility and Boeing's Canadian factories have been eligible for provincial government industrial assistance.[70] By the same token, neither Boeing nor MDC objected to other governments providing aid for subcontract work on their aircraft.[71]

In the final analysis, the most important 'aid' available to the US commercial aircraft industry has been the role of the dollar in determining aerospace prices. The international airline industry works in dollars and buys its equipment in dollars. This has meant that European manufacturers have been obliged to carry an exchange risk largely absent in the US. The downward trend in the value of the dollar from the mid 1980s placed considerable pressure on the profitability of European programmes such as Airbus. As this would be difficult to counter without a major realignment of the international economy, direct aid by European governments to civil programmes has been justified as a counterweight to this structural advantage afforded to the US aerospace industry.[72]

The Airbus dispute

The difference in philosophy between the US and Europe in respect of government support for civil aerospace was brought into sharp focus by the success of the Airbus programme. The challenge to US industrial interests represented by the Airbus blossomed into a full scale trade dispute which threatened to disrupt the whole structure of trans-Atlantic aerospace relations. The publicly-funded Airbus was seen as a major threat to the US civil aerospace industry - a market distortion which had already helped to force one US firm (Lockheed) out of the civil sector and threatened to do the same to MDC; had unfairly reduced the profitability of Boeing and MDC airliners; and which increased the risk generally of launching new projects for US industry. As the Chairman of MDC put it, 'there is no more blatant example in the world today of a tax-supported entity engaged in unfair and predatory trade'.[73]

Initially, US objections to European support for civil aircraft centred on the misuse of export credits to finance aircraft and engine sales.   This was largely resolved by the so-called 'Commonline Agreement' of 1985.[74] By then, however, the issue had moved on to the direct question of launch aid and other direct supports for civil programmes. The turning point was the launch successively of the A320 and A330/340 which confirmed Airbus as a major contender in world markets and which threatened to overwhelm MDC as the weaker of the two remaining US firms. But even Boeing felt threatened by the possibility of Airbus launching a competitor to the 747 and has stated that the launch of the 777 was adversely affected by the government funded A330.

The formal GATT position, based on a 1979 agreement governing civil aircraft export credits, was decidedly unhelpful on the question of what constituted an 'unfair subsidy'. The Agreement states that:

> signatories agree that pricing of civil aircraft should be based on a reasonable expectation of recoupment of all costs, including non-recurring programme costs, identifiable and pro-rated costs of military research and development on aircraft components and systems that are subsequently applied to the production of such civil aircraft, average production costs and financial costs.[75]

Neither side was able to agree on what constitutes a 'reasonable expectation' of recoupment or satisfactorily to calculate the value of defence work. In the negotiations leading to the 1979 GATT agreement, the US tried and failed to outlaw launch aid, largely because the Europeans and others successfully argued that defence interests complicated any trade aspect and that state aid facilitated rather than undermined global competition. As a senior Airbus executive later asserted, 'Airbus stands today as the only recourse against the monopoly of the civil aerospace industry by US manufacturers.'[76]

The dispute was accompanied by an often bitter exchanges of propaganda, assertion and counter assertion. Both sides commissioned studies to 'prove' the perfidies of the other. In 1990, the US Commerce Department sponsored the Gelman Report, which outlined in considerable detail the nature and extent of European aid for Airbus - although some of the data referred in fact to total government aid to civil projects and not just to Airbus. Gelman confirmed that European governments had collectively invested over $13.5 billion in the Airbus family - a figure which, according to Gelman, should have been $25.9 billion if the money had attracted a commercial rate of interest (see Table 3.1). Although the Europeans claimed that the greater part of their investment had been, or would be repaid through sales levies, Gelman argued that much of the initial Airbus investment would have to be written-off. More contentiously, using data from unattributed US sources, Gelman claimed that even the latest Airbus projects such as the A320 and A330/340 would be unprofitable.[77]

The response to Gelman was a counter-blast from an EC-sponsored report by the US firm of Arnold & Porter, which claimed that between 1978 and 1987, MDC and Boeing had received more than $41.5 billion in direct and indirect subsidy from the US government. As we have noted earlier, support had come in the form of DoD and NASA contract awards, tax breaks, export incentives and independent R&D reimbursements. More important, Arnold & Porter's analysis challenged the argument that US firms had paid in

Launch Aid for Airbus Members *
($ billion)

	France	UK	Germany	All Airbus
Commitments	2.7	1.2	5.5	9.5
Disbursements	2.1	0.8	2.8	5.6
Value at Govt.	4.8	1.3	4.7	10.7
Value at Co.	9.6	1.3	7.1	18.0

* Figures include launch aid for non-Airbus projects.
Value at Govt. assumes government rates of interest over 10 years
Value at Co. assumes corporate prime rates

Table 3.1   Source: Gelman, derived from national data

full for any such aid through recoupment procedures.[78] Airbus Industrie's (AI) own response to Gelman noted that substantial sums were being repaid to the four governments through royalties - around $500 million in 1990 and likely to increase substantially through the 1990s. According to AI, if MDC had particular problems, these were as much to do with its own managerial and technical weakness as any 'predatory' competition from Airbus.[79]

As market conditions deteriorated during the early 1990s, American fears of a 'subsidised' attack on the US market share intensified. In addition to the question of development aids, there were some signs that sales 'inducements', which had been contained by the Commonline Agreement, had begun to reappear. Japanese customers were 'reminded' of their responsibilities to redress the US-Japan trade balance and Swissair bought Airbuses with a clear eye on its relations with the EC. The 1990 deal between Airbus (together with GE) and Northwest Airlines, where the airline received a $500 million loan to help secure an order for A320s, and the favourable leasing arrangement which Delta obtained from Airbus in 1992, were felt to be non-commercial inducements by Boeing and MDC. Airbus retorted that this was only a type of discounting practice which Boeing and MDC also used to win orders. However, with many US airlines in a parlous financial state, Airbus's apparent ability to raise cash to finance sales gave it a significant advantage and overall, Airbus was better placed to obtain credit than its American competitors, primarily because of the backing its partners were seen to have from their national governments.[80]

By 1991, talks between the US and the EC had reached a stalemate. The US had successfully challenged the German government's exchange rate guarantee to Daimler under the 1989 GATT agreement, but had failed to obtain a favourable ruling against the principle of European support for Airbus. The US side was prepared to concede the principal of launch aid, but wanted to 'cap' the extent of its application to 25 per cent of non-recurring costs. The Europeans would also have to abandon other forms of aid, including production credits and exchange rate guarantee schemes. In turn, the EC negotiators were willing to accept a limit to launch aid, but not less than 45 per cent. In addition, the EC wanted full 'transparency' of aid given to civil programmes through the US defence budget. There were also differences over what size of airliner was to be covered by the agreement: the US requested the ceiling on development support to apply to aircraft over 100, seats whereas the Europeans felt that this should remain at 150 seats, the threshold accepted by the 1989 GATT agreement. Failure to reach agreement triggered a second, more general complaint to GATT from the US. Even if it had been proven, GATT could only have demanded the cession of support for the Airbus, and could not have required repayment of past subsidies. But more seriously, as relations between the US and the EC deteriorated, the American government threatened to take unilateral action under its own domestic trade laws.[81]

The Airbus dispute with the US was further complicated by the EC's position in respect of subsidies towards industry in general, and towards small airliner development in particular. The Commission, encouraged by the Single European Act, sought to reduce the market distorting effects of national industrial subsidies. As a report from the Directorate responsible for encouraging aerospace development noted, the maintenance of 'free undistorted competition' was one of the 'cornerstones of the Community', and it was essential to have full transparency in public financing. On the other hand, while improved competitiveness in the aeronautics industry implied a progressive reduction in public support, 'the timing and the extent will depend on the efforts made by European industry's competitors.'[82] Projects such as the Airbus were regarded as special cases - in this instance, internal European competition in large airliners was clearly imposible. But the development of smaller civil aircraft where there were several European contenders was a different matter and the Commission has been forced to take a stand against the prospect of government-funded programmes competing with other European projects which did not attract state aid.[83]

The rest of the aerospace industry on both sides of the Atlantic tried to kept a low profile in the Airbus dispute. European and American engine and equipment firms supply both sides, and neither the Europeans nor the US would have benefited from a trade war with the imposition of tariffs depressing still further demand for airliners. For its part, Airbus Industrie had conceded that it would have to look for more commercial sources of launch capital and raised the $480 million needed for development of the A321 privately.[84] Airbus Industrie and its industrial partners recognised that in the future its programmes would have to be increasingly financed from revenue and by adding risk sharing partners to the team.

The April 1992 GATT Agreement

In the event, after another period of intense negotiations during the early spring of 1992, the two sides finally achieved a compromise agreement. Although there were hawks on both teams who seemed prepared to push matters to a break, neither side was willing to take aerospace trade into the unknown territory of a full-blown trade war.   Under the terms of the agreement reached in April 1993, direct development aid would be limited to 33 per cent of launch costs and indirect aid from agencies such as NASA and DARPA pegged at a ceiling of four per cent of a manufacturer's civil aircraft annual sales. There would also be new rules preventing inducements to buy airliners. The agreement will be monitored and details of current aids and future plans will be revealed at regular meetings between the two parties. Although the US admitted for the first time that indirect state aids do play a significant role in civil aircraft development, the Europeans made the more concessions.   In the absence of an integrated, European-wide civil aerospace R&D programme, the Americans would still have an edge afforded by NASA and DoD technological support. Moreover, they also retained the advantage of dollar pricing. The 1992 agreement left plenty of room for debate about the nature and value of indirect aids and governments would be allowed to 'suspend' the GATT provisions in the event of a major problem for a national supplier.   Further negotiations would also be needed to extend the new GATT regime to smaller airliners, aero-engines and state-aided sub contractors. This has entailed a broader format, with, for example, Canadian and Japanese participation.[85]

Reactions to the 1992 agreement were mixed. Many on the US side, including Boeing, felt that any agreement was better than none. There was some disappointment that the agreement only applied to future programmes. A number of European industrialists felt that the 33 per cent limit was dangerously low - 'peace was not worth this price' - and European aerospace would require a substantial increase in indirect assistance to compensate. By the same token, NASA was urged by US firms to spend more money on civil aeronautics to match increased European and Japanese activity. With some dissenters in Congress prepared to continue the fight, there is no guarantee that the accord will be an end to the Airbus subsidy dispute.[86] The 1993 agreement did not end sniping across the Atlantic: the US claimed that Airbus repayments had not been made or were not reflecting a market rate; the Europeans asserted in turn that the US is already in danger of violating the limit on indirect aid.[87] On balance, the US probably won more from the 1993 agreement than the Europeans. The 'cap' on launch aid will be far easier to monitor than ambiguous definitions of defence-related assistance. It will require Europeans to increase spending on basic R&D and, perhaps, to coordinate more effectively R&D activities at a European level.[88]

During a decade or more of dispute, the debate over Airbus subsidies often seemed like a dialogue of the deaf. Each side viewed the issue from a pungent combination of ideological principal and commercial vested interest. The Europeans had determined individually and collectively that they would challenge the US 'monopoly' in large civil aircraft. At heart, this was as much a political as an economic argument, based on long-term strategic interpretations of industrial activity. If this perspective ran counter to US preferences and politico-industrial philosophies, it was simply unfortunate. US 'arm twisting' was not going to sway European commitment to the Airbus. Nevertheless, European government support for civil aerospace cannot avoid questions about its long term validity. If support for the early Airbus types was justifiable under 'infant industry' arguments, after twenty years of aid extended to some of the largest European aerospace companies, enough may have been enough. As one Boeing spokesman put it , 'Airbus is 21 years old ... it is time for it to leave home'. However, Airbus had become something of a symbol of European industrial cooperation - a 'flagship EC industry'. According to Airbus chief Jean Pierson, the US could not expect to retain a guaranteed share of global sales, 'we want a more balanced redistribution of the world market in civil aircraft. This implies an acceptance of modifications to existing transatlantic trade relations.'[89]

In all the conflicts over state-aid and the promotion of aerospace technology - especially those involving the US and Europe - raw self interest has never been too far from the principled stands taken by both sides. There has been much hypocrisy here; the Europeans do subsidise - the Airbus would never have survived or prospered without it. That is the European edge. The US has the strength of the world's largest civil and military aerospace market and the benefit of dollar pricing. That is theirs. And, it should be noted, the US has directly subsidised commercial aerospace when important technological interests have been at stake. In the 1970s, for example, there was much embarrassment in Washington when an American company wanting to build a commercial satellite launcher charged Ariane with subsidised pricing, but NASA had to admit that it was boosting Shuttle launch prices even more flagrantly than the Europeans.

Aerospace in general and civil aerospace in particular, does not operate in a free market - it is unlikely ever to do so. As one respected aviation journal observed in respect of the Airbus dispute, 'the argument is unwinnable because the figures are indefinable'. The author went on to ask 'what is so evil about government funding anyway?'. No aerospace industry could exist without some form of state aid and the internationalisation of development has ensured that all recent civil aircraft receive government funds from somebody.[90] Although part of a dubious exchange of propaganda, the Gelman and Arnold & Porter reports have clearly shown the extent of state intervention in the aerospace sector. The real question is, perhaps, which of a range of policy instruments the state might most effectively use to promote its industry.[91] Nor should one expect the definition of effectiveness to be readily subject to quantifiable economic analysis; the interests at stake here are more often to be found in the subjective realms of political goals and generalised beliefs about the value of technological leadership.

4

The Defence Market

Introduction

Historically, the health of the world aerospace industry has depended on the level of defence spending. Few companies have made their living from the sale of civil aircraft and equipment alone. Even Boeing, which currently earns nearly two-thirds of its turnover from civil sales, has been (and still is) a major defence contractor. The bulk of industry R&D has been largely sustained by defence contracting and military programmes. In the early 1990s, the 'End of the Cold War', and pressures throughout the US and Western Europe for a 'Peace Dividend', began to have a profound effect on the structure and operations of defence/aerospace companies. Few of the prime contractors escaped job cuts and plant rationalisation. A surge in demand for civil aircraft and systems provided some compensation. Other opportunities were found in expanding space programmes and new defence technologies associated with arms control and verification.[1] But the sharp drop in defence requirements at the end of the 1980s precipitated a crisis of over-capacity and triggered structural upheaval throughout the world aerospace industry.

The defence aerospace sector was already facing problems: the Soviet Union's economic problems had already begun to hint of a slowing down in the arms race; defence budgets began to decline as a series of arms control measures took effect, and were under pressure; and several western governments also wanted to obtain greater value for money in defence procurement. Even without the unpheavals of the early 1990s, the defence business was growing tougher for aerospace firms. US and British defence/aerospace companies faced particularly stringent periods of procurement reform which, in the case of the US, had a profound effect on the financial health of many major companies. But other governments, including those of France and Germany, had to make their defence budget stretch further. In Europe generally, moves to open up hitherto tightly controlled domestic markets also implied changes

65

in the regional defence market.   Finally, the entry of second tier defence/aerospace firms threatened even more competition in world defence markets.

The defence market

The aerospace industry has always followed a 'boom and bust' pattern reflecting periods of heightened tension and detente (see Fig. 4.1).   Each of the two major wars this century marked a watershed in the expansion of the industry.   Military spending in World War One effectively transformed aviation from an enthusiast's eccentricity into an industry of considerable size and importance.

Defense Department Budget Authority, 1946-95–
Estimated
(in 1991 constant $ billions)

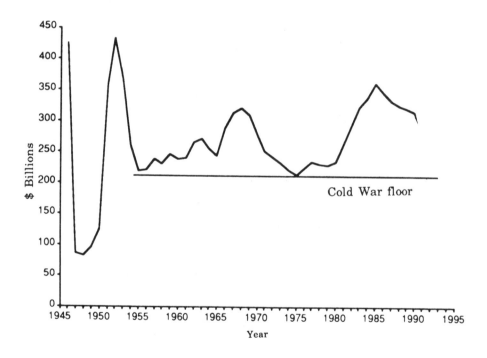

Figure 4.1   Source: Department of Defense, and Office
                                     Management and Budget, 1990

At the end of the war, rapid demobilisation brought immediate recession. During the inter-war period, defence contracting sustained the aircraft industries of Britain, France and the US, albeit at a much lower level. Rearmament and the Second World War again brought unprecedented rates of production and accelerated technological development. In 1945, demand again fell and industries contracted. But the onset of the Cold War, and particularly the Korean War, led to conditions of near permanent growth, while the arms race between the US-USSR sustained increasing levels of expenditure on R&D. Post-war regional tensions also generated a strong demand for defence exports.

Even during the Cold War period, there were cycles of higher demand and temporary recession. US defence expenditures fell during the early Eisenhower years to rise again during the Kennedy Administration and to peak during the Vietnam War. The trough following the end of Vietnam, in many respects, hit the US aerospace industry harder than the current recession. But overall, Superpower competition sustained long term commitments to R&D and a regular cycle of production. European countries experienced similar patterns of Cold War build-up and re-armament, followed by budgetary retrenchment. In the case of the UK, several military aerospace programmes were cancelled following the 1957 Defence White paper and the Defence reviews of the mid-1960s.

During the 1980s, although generally good years for the defence/aerospace industry, signs of deeper structural problems started to appear. In particular, concern over the rising inter-generational costs of weapons and the efficiency of defence industrial production began to fuel demands for procurement reform and to obtain more 'value-for-money' from defence spending. There was also a growing fear that ever higher unit costs would reduce orders to a point at which military effectiveness and production efficiency would be seriously threatened. For some states, particularly in Europe, international collaboration was a partial answer to the problem of rising development and unit costs. But changes in the context of defence were already hinting of tougher market conditions for defence manufactuers. Even before the collapse of Soviet Communism, the problems facing the USSR, and the pace of reform triggered by President Gorbachev, were such as to reduce the credibility of 'the Threat' and the need for Western states continually to arm themselves in response. Although world expenditure on arms touched $1 trillion in 1987, and while many governments marked time in the later part of the decade with a modest two per cent reduction in global expenditures, the rate of contraction began to accelerate in the early 1990s. But inititially, the first set of problems stemmed from changes closer to home -

governments wanting increased value for money in weapons procurement.

Procurement reform and the aerospace industry

As the aerospace industry's main customer, the state has inevitably had a major influence over its health and commercial viability. By changing the terms under which it does business, the state-as-customer can dramatically affect the risk and profitability of defence contracting. This relationship has been the source of tension and dispute for as long as aircraft companies have sold aeroplanes and equipment to the armed forces. The regular cry of 'fraud, waste and abuse' in the defence sector has often triggered demands for reform and for measures designed to squeeze greater efficiency from defence contractors. The heart of the problem is the extent to which defence companies should carry the risk of developing long-term, technologically advanced projects for a single, often fickle customer. In a commercial environment, the risk of any new investment is carried by the firm which is rewarded by a market-defined price for its products. Efficiency should be encouraged through competition. Defence procurement rarely has the characteristics of a free market; the customer, usually in collaboration with the supplier, sets specific demands and requirements which the contractor seeks to fulfil. Many are so exotic and customer-specific that there may be no other market for the product. The technological demands can be so great, the development risks so huge, and a return only possible over a very long term, that the state must carry the financial burden of development. By the same token, few companies, certainly within a single state, may be able to compete for the business. Such a system, with outcomes dependent on a mixture of negotiation and political influence, inevitably contains dangers of abuse and inefficiency. The trick is to find procedures which achieve a balance between these different pressures and needs. The difficulties in framing rules governing procurement have grown with the increased costs and complexity of weapons. No weapons acquisition system has yet been devised which can fully satisfy the competing demands of economic efficiency, technological complexity and political accountability.[2]

In the 1980s, another wave of reform began, as it often has, in the US; but the 'value-for-money' doctrine rapidly gained adherents in the UK and elsewhere. The underlying idea was to introduce a greater degree of competition and other 'free market' characteristics into the weapons acquisition process. This, in turn, would hopefully increase the efficiency of defence procurement and drive down costs. But the effect of procurement reform, certainly in the United States, precipitated a financial crisis which had a lasting impact on the defence-aerospace industry.

The United States

Weapons acquisition in the US has evolved into a highly complex, hugely bureaucratised and heavily politicised process. It has become a 'four-handed' game with players drawn from industry, the armed forces, political leadership and the Congress. Change has often coincided with the advent of a new Administration looking for a 'new broom' to sweep away real or imagined weaknesses in the system. Equally, Congress, representing the tax-payer, constituency interests and the industrial lobbyist, has rarely been able to resist the 'micro-management' of defence programmes under its budgetary control. Finally, bureaucratic pluralism and the persistent effects of inter-service rivalry, have further complicated the procurement system.

The latest phase in the cycle of US procurement reform began in 1984 with the Competition in Contracting Act. The 1984 Act followed a series of revelations about overcharging and programme failures during the Carter-Reagan defence build-up. Concern over the burgeoning Federal deficit and the need to pay for the Reagan defence programme led to further pressure for efficiency in procurement. Congress also intended to give Secretary of Defence, Casper Weinberger a political lesson; his refusal to negotiate over his defence budget had so outraged Congressional figures that many were determined to force him into 'exerting greater control over Pentagon operations'.[3] Inside the Pentagon, procurement reform was seized upon by some senior officials as a way of achieving ambitious service goals. In particular, Secretary of the Navy John Lehman wanted to finance substantial increases in force-levels as well as new, advanced technology weapons systems within tight budgetary limits. As a result, procurement reform affected naval aerospace with particular intensity, but the pressure to squeeze more out of the contractor base was felt throughout the industry.

This round of procurement reform had many detailed features, but overall the aim was to shift the balance of financial risk in large defence programmes from the Pentagon to the contractor. The main device was the competitive, fixed-price contract to be used even during the development phase of advanced technology weapons systems. Other devices, such as 'second sourcing' (competition for repeat production awards) were similarly designed to limit cost growth throughout the development and production cycle. Defence companies had to accept lower profit margins, stricter curbs on allowable overheads and less generous progress payments.

Contractors also faced more elaborate and consequently more costly demands from Pentagon and Congressional oversight procedures.⁴

These pressures were, of course, on top of the endemic problems of single-year funding and the annual battle for Congressional authorisation, changing military requirements and budget-driven programme 'stretch-outs'. The industry's ability to defend itself was undermined by the limited number of large programmes which the Pentagon could afford. The result was to force firms to assume greater risks in order to stay in the business and to accept 'teaming' for major development and production contracts. It is, perhaps, difficult to sympathise with an industry that had benefited from a massive rise in defence spending during the late 1970s and early 1980s, and whose reputation for inefficiency and ruthless lobbying was often justified. Nevertheless, during the late 1980s, defence contracting became an increasingly expensive and frustrating exercise. The US procurement process had always been more adversarial than is the case in Europe, but at times it appears that the two sides were fighting a bitter guerrilla war.

Competing for a diminishing number of contracts under this regime, drained corporate resources. The effort threatened to reduce independent spending on basic R&D. As one industrialist put it, 'eventually US industries will be spending as much competing for contracts as they do in developing new projects.'⁵ The Pentagon was also constrained to reduce production targets. Together with the possibility of cancellation, firms which were competing for new development contracts faced the prospect of much reduced returns from production, or none at all. In the case of very large and very important programmes such as the Advanced Tactical Fighter (ATF), both teams competing for the contract sank over a $1 billion in building the two prototypes. Even winning a contract like the ATF could prove to be a Pyrrhic victory. As a former ATF project manager put it: 'it's like gladiators in a ring fighting to the death and even the winners are thinking about how to recoup their investment'.⁶ Many companies opted out of major programme competitions because the risks were not justified by the potential return and by the fear that their R&D would be handed over to a 'second source' competitor. In the view of Grumman president John O'Brian, 'fixed price contracts and other Pentagon procurement changes are gradually liquidating military contractors. It's like lemmings heading to the sea'.⁷ But for the prime contractors, there was little alternative; they had to bid or face long term 'relegation' as design teams and watch production skills wither through lack of business.

Other changes in US company taxation rules ended deferrals on defence programmes which added several billions of dollars to the aerospace industry's tax liability. Investment in R&D competitions also led to increased borrowings as interest rates began to rise rapidly. The result was to add considerably to corporate debt burdens. Northrop's debts, largely incurred as result of the B-2 and other 'black programmes', rose from $65 million in the early 1980s to $1 billion in 1989. Similarly, over the same period, MDC's debt increased from $40.5 million to $2.3 billion. By 1990, the industry overall owed $6 billion in taxes alone and the Standard and Poors' Aerospace index showed a deterioration in corporate debt/equity ratio from 14 per cent to 37 per cent between 1983 and 1990 (see Table 4.1). Credit ratings for the defence sector plummeted which only served to raise their interest charges in order to compensate investors for the increased risk reflected in lower ratings.[8] As a result of these difficulties the defence/aerospace sector began to record huge losses. In 1989, three firms, Lockheed, Northrop and MDC, wrote-off $853 million on aircraft and associated systems under development for the Pentagon. According to AIAA figures, the profitability of defence programmes was cut by 23 per cent with commensurate impact on corporate cash-flow. [9]

The ATF programme exposed the limits of fixed-price contracting in the case of highly advanced programmes. It involved the concurrent development of several high risk technologies - a task made worse by the need to reconcile both USAF and USN requirements. This complicated the design task and immediately put additional pressure on the contractors bound by 'not to be exceeded' limits on weight and fly-away costs. The situation was recognised by DoD officials as impossible.[10] Many of the resulting difficulties were predictable and, in private at least, predicted. As one former USAF ATF programme director admitted:

> there were signals that we would be heading into projected moderate (defence budget) growth .... in hindsight, we perhaps should not have embraced the concept of firm, fixed price R&D contracts. But senior personalities were behind that type of contract and it was almost impossible to do anything else.[11]

By 1989, it was evident that the contractors were struggling to meet the programme's tough technical requirements and development schedule; both teams found it difficult to stay below the weight limit without significant performance losses. However, budgetary constraints forced the USAF to reduce some of its ambitious requirements and development schedules. Under further pressure from the ATF teams, the USAF also agreed to pay an additional $550 million for the 'Dem-Val' stage. The DoD also conceded that full-scale development and early production contracts would be based on a cost-plus-award fee contract.[12]

US Aerospace Companies Debts (1989)
($ millions)

Company	Equity	Long Term Debt	% Debt to Equity
Boeing	6,131	275	4
Gen. Dyn	2,126	906	43
Grumman	818	884	108
Lockheed	2,060	1,835	89
Martin Marrietta	1,355	477	35
McDonnell Doug.	3,994	2,597	88
Northrop	875	584	67
Raytheon	2,426	48	1
Rockwell	3,978	552	14
UTC	4,740	1,960	41

Table 4.1   Source: *Defense News   23 April 1990*

Contract conditions were improved for the winning ATF team
(led by Lockheed); under the terms of an eight year engineering and
manufacturing-development contract, they will earn four per cent
on every dollar spent on ATF (F-22) development. In addition, the
companies could earn up to nine per cent for exceeding contractual
targets.   As a result, the contractors were assured that future
development costs will be covered. As one Lockheed executive put it,
'this is a no risk contract....We're going to let the Air Force spend its
money this time...We've spent all the dollars we're going to spend'.[13]
The losers, of course, had to write off nearly $500 million on the
Dem-Val stage and the loss of important technological and market
opportunities. Total private investment in the ATF competition
amounted to over $1 billion.[14]

Moreover, there was no guarantee that the F-22 would be built
in sufficient numbers to produce a profit, nor, despite its
importance to the USAF, whether it would be produced at all.
Malcolm Currie of Hughes has argued that on a discounted cash-flow
basis, the successful team might never be able to break even, being
paid in de-valued mid 1990s dollars in return for investments it
made in 1980s money. As a senior GD executive recognised, 'from a
business standpoint, as far as a reasonable return on investment,
nobody is going to do business on the F-22; not the primes nor the
sub contractors'. The earliest anybody is likely to see a return on
the programme is well after the Year 2000. However, participation
in the programme was viewed as a strategic investment in new
technology.   Currie again saw this as the only reason for his

company to bid: '...if we didn't make it we would have been out of business. So it was very vital for us strategically to invest in that programme'.[15] But as a senior Pentagon official observed in 1988:

> to structure the competition so that the only way the contractors can compete is to put in all of this up-front money when, even if they win, they may end up with an empty bag is, I think, very questionable government practice. [16]

The LHX (later LH) Comanche programme was less problematic. The two teams (Boeing-Sikorsky and MDC-Bell) were again required to invest their own money in a fixed-price 'Dem-Val' competition. The original specification was also demanding in terms of both cost and performance requirements. But the US Army recognised early in the programme that fixed-price contracting had its limits and took steps to reduce the risk that the companies would incur huge losses as a result of entering the design competition. Originally, there was a temptation to take a risk on development commitments in order to secure the contract. In the event, the Army decided to ask for a 'reasonable' contribution to the risks and stated that unrealistically low bids would be rejected. The eventual award to Boeing-Sikorsky was based on a two-stage contract in which both sides would cover any extra costs or share any savings achieved during the prototype phase.[17]

The ATA (A-12) programme, on the other hand, was an unmitigated disaster. A winning team was selected in 1987 after a design competition involving GD, Northrop and Lockheed. All had the necessary stealth technology, but the Navy required them to team with companies experienced in carrier-qualified aircraft. Northrop, already developing the B-2 bomber under a 'black contract', teamed with Grumman and LTV, while GD linked up with MDC. This left Lockheed, builders of the F-117 Stealth bomber, out in the cold. Northrop's bid for full-scale development was close to the Navy's target, but the team refused to accept a fixed-price contract. MDC and GD, on the other hand, submitted a fixed-price bid $1 billion below Northrop's, and won the contract. This meant that the two most experienced stealth technology companies were excluded from ATA development. In the event, GD and MDC found that they had seriously underestimated the costs of building a stealth aircraft.[18]

As a 'black programme', details of the A-12's problems were slow to emerge. In March 1989, the USN reported that the programme was on schedule and progressing as expected. But by early 1990, the programme was reported to be a year behind target and nearly $1 billion over cost.[19] The ATA team offered to restructure the programme and to assume nearly $2 billion of a total cost overrun of over $3 billion; but in January 1991, Secretary of Defence Dick Cheney declared the contractors in default and terminated the programme, the largest cancellation in US procurement history. The DoD demanded repayment of nearly $2 billion in progress payments to the two contractors, but in order to stave off possible Chapter 11 bankruptcies (especially the financially weak MDC), these were deferred until 1992.[20]

The Navy was left without a desperately needed new attack aircraft and the two contractors faced a large hole in their finances and a big gap in future production. The ATA had been considered to be a relatively low risk project, but obsession with fixed price contracting and competition had left the two most experienced stealth companies on the sidelines. Given Northrop's later difficulties with the B-2 Stealth Bomber and Lockheed's management problems with the P-7 patrol aircraft, an alternative combination might not have fared much better. But the decision to choose the technically least experienced combination on the basis of low bid proved, in retrospect, to be a false and ill-judged economy.[21]

Fixed price-contract development could be appropriate if the level of risk involved was reasonable. Resulting problems were often due more to internal weaknesses and inefficiency than to over-stringent contracts. MDC, for example, underestimated the difficulty of converting an established design (the BAe Hawk) into the T-45 Naval trainer. The company's problems with both the T-45 and the C-17 tactical transport were compounded by poor management.[22] Lockheed's experience with the P-7A patrol aircraft, also cancelled for contractor default, was more ambiguous. In this case, all concerned again felt that the technical risks of the $600 million programme were low. Lockheed had developed the P-7A's predecessor, the P-3, and with between 30-40 per cent commonality between the two aircraft, the company regarded the P-7A as a relatively straight forward up-grade. However, Lockheed underestimated the complexity of the P-7A requirement and found that commonality proved to be less than four per cent. Lockheed fell steadily behind cost and delivery targets and the USN finally decided to end the programme, leaving Lockheed with a $300 million write-off. Ostensibly, the responsibility for the failure was Lockheed's, but the US Navy had again cheerfully accepted the Lockheed bid after a fierce competition and should bear some of the blame.[23]

Some of these cases (as well as other problems with cost-plus awards such as the B-2 bomber) exposed genuine and deep-seated management weaknesses in the US defence-aerospace industry. Nor can there be any excuse for corrupt practice in public procurement. As McNaugher puts it, 'that one firm was caught claiming the kennel fees for its president's pet dog suggests that the game needed a sharp corrective'.[24] A USAF report into Northrop's mismanagement of the B-2 and Tacit Rainbow programmes was a scathing indictment of contractor ineptitude. Pleading guilty to 34 counts of fraud for falsifying test data hardly helped its reputation, or that of the defence industry at large.[25] Significantly, the USAF's decision in favour of the Lockheed-Boeing-GD team for the ATF contract, was based partly on an assessment of management ability. According to one senior Pentagon official, the winning team's proposal offered 'a greater capability to execute this programme successfully than we judged was the case with the other alternatives'.[26] Large, politically well-connected companies choosing freely to take on impossible targets should not necessarily complain about the terms of the contracts they accept. Past evidence of contract-padding and excessive profits should also limit one's sympathies for their plight. But the fixed price contract and winner-take-all competitive regime that dominated the 1980s, often left firms with few options but to 'tender or die'. In a situation where the Pentagon fixed the ground rules for competitive, fixed-price tendering it had to assume some of the responsibility for the resulting mess.

Procurement reform, and the disciplines it engendered, did force the US defence and aerospace industries to put their own house in order. The 'great engine war' between GE and P&W may not have produced large cost savings for the Pentagon, but it galvanised a complacent P&W into much needed managerial and technical changes.[27] MDC's 'second-source' bid for Tomahawk production had a similar affect on GD. The widespread introduction of new management techniques, often derived from Japanese commercial practice emphasising cost and quality control, was another sign that procurement reform and budget stringency had had a salutary effect on attitudes within the US aerospace industry.[28]

By the early 1990s, there was a widespread feeling throughout the US defence and aerospace industries that the relationship with both government and Congress had become too adversarial. Many firms believed that the DoD had used their money to solve its budgetary problems and that they had carried too much of the blame for past blunders and mistaken defence requirements. Procurement officials admitted that many of the reforms had been adopted without due regard for their long term consequences and against the better judgement of full-time programme managers. As one official put it, it was a 'meat-axe approach to management' with no regard for either the complexities of developing high-technology weapons or for the broader health of the US defence industrial base. Objective analysis demonstrated, in some cases, that competition and second sourcing had even increased procurement costs.[29] If firms were forced out of the business by the high cost of defence work, the scope for future domestic competition would steadily diminish. It could

also lead to the loss of important technological assets.[30] GD's Chuck
Volmer summarised the problem in these terms:

> Never has competition been endorsed by so many in the defence
> procurement community, but never have the trends been so averse
> to this principle.   The high cost of competition is reducing the
> number of viable competitors in all sectors of the defence industrial
> base.   Cost consciousness is forcing firms away from technological
> risk toward evolutionary product improvements.   The competitive
> trends point in the direction of a loss of US technological
> superiority.   The US cannot compete on cost alone.   Technology is
> the grist of competition.[31]

The advent of the Bush Administration led to some relaxation in
the pace of reform.   Donald Atwood, the DoD's new procurement
chief, recognised that the 'poisonous atmosphere' in Pentagon-
Congress-Industry relations had to be improved: 'if AT&T, Ford or
General Motors had the kind of relationship with their suppliers
that we (have) with ours, they'd be out of business'.[32] Atwood and
other Pentagon officials accepted that steps had to be taken to protect
the US DIB. He held out the prospect of greater stability for long
term programmes and less 'micro-management', with its continual
and expensive audit requirements. Atwood also conceded the need to
restore a proper balance between risk and reward in defence
contracting.[33]

More generally, the DoD began to appreciate the long term
dangers of over zealous procurement reform. As one official put it
'we're the only game in town.   If we do something that's not fair, it
very hard for aerospace companies to walk away.   Our leverage is
enormous.   We must be fair because of that leverage'. Competition
was important, but the Pentagon should not force firms into taking
unnecessary risks: 'when they start hurting very much, they don't
do as good a job for us, they cut corners wherever they can ... It
doesn't work to our favour or to theirs when these big overrun
situations occur'.[34]

The new approach was signalled in a 1990 DoD memorandum,
'fixed price contracts will not disappear, but they will have to be
used in the right order.   When risks depend on execution as opposed
to creation, then fixed price may be perfectly appropriate'.   This
was a crucial distinction; where a contractor had to extend the
frontiers of technology, and where the risk of failure was high,
fixed price contracting was asking for trouble. Production, or more
modest development programmes, on the other hand, should be more
predictable and were thus more suited to stringent contractual
obligations. Furthermore, Atwood recognised that if the risk for the

contractor was high, progress payments and opportunities to make a satisfactory profit had to be commensurately generous.[35]

As a result of the change in policy the number of major fixed price awards dropped and several second source competitions were abandoned.[36] However, some equipment firms were still expected to perform quite advanced development work under fixed-price contracts. More important, the new rules applied only to government contracts and not to subcontracts issued by the primes. In many instances, the responsibility for cost control was passed down the supplier chain to firms less able to sustain the costs and risks of fixed price development. As a result, many of these companies began to avoid defence work unless the job called for a well established product where the risks were more predictable.[37] The era of procurement reform has also left a messy legacy of litigation as firms such as Northrop and MDC have challenged DoD default decisions and the extent of their corporate liability under fixed-price contracts.[38]

Some have continued to argue that the industry still needs lessons in commercial risk-taking. John Lehman felt that defence firms did not have the attitudes and the procedures to cope with a commercially orientated procurement system: 'the moans you hear from industry in the past few years are the moans of people facing up to the free enterprise system'. Cost-plus regimes provided no incentive for efficiency and the old weapons procurement heritage blinded some companies to danger: 'they don't have a culture of managing to cost'. Similarly, in 1991, Eleanor Spector, a senior DoD procurement official, blamed 'dismal management' for MDC's continuing problems.[39] On the other hand, the pressure did force several firms to re-think their entire management system, with increased emphasis on quality and cost-control.

In any event, over a decade of procurement reform has left the US defence-aerospace industry in a poor state. During the early 1990s, the profitability of US firms fell faster than those in Europe, a phenomenon largely attributed to the effects of fixed-price contracting. This was especially so for the airframe companies. As systems integrators, their margins were lower than, for example, missile companies, and were also more vulnerable to cost overuns and write-offs.[40] As Ken Kresa of Northrop put it, 'we're now seeing the projections come true that we saw coming when some of these bad contracts were set up that could not be effectively handled...We have to get those programmes flushed out of the system before we can put a strong industry back in place'.[41] Quite apart from the immediate impact of R&D write-offs on corporate finances, several industry spokesmen deprecated the increasingly defensive attitude towards R&D commitments. US aerospace companies felt that the cycle of reform was turning once

more in their direction.   But there was a good chance that several
major contractors might not survive the effects of past decisions.
Those that could weather the storm with new technologies and
products should recover.   As Bill Anders, head of GD put it, 'the
winners will emerge stronger than now, the weaker ones will fall
by the wayside'.[42]   Similarly, the move announced in 1992 to focus
future procurement on 'technology on the shelf' strategies, might
exacerbate rather than improve the position of US defence-
aerospace contractors.[43]

The uncertainty affecting the future of defence procurement in
the US continued with the election of President Clinton.   By the
spring of 1993, no major change had been made to the procurement
system, but the overhang of mistakes, misjudgements and pressured
decisions made in the 1980s, continued to have a deleterious impact
on the performance of the major contractors.   On the other hand,
the new Administration did adopt a more sympathetic attitude
towards high technology industries such as defence and presented
measures designed to help firms diversify out of defence production.
Most of the major defence contractors had also been galvanised into
taking steps to improve their own productivity and efficiency.[44]
Although a major review of defence needs by the new Secretary of
Defence, Les Aspin, proved to be less damaging than feared to US
military aerospace, President Clinton's determination to rein back
defence spending during the late 1990s will cast a cloud over US
defence aerospace firms.[45]

Procurement reform in Europe

The relationship between customer and contractor in European
defence procurement has usually been less adversarial than in the
US.   This was due in part to the closer association between defence
and industrial policies and a higher degree of concentration in the
defence industrial sector which has made domestic competition less
feasible.   The growth of international collaboration has also
complicated the management and administration of large defence
programmes, reducing the impact of individual procurement
regimes.   However,   problems of cost escalation and technical
failure have also dogged European weapons programmes and there
have been a number of cases of fraud and malfeasance.[46] In recent
years, the rising costs of weapons development and the need to make
the defence budget stretch ever further to meet commitments,
prompted a closer examination of defence contracting.   None have
gone as far down the road as the Pentagon in seeking competition or
in the application of fixed price contracting, but similar principles
were increasingly applied to weapons programmes.

The British government led by Mrs Thatcher, was amongst the pioneers in using procurement reform to obtain greater 'value-for-money' in defence procurement. The Thatcher administration was ideologically inclined towards 'good housekeeping' in government, but the inherited crisis over the Nimrod AEW aircraft helped to fuel the Prime Minister's determination to 'sort out' the defence industry. Responsibility for the problems affecting the Nimrod was disputed between the UK MoD and GEC, the contractor responsible for the radar and systems integration, but neither side managed the affair with distinction. Although greatly over cost and with a doubtful technical prognosis, termination was still felt to be out of the question on defence industrial grounds. However, its cancellation in favour of the US AWACS was widely seen as a warning *pour encourager les autres*, and a signal that under certain circumstances the UK would buy even a major weapon system from abroad if there was no cost-effective alternative.[47]

The appointment of Peter (later Sir Peter) Levene of United Scientific, to head the MoD Procurement Executive, was a clear case of setting a poacher to act as gamekeeper. His brief was to bring a 'more commercially minded' approach to the Procurement Executive, and was enshrined in the 1982 report on *Value for Money in Defence Procurement*. Competition was identified as the key dynamic which would structure procurement policy. During his period in office, the number and value of competitive awards increased markedly. Cost-plus contracts were rejected for all but the most risky and uncertain types of development work, although even here, companies would be expected to negotiate incentives. Where possible, existing cost-plus contracts were re-negotiated.[48]

In general, the British fell short of applying the same kind of stringent competitive framework as had the Americans during the same period. This reflected the facts of British and European national defence industrial life: the scope for competition amongst aerospace primes was very limited. BAe dominated the combat aircraft and missile airframe business and Rolls-Royce was the sole supplier of high performance aero-engines. To some extent, the government also accepted some responsibility to defend British 'national champions' in collaborative programmes. However, the MoD made it clear that it rejected any overt and generalised commitment to the protection of the national DIB and frequently stressed the importance of maintaining an arms-length relationship with UK contractors.

The main impact of UK policy was on the avionics and defence electronics sector. The UK had a unparalleled range of electronics suppliers and the government could act to maintain existing competition through the application of British anti-trust law, as well as by encouraging new firms to enter specialised markets.

The government also sought to foster competition for key equipment contracts in European collaborative projects. However, the presence of European 'national champions' tended to nullify real competition for all but the British participants. But with the continuing consolidation of both the British and the European electronics industry, the British government had to accept that scope for domestic competition would narrow over time.

The British government also began to encourage more open international, or at least intra-European competition. Practical politics ensured that the British market would not be thrown open in advance of comparable concessions in Europe or the US, but the Nimrod and other high profile overseas purchases rammed home the prospect of a less protected British home market. The Thatcher government encouraged the development of *contra achats* deals with France and other arrangements with European countries to make bidding easier for domestic contracts. It also led moves to encourage a more open defence market within NATO's Eurogroup. As Levene noted, 'we can't expect more competition within the country but, seen from a wider perspective, competition will increase between countries.'[49]

Although the impact of procurement reform on the UK was less radical than in the US, British defence/aerospace firms complained that the policy, combined with a general neglect of R&D funding, undermined their global competitive position and placed them at a disadvantage compared to their European and US counterparts.[50] The electronics sector again led the pack. From its perspective, the very strength of British industry had been based on previous generations of government supported R&D. Fixed-price, competitive contracting had eaten into this 'seed corn.' Even the larger contractors expressed their concern at the neglect of broader-based R&D. The electronics industry was also worried that competitive bidding could leave the UK industry increasingly vulnerable to foreign ownership, with a possible loss of technological autonomy.[51]

Nevertheless, Sir Peter Levene was able to assert that greater competition at home had forced British companies to become more effective and sharper in international markets.[52] The changes in the procurement process had delivered a shock to UK companies by underlining the fact that defence was a shrinking market in which 'no one had a birthright to a contract'. Levene also felt that the new system, with its concept of 'cardinal points' specifications, had given defence contractors more freedom to run their own programmes. The MoD PE would still need to monitor performance, but this would be 'eyes, not hands on'. On his retirement from the Procurement executive in 1991, Levene believed that procurement had become more efficient: 'after six years, we looked at all our contracts over £100 million and saw that they were all under budget and on time. Those that weren't were not going to cost us any money.'[53]

In 1991, the UK National Audit Office reported that competitive tendering had led to savings of nearly 70 per cent on some projects, and the proportion of fixed price contracts had risen from 36 per cent in the early 1980s to 67 per cent in 1989-90. The role of cost plus awards had also shrunk, falling in value over the same period from 16 per cent to four per cent.[54] On the other hand, the much vaunted competition for a new RAF trainer which had been won by the Embraer/Shorts Tucano proved less successful. As the UK Parliamentary report observed, it was 'not an example we wish to see emulated'. Problems in adapting the Tucano for RAF use had led to substantial overruns for which, in theory, the nationalised Shorts was liable. These were, however, absorbed in the debt-write off which accompanied Shorts' sale to the Canadian firm Bombardier. This provision effectively wiped out the notional £60 million the government had saved in the original competition. According to the House of Commons Defence Committee, 'the Tucano programme shows that a firm or fixed price driven down by iterative tendering is not necessarily in the MoD's interests if it jeopardises the successful completion of an equipment programme'.[55]

In practice, even closely controlled applications of full fixed price contracting and complex technological development underlined the need for a strong capital base. This again favoured the big battalions such as GEC and BAe. As one senior BAe executive put it, 'defence margins have been reduced as the competition policy of the UK government has worked. We have to put more of our own money in to trigger programmes'.[56] In 1991, for example, Westland was in danger of losing responsibility for EH101 avionics integration to a BAe/GEC partnership because it lacked the financial resources to take on the strict fixed price contract demanded by the MoD. The Ministry evidently required a minimum of £100 million in cash reserves to cover any cost escalation. In order to compete effectively against the BAe/GEC combination, Westland had to team with IBM.[57]

The EH-101 contract presented the British government with a dilemma. Awarding it to BAe/GEC - the two largest UK defence/aerospace companies - would further concentrate the UK defence industrial base. But the alternative again raised the question of foreign control over an important defence technology. From one perspective, this would continue the logic of competition - that national barriers would have to go if declining defence budgets were to cover military commitments. From another, while this may well be the future for the defence sector, Britain could not afford to do it unilaterally without incurring the risk of losing its

competitive edge in European and world markets. In the event, the
contract went to the Westland/IBM team which, according to the
MoD, offered the better 'value-for-money'. The contract was a £1.5
billion fixed price contract which was clearly designed to insure
that industry carried the greater part of any risk. For its part, IBM
was confident that it had done its sums correctly and had weighed up
the balance of technological uncertainty against potential profits;
'the government is buying IBM risk and management'. From
Westland's perspective, the alternative would have been to have lost
a key contract and the prospect of staying in the high-value systems
integration business.[58]

The rest of Europe was slower to introduce more stringent forms
of contracting. This was due partly to the continuing influence of
more explicit links between defence procurement and national
industry and technology policies. But by the late 1980s, even the
French government faced problems in matching resources to
defence commitments and was looking to increase efficiency in
procurement. The cost of developing the Rafale fighter, for
example, was a huge drain on defence resources - described by one
French parliamentary report as a 'bottomless pit for billions'. In
1991, the Rafale programme was hit by budget problems, forcing
the cancellation of one prototype.[59] As a result, defence-aerospace
companies - even those in the public sector - had to assume a
larger proportion of funding for R&D and accept tighter contractual
terms. The French government required Dassault and other
important Rafale contractors to carry 25 per cent of the
development risk.[60] The Swedish government employed fixed-price
contracts to develop the Grippen, and the contract team suffered
large losses as a result.[61]

The pressure for greater value for money in procurement was
also extended to international programmes. Companies working on
both the EFA and the PAH-2 Tiger were required to work within
price ceilings during the development phases and under fixed price
contracts for production. In the case of the EFA, German
procurement and industry officials had to be prodded hard by the
British. But the vulnerability of EFA to domestic political criticism
helped to overcome German reluctance to abandon the protection and
comfort of cost plus contracting.[62] Both the Tiger and EFA offered
some contracts for competitive tendering between international
consortia, although this was largely nullified by rationalisation and
the need to maintain *juste retour* within work sharing agreements.[63]
This problem was highlighted by the UK House of Commons Defence
Committee which noted that in the case of EFA lower price bids from
British firms for equipment sub contracts might be over-ruled by
the need to redress imbalances in work-sharing. Even the British

MoD was willing to pay 'a little more' in order to maximise British industry participation in as many technology areas as possible.[64]

For its part, as the EH-101 award confirmed, the British government showed few signs of relaxing its search for value for money in procurement. The clear identification of a prime contractor would facilitate clearer lines of accountability and responsibility for over-spend.[65] Levene himself, when asked about US recantation of fixed price contracting, argued that 'we're right and they are wrong'.[66] Nor was his successor, Dr Malcolm McIntosh, to be diverted by pleas from defence companies under pressure: 'defence contractors will simply have to adapt to the way markets and the structure of industry in general are changing. And I think many of them are starting to do that in a quite realistic way, but it will be painful'. McIntosh believed that companies had to seek their own salvation through rationalisation and collaboration.[67] Other officials felt that the changes had forced the UK defence-aerospace industry into becoming one of the most efficient in the world.[68]

On the other hand, the British defence industry lobbied hard to show how the government was failing to recognise the long term dangers posed by falling budgets and tighter controls on margins in defence contracting. Their complaints were not intended as a lament for the days of 'cost-plus' contracting, but to warn of the erosion of technology and the loss of export sales which would follow from a narrow, short term policy designed only to maximise returns to the Treasury.[69] British firms contended that they faced extra pressure to compete for domestic and collaborative business while their European colleagues were still protected by government policies. By 1992, with the general level of defence spending falling fast, the British MoD began to modify its position. While retaining the general principles of value-for-money, ministers and officials began to stress the importance of a partnership between customer and contractor. A number of measures were announced designed to help the UK defence industry maintain its technology base. But this was seen by the defence industry as only a start in the process of re-building relations between the Defence Ministry and its major contractors and, in the short term, it would not ease their situation.[70]

In general, the Anglo-Saxon countries, with governments committed to non-interventionist industrial policies, saw the most stringent applications of procurement reforms. Neither the French nor the German governments went to the lengths which the Reagan-Bush or Thatcher Administrations pursued to squeeze efficiency gains from their defence contractors. The Japanese also maintained a pro-industry approach to defence procurement during this period.[71] These differences reflected distinct ideological differences between governments with clear views on the wider strategic value of the defence sector and those whose first instinct was to trust the market.   The   aerospace industry unquestionably possessed the inefficiencies and complacent managerial attitudes born of Cold War defence spending, but some of the changes imposed by the US and UK governments during the 1980s smacked of throwing the baby out with the bath water.

Aerospace and the 'Peace Dividend'

The early 1990s saw the end of Communist control throughout Eastern and Central Europe, the fall of the Berlin Wall and German re-unification. Even before the dramatic events of 1991, the thaw in East-West relations and the likelihood of disengagement had already raised hopes of a 'Peace Dividend' - a wholesale shift in national priorities amongst the hitherto hostile states towards less spending on arms of all types.   The break-through in regional nuclear arms control brought by the 1987 INF treaty was followed by the Conventional Arms Control in Europe (CFE) agreements and by progress in strategic nuclear arms reduction culminating in the START treaty of 1991. All of these agreements pointed the way to a much reduced need for military aerospace products. The subsequent winding up of the Warsaw Pact and the retreat of much of Soviet military power removed much of the immediate threat to Western security. Even nationalist turbulence and political instability in East Europe, the Balkans and the Soviet Union itself, had little impact on the trend towards lower defence expenditure.

The Gulf War of 1991 was a reminder that there could still be more generalised threats to security and world peace, but their impact on the downward drift in defence spending was limited. The Gulf conflict reinforced the need for weapons capable of sustaining 'out of area' commitments which could cap the extent of the 'peace dividend'. The prospect of missile technology and warheads of mass destruction becoming more readily available further indicated the potential of sophisticated tactical missile defence systems. More extensive and elaborate arms control also brought a need for verification technologies. Finally, there was the prospect that the possibility of violence in East and Central Europe could lead to renewed military tension in Europe. In such cases, continued vigilance remained a prudent policy for western government, necessitating the maintenance of high-technology defence capabilities.

But overall, the end of the Cold War removed much of the driving force behind post-1945 defence development. As a 1991 Deutsche Bank report put it, 'the 'peace dividend' is not a hollow phrase, but a real possibility'. Such a dividend would not be immediate, nor wholly available for alternative public needs. The transition would inevitably entail costs associated with the disposal of unwanted weapons, expenditure on new technologies of verification and the 'social adjustment' costs of armed forces and defence industries converting to a less militarised future. But the new conditions meant that each member of the NATO alliance could begin to reduce defence expenditures without adversely affecting national security.[72]

National responses

The United States

Any move to secure a 'peace dividend' was bound to have serious implications for the US aerospace industry. The DoD was the industry's most important customer and the health of most of the major US aerospace companies largely depended upon the level of domestic defence expenditure. Domestic sales comprised the greater part of the industry's turnover; compared to the largest European manufacturers, where exports accounted for over 60 per cent of sales, US aerospace companies commonly sold less than a quarter of their output abroad.[73] Defence spending in the US has also been under pressure from policies designed to reduce the huge Federal deficit. Total US defence expenditure for FY1991 amounted to $300 billion and supported about 26 million jobs in the US defence industry. But defence spending had been falling in real terms for the five years between 1985 and 1990. FY92 proposals continued the downward trend, posting the lowest request since 1985. President Bush's 1992 State of the Union message announced a five year reduction of 20 per cent in the US defence budget. Several programmes, such as the small ICBM and the B-2, were either reduced in number or cancelled outright. The election of President Clinton brought little respite: although more sympathetic to industrial needs, the need to cut the deficit as well as new set of domestic priorities continued the attack on defence spending. The Aspin review published in September 1993 was less drastic than expected, but planned reductions in defence expenditure will mean that by 1996 the US should be spending less on defence as a proportion of GNP than in any year since 1939. By 1996, the defence budget is expected to be below 22 per cent of total Federal Expenditure, its lowest share since 1940.[74]

Although the aerospace industry conceded that change was inevitable in the 'post Cold War' era, many industrialists argued that this had to be set against a broad review of US strategic objectives and defence equipment needs. This would have to encompass wider defence industrial and technological questions.

Companies needed some idea of future requirements to make the necessary adjustments and capital investments, including rational decisions to downsize if that was inevitable.[75] As the pressure to generate large savings grew, a key issue was the extent to which investment in new technology should take priority over production. During 1990-91, several long-running production programmes were cut to make room for new projects. A more radical suggestion was to move towards an R&D-based procurement process, with new technology developed as far as the prototype stage and, unless there was an obvious need for production, 'put on the shelf'. This approach this would seem to save money, but industry argued that separating development from production would be a false economy. It would lead to the dispersal of key production skills and would retard the development of new cost saving process technologies, as well as certainly requiring an enhanced commitment to defence R&D. Defence contractors would also need financial incentives to maintain design teams and integration skills without the promise of 'gravy' from production contracts.[76]

The downturn in demand for defence equipment had a dramatic impact on the major US aerospace companies. The reduction in demand threatened to trigger a large-scale rationalisation of aerospace primes, with a commensurate impact on the subcontractor base. During 1990-2, all of the major US aerospace companies announced large job cuts, with 45,000 in the first nine months of 1990 alone.   LTV announced 1,500 redundancies associated with cuts to B-2 production and Boeing declared 8,000 job losses from its defence divisions. But overall during the 1980s, employment in the industry, which peaked at 1.3 million in 1987, at the height of the Reagan defence build-up, contracted by one to two per cent every year.   MDC lost nearly 17,000 employees, despite a strong civil order book, and GE cut 10,000 from its 45,000 total.   Even winners of major contracts, such as Lockheed and GD, reduced employment in order to improve productivity; GD's plans included a cut of 30 per cent of its workforce, some 30,000 people. These cuts were less sweeping than the layoffs which followed the end of the Vietnam war when employment dropped from 1.5 million to 820,000, but the speed of retrenchment was still devastating and precipitated a major restructuring in the US aerospace industry.[77]

The impact on Europe

The era of shrinking defence markets affected European states in different degrees and at different speeds. Of the major powers, the German government was under the most political pressure to declare a 'peace dividend'. The German government planned to cut defence spending by three per cent annually between 1991 and 1994 and the 1991 budget was the lowest share of Federal expenditure since 1956. Although manpower was the main target for cuts, a smaller military establishment would need fewer weapons. The immediate impact on major procurement items such as EFA, the Tiger and other aerospace projects was slight, but procurement expenditure would be cut by 26 per cent and spending on defence R&D by 8.6 per cent by 1994.[78] In Germany, DASA's order book shrank by 43 per cent in 1990, with few guarantees that the future would be much better. The downturn forced DASA to re-organise its military division and led to 1,000 redundancies.[79] In 1992, the pace of retrenchment picked up, with the German government announcing production cuts in several programmes, this time including the Tiger helicopter and the European Fighter. DASA predicted that the German defence budget would entail an annual reduction of between 15 and 20 per cent in its business.[80]

In the UK, there had been no real growth in the defence equipment budget since the mid 1980s. But the British government's *Options for Change,* published in July 1990, triggered a more extensive debate. Opinions were divided on the extent and location of UK defence cuts, but the initial target was aggregate force levels, especially in the size of the army. But with deeper cuts expected, several defence industry trade associations suggested that an expected average decline of four per cent per annum over five years, would mean a fall in demand for UK defence equipment by as much as 25 per cent. This would cost UK defence contractors over £408 million a year. Although land systems would initially bear the brunt of the cuts, the aerospace industry also began to lose business.[81] Britain's extensive role in the Gulf War made little difference to the long term trend in UK defence spending and plans to curtail production and subsequent defence budgets led to a further reduction in requirements for military equipment.[82]

Although the British aerospace sector was initially affected less than land or naval systems, most of the major aerospace companies retrenched. Overall, 4,800 defence-related jobs were lost after the publication of *Options for Change.* Reduction in planned Tornado production and other problems entailed closure of two military aircraft factories with the loss of 5,000 jobs and four out of nine factories involved in missile work were closed. Further job losses were announced in 1992, including 5,000 in the company's military aircraft division.[83] Like BAe, Rolls was affected by the Government's decision to cut Tornado production. and a shortfall in helicopter orders - in particular a delay in ordering the EH-101 - had a similarly depressing effect on business. In the spring of 1991, Rolls announced a series of job cuts totalling 6,000 from a workforce of 34,000, including the closure of a dedicated helicopter engine plant.[84] Similar job losses and poor results were recorded by the UK avionics and defence electronics sector. The decline in defence work and associated R&D also meant that civil programmes had to carry a higher proportion of research overhead - a particularly problematic issue for a company such as Rolls-Royce competing against much better funded US firms.

Initially, the French took a less sanguine view of European security and the French military pressed for a four per cent increase in the 1991 defence budget.   Although the French government only accepted a three per cent increase (a small cut in real terms), it remained committed to nuclear force modernisation and to key conventional programmes such as the Rafale fighter for industrial reasons. According to the French Minister of Defence, 'maintenance of a competitive world-scale French aeronautics industry is part of France's defence'. The French also supported the development of independent European space surveillance systems. As a result, in the short term, the French aerospace industry was the least affected by the downturn and while there were some cuts in production, French firms were able initially to avoid large job losses.[85] But even the French have had to face some hard choices. Rising costs forced cancellation of a new land-based strategic missile and cast doubts over French participation in the international NH-90 helicopter programme. The Defence Ministry was able to hold defence expenditures for 1992-3, which would protect commitments to new programmes, but current and future production levels had to be cut. There was also a strong hint that France would buy more defence products 'off the shelf' from foreign manufacturers and would collaborate even more extensively to develop major systems.

The French aerospace industry was, therefore, better placed than many in the west, but in 1990 falling demand forced Dassault to restructure its military operations   and shed 4,000 jobs.[86] B y early 1991, Henri Matre of Aerospatiale was warning that unless the trend towards defence cuts was halted, the French aerospace industry turnover would drop by 25 per cent by the mid 1990s. By the spring of 1992, even the French had to concede the need for a significant reduction in equipment spending and the Rafale programme was stretched-out by two years and the NH-90 helicopter by three years.[87] By early 1993, the situation had further deteriorated, and a number of new programmes such as the NH-90 and the Helios military satellite looked vulnerable to cuts. Up to this point, the French defence industry overall had seen employment drop by seven per cent over two years and both Dassault and Aerospatiale announced plans for further large scale redundancies.[88]

The rest of the world

Outside Europe and the US, the impact of the 'peace dividend' was less marked, although economic recession had a depressing affect generally on demand for military hardware. Although Super Power disengagement affected some military dispositions outside Europe, there were plenty of other external threats facing states in the Middle East and in the Far East. The Japanese defence budget, small as a proportion of GNP, grew in FY92 by 5.38 per cent. Although in 1993, the Japanese government announced plans for a reduced future spend and cuts were made in current production programmes, the commitment to the FSX still remained firm. Elsewhere in the Far East, governments scheduled large increases in defence spending, with Malaysia, for example, budgeting a 230 per cent increase between 1991-5.[89] Arms spending in the Middle East was also expected to grow by three per cent, and despite pressure to resolve some of the region's problems, continuing threats to the oil-producing states would provide opportunities for the hungry aerospace firms of the US and Europe. In general, the major aerospace firms looked to increased levels of military exports as a way of improving their chances of survival.

Arms sales

Since the Second World War, the world arms market has been dominated by the US. Although overseas sales were not usually essential to US military aerospace manufacturers, exports were often highly profitable and augmented production runs, allowing US firms to recoup more of their development costs over a longer period. This, in turn, helped to reduce the unit costs for US domestic procurement. Several US military aircraft, such as the F-4, F-16, F-14 and the Patriot, have been very successful in world markets. A few, such as the F-5, built by Northrop, were deliberately aimed at foreign markets and also sold in large numbers. For others, especially European firms, foreign sales have long been seen as vital to the economic viability of major weapons programmes, and special efforts have been made to maximise export potential (see Table 4.2). From the early 1960s, the US had encountered increasing competition, especially from European defence/aerospace contractors. In particular, with the advent of large scale collaborative programmes such as Tornado, the Europeans made great efforts during the late 1960s to 'recapture' their home market. Although the US still has a positive balance of trade in defence equipment with Europe, by the mid 1980s, European firms had clawed back a significant share of European business.[90] However, the extent to which US aerospace firms lost

Export dependence of Defence Production (1989)

Belgium	36%
France	31%
Germany	8%
Italy	17%
Holland	42%
UK	23%
Spain	9%
EC 12	23%
USA	9%

Table 4.2   Source: US ACDA

ground should not be overstated, particularly when set against the difficulties faced by foreigners in penetrating the US domestic market (see Table 4.3).   Over the same period, European firms certainly became increasingly formidable competitors in international markets, most notably in the Middle East, where they were able to take advantage of US restrictions on arms sales. For example, in 1980, the US had 60 per cent of the Saudi arms market; in 1990 this had sunk to ten per cent, largely due to Congressional support for Israel.[91] US government attempts to control sales to third parties also led to discrimination against US sub contractors and equipment companies bidding for European contracts.   But, as Table 4.3 confirms, as of 1988, US designed equipment rarely accounted for less than 40 per cent of world military fleets and were even better represented in the more expensive categories.

Most arms deals are government-to-government agreements and reflect political as much as commercial interests. During the 1950s and 1960s, the Europeans felt that the US aerospace industry was an arm of US foreign and security policy, with an active programme of support for overseas defence sales. In recent years, the position has been reversed; American companies have complained bitterly that the US government, particularly the Carter Administration, provided less help to defence/aerospace sales than the Europeans. Since 1974, for example, the US Eximbank has not supported defence-related sales, whereas European companies were eligible for government credit packages. US companies and trade officials noted with envy the role played by Prime Minister Thatcher in securing the Al Yamamah deal with Saudi Arabia and the support given by French Presidents for the French aircraft industry.

US and European Military Aircraft Fleet Composition (1988)

Type	US Fleet	US design	EC Fleet	EC design	World Fleet (excl SU)	US design	EC design	per cent US design	per cent EC design
Air Superiority	1,310	1,310	240	221	2,229	1,621	287	72.7	12.0
Fighter/Attack	3,213	3,200	2,225	909	14,956	7,637	2,163	51.1	14.5
Attack	2,568	2,427	477	379	4,911	2,948	662	60.0	13.5
Advanced Trainer	1,112	1,110	921	771	4,838	1,991	1,758	41.2	36.3
Helicopters	10,205	10,115	4,103	2,453	23,570	16,910	5,141	71.7	21.8
Transport	2,135	2,096	583	390	5,266	3,335	936	63.3	17.7
Maritime	1,160	1,119	179	149	1,791	1,525	214	85.1	11.9
Bomber	757	757	649	649	1,689	779	764	46.1	45.2

Source: European Community 1992

Table 4. 3

Within Europe, the French were once regarded as having the most aggressive approach to arms sales, often formulating specifications and gearing procurement policies to emphasise the 'exportability' of military aircraft projects. But in recent years, the UK has built up the more aggressive and a better coordinated system which has acquired an edge over increasingly bureaucratised French procedures. French arms and military aerospace has also fallen behind the UK (and the US) because its less advanced products are no longer so attractive in world markets and have been especially vulnerable to competition from 'second tier' countries. In recent years, French military aerospace sales have slumped: Dassault failed to sell an aircraft outside France between 1988 and 1991, despite a private investment of $714 million (shared with Thomson and Matra) in an export version of the Mirage 2000.[92]

German, Swedish and Italian aerospace firms have faced stringent controls over defence exports, although involvement in collaborative programmes helped both the German and Italian industries to become significant arms exporters. Membership of international programmes led Germany to soften some of its restrictive regime, but several cases of illegal arms and defence technology transfers caused the German government considerable embarrassment and led to calls for even stricter controls.[93] On the other hand, German industry has pressed for some relaxation, or at least a consistent application, of the existing regime. German arms sales policy also created problems for German firms collaborating with French or British industry. Although several inter-government agreements served to reduce the impact of German sensitivities, as Johann Schaefler of DASA put it, German arms export policy was a 'Sword of Damocles' over German participation in joint ventures.[94] The Japanese have also had informal but equally strict prohibitions on the sale of combat aircraft and other lethal military systems. These limitations will inhibit the growth of a domestic aerospace industry, although the Japanese component industry has benefited from sales of foreign military aircraft using their parts.

However, government policies and attitudes are not the only reason for European success - commercial realities have played a key role in shaping European approaches to defence-aerospace exports. The problems of developing aircraft on the basis of limited domestic markets sensitised European producers to the demands of export customers. In the US, however, easier conditions at home, especially during the Carter-Reagan defence build-up, made selling to the US government much easier and more profitable option than foreign sales. As Chuck Volmer of General Dynamics put it:

> European corporate cultures, policies, top personnel, as well as products are orientated to the export market. US defence companies, accustomed to a robust domestic market, are not

prepared to compete internationally when the foreign competition has technological equality and comparable levels of production.[95]

BAe, for example, restructured its defence and military aerospace business in order to improve the coordination and commercial effectiveness of its overseas marketing operations. BAe has developed expertise in selling complete defence sales packages, including weapons, training, construction and long term support. In the case of the Al Yamamah deal, BAe has acted as the programme manager on behalf of several UK companies. As a result of this sales activity, by 1991 Saudi Arabia had become the largest single customer for BAe's military aircraft division.[96]

The increasing complexity and cost of some US aerospace products began to put them beyond the budget of all but a few wealthy customers. The nature of much of the technology used in US aircraft also reduced their exportability. Northrop, for example, has ruled out export sales of its current projects because of the sensitive technologies involved and aircraft such as the F-22 will not be available for export until well into the next century. Although Lockheed has suggested that a 'lower technology' version could be produced for export, because of the advanced process technology involved, co-production agreements would be out of the question. This situation has led several commentators to wonder if any of the most recent frontline US aircraft will ever have substantial foreign sales.[97] There are aircraft like the F-16, some US helicopters and guided weapons which are still attractive, cost-effective, state-of-the-art exports. However, many are old designs and are reaching the limit of further development and new European projects such as the EFA, Rafale and Tiger helicopters, will be powerful competitors in export markets.

In the future, both the US and European companies will face increased competition from the former Soviet Union and new entrants offering 'cheap and cheerful' weapons to less wealthy customers. Brazil, Israel, South Africa, Indonesia and China have all entered the defence aerospace market to some extent, and their presence will be increasingly evident as defence budgets become tighter and price more important than performance. Aircraft such as the Embraer Tucano have also won sales in the developed world. On the other hand, since the Gulf War, the second tier countries have found it harder to make headway against a revitalised US arms industry and demands for the more sophisticated types of military hardware available from the US and Western Europe.

The former Soviet Union was a different matter again. Russian aerospace products offer a level of technology comparable to US and European companies, and at a significant price discount. The USSR has always been a major arms exporter, but mainly for political reasons. Since the end of the Cold War Russian sales have been motivated by the country's desperate need for hard currency. Military aerospace remains one of the few areas of exportable manufacturers where Russia and some of the other members of the CIS can compete on equal terms with the west. Even before the collapse of the Soviet state, the basic Mig-29 was being offered to potential customers at $11 million a unit and an advanced version at $29 million. This compared very favourably with an aircraft such the MD F/A-18, priced at $39.6 million. In 1993, the Thai government was quoted a price of $3.7 million per aircraft for the Mil 17V helicopter, undercutting the Bell 212 by $1.4 million.[98] Although there are question marks over the reliability and life-cycle costs of Russian aircraft, such prices for advanced military equipment are very tempting for poorer customers in the Third World.

The long term implications for the US of declining defence aerospace sales were viewed with growing concern by US industrialists and analysts. If US military exports were to decline too far, the cost of weapons acquisition in the US would rise and the profitability of US firms would be even more depressed. The US trade balance would suffer and the US government would have less foreign policy leverage. The extent of the decline in US defence aerospace exports can be overstated. Throughout the 1980s, the US remained the world's most important arms exporter and much of its own market was largely untouched by external competition. Nevertheless, as defence budgets shrank, US firms began to see the need for an increased share of overseas markets and to put greater emphasis on exports. In the early 1990s, they started to act more aggressively in looking for overseas markets. The US Congress had seemed to learn that denying friendly states US aircraft only benefited European companies. There were moves to authorise export credits, at least for sales to NATO and other allied states as US aerospace firms, a senior Eximbank official observed 'faced real economic adjustment problems' and '(export) finance would be a way for the government to be of some help'.[99] Undoubtedly, the Gulf War acted as a shop window for US products with a gratifying upsurge in interest throughout the Middle East for US weaponry with Saudi Arabia negotiating a $20 billion arms package with the US. As a result of this interest, US firms began to lobby more aggressively to secure political support for arms sales.[100]

The Gulf War, while cheering some US and European defence companies, underlined the dangers posed by aggressive 'Third World' states armed by the industrialised world. As a result, the need for more extensive controls over arms sales and, more important, the transfer openly or illicitly of critical technologies such as missile guidance systems, was now high on the international policy agenda. In October 1991, the five permanent members of the UN Security Council began to discuss cooperation on limiting arms sales to the Middle East. Other UN and similar regional initiatives were also under consideration, including a common EC policy on arms sales regulations.[101] The extension of arms transfer control regimes to conventional equipment would have made the business of selling military aerospace more difficult and would have added to the long term contraction in the defence market. But as defence cuts began to bite the countervailing pressure on governments to support arms sales or to protect national companies was growing. By 1992, there were already signs that concern for conventional arms transfer controls was losing out to the need to protect national defence companies, and both the US and European governments seemed more eager to promote rather than to control arms sales to the Middle East and elsewhere. The watershed was the decision by the Bush Administration to authorise sales of F-15s to Saudi Arabia in the autumn of 1992. Clearly designed as a move to help his re-election campaign, the deal was also endorsed by Candidate Clinton. As President, Clinton took an equally robust line on the value of US defence exports.[102] It would seem, therefore, that a 'business as usual' attitude towards arms sales will continue to carry more weight with governments in the 1990s than any pressure to constrain regional arms races.[103]

The 'peace dividend' - a return to normality?

The late 1980s were hard going for most defence contractors, especially those in the US. The 1990s have already proved to be worse. The combination of tighter procurement procedures, shrinking defence budgets and problematic defence markets left the industry reeling and facing significant changes to its structure and operations. The new environment did have some positive effects: for example, although US defence aerospace companies might be smaller, financial analysts believed that they might be more profitable and by late 1993, US defence stocks were rising in value.[104] But throughout the major aerospace nations, there were still long term re-structuring issues to be resolved; defence markets were shrinking and the continued survival of several US primes was doubtful. The closing of the Cold War era had, perhaps, brought a return to 'normal' times and an end to cyclical increases in defence spending.[105]

   With so many threats to the defence-aerospace industry, there were growing calls on both sides of the Atlantic for state aid in the 'conversion' process. In Germany, the Daimler Group chairman, Edzard Reuter, warned the German government that it would seek 'compensation' for the long term investment in defence production that DASA-MBB had made on behalf of the state:

> capacities have been built up, development and production capacities for military aircraft, as the result of political decision. This means that the state would have to help shoulder the consequences if the political decision is now made that these capabilities are no longer required.[106]

In 1993, President Clinton announced a $1 billion conversion fund to aid US industrial diversification. The Aspin Review of September 1993 was also designed to encourage the commercialisation of defence R&D and to preserve key defence/aerospace technologies, even if individual companies might still be allowed to go to the wall.[107] The EC began to consider measures designed to help affected companies and in several countries, political and Trade Union groups published plans and proposals for 'defence conversion agencies' to ease the transition. But for the most part, companies will have to find their own salvation. Although some firms could look to a growing demand for civil aircraft or space systems, defence-dependent companies would either have to develop new markets or face significant cuts in size and capacity. This might entail a more focused approach to core aerospace and defence activities. For others, it would mean exit from the market or acquisition by a stronger survivor. But as we will consider in the next chapter, re-focussing on the civil market and space is also unlikely to be an easy option.

5

The Civil Aircraft and
Space Markets

Introduction

The end of the Cold War, and the growing clamour for a 'peace dividend' left defence contractors with a shrinking market. The civil sector, on the other hand, looked as though it was set for a period of continual growth. The prospect of ever increasing air traffic and the need to retire a generation of aging, inefficient and environmentally unfriendly aircraft gave rise to expectations of a bonanza for civil aerospace. Understandably, firms with existing civil interests began to place more emphasis on the commercial market and those without began to look for ways of entering the business. Equally, the space market, although smaller in absolute terms than commercial aircraft and systems - offered the possibility of very high value business. Even military space - the largest segment - promised to have some immunity from the general downturn in defence activity with an increased demand for space-based surveillance and communication systems. But neither the civil aircraft nor the space market has proved be an easy or complete answer to the decline in conventional military sales.

The civil market - introduction

Civil aviation grew and matured after the First World War. In the first instance, converted bombers were used to pioneer long distance routes. The aircraft industry, reeling from de-mobilisation, soon began to produce aircraft designed specifically for airline use. By the mid 1930s, with the development of aircraft such as the DC-3, the era of commercial aircraft manufacturing and operation was well established.   During the 1950s, with the advent of the jet-powered airliner, the market for civil aircraft and engines began to expand dramatically.   This continued through a succession of technological advantages including wide-bodied aircraft, turbo-fan engines and computer-driven control systems.

However, the market for civil aircraft has always been uncertain, like the defence sector, characterised by cycles of 'boom and bust'.   Few companies since the 1950s have found civil aerospace consistently profitable.   Nevertheless, civil production has always been prized for its counter-cyclical effect, balancing the oscillations of the more important defence market.[1] With the outlook for military aerospace now so poor, certainly far worse than at any other time since 1950, access to civil markets has become particularly significant, the more so because from the early 1980s, the civil sector was experiencing an unprecedented burst of orders. The combination of increasing airline traffic and the need to replace a whole generation of aging and environmentally unacceptable airliners, implied an apparently continuous period of growth.   In the late 1980s, the main problem for the civil sector was to build enough aircraft, engines and associated equipment to keep up with the demand.[2]   Indeed, as the pace of production increased, even Boeing encountered embarrassing delivery and quality control deficiencies which dented its reputation for unblemished production efficiency.   All the major manufacturers had to face challenging demands of increased volume.   New production capacity was needed; this entailed heavy investment by the major civil primes, and several defence companies were approached as possible additional subcontractors.[3] But within three years, the situation had again changed, with orders subject to deferral and cancellation.   Although the long term prognosis remained buoyant, volatility had returned to the civil market.

The market for civil aerospace since 1945

General characteristics

The main end customers for civil aircraft are, naturally enough, the world's airlines, although in recent years many have tended to lease their aircraft and engines from financial groups who have actually bought the equipment. Although there are only a limited number of airlines, and a few really large carriers whose procurement decisions may have a disproportionate effect on the market, selling civil products requires a very different set of skills and a corporate culture far more commercially sensitive than the defence aerospace business. Although a large number of airlines are state-owned, with some of the characteristics of a controlled public market, most are driven by commercial pressures and demand tight prices and solid delivery and performance guarantees.[4] In the past, European nationalised airlines have been required to support their local product; this has not always been a happy relationship and most have now escaped this requirement. But in general, the civil aerospace market has rarely been a cost-plus environment.[5]

Before the 1960s, engines and airframes were usually bought as a package, but following the development of three families of turbo fans in the 1970s, each airliner sale was almost inevitably accompanied by an equally fierce competition for the engine contract. An airline's decision to buy a particular aircraft or engine is based on a number of related factors. There are certain fundamental economic criteria: range and payload, combined with capacity and frequency demands; airport and environmental requirements; the capital costs of acquiring the aircraft, training crews and maintenance; and especially important since 1973, fuel efficiency. Similarly, fleet standardisation and commonality, as well as favourable financial packages offered by the manufacturers will be important factors in securing sales. Other, more political inducements, may have some impact on individual customers.[6]

Civil aerospace has required a greater commitment to reliability and cost-effectiveness than the performance-driven military arena. Equally, firms involved in civil production have had to be more cost conscious in production and marketing. Yet over the years, civil aircraft have become increasingly complex and expensive, involving huge investment on the part of the civil companies. As we have noted in Chapter Three, in Europe much of the financial strain has been covered by government subvention, but few civil aircraft have sold enough or fast enough to cover costs. As in the case of military aviation, these pressures have forced civil manufacturers to spread the risk either through collaboration or through a network of risk-sharing sub contracting. There has been a direct relationship between technological innovation and demand. New technology - the jet engine, wide-bodied airframes, fly-by-wire control systems - has consistently improved airline productivity and competitive pressure has forced airlines continually to invest in new equipment. In recent years, the attractions of new technology for its own sake has lessened, and customers have had to be convinced that the price they would pay for innovation would be economically justifiable over the lifetime of the aircraft.

The market for civil aircraft since 1945 has followed a cyclical pattern of high demand and precipitate slump (see Fig.5.1). This was, in part, a reflection of general movements in the international

Commercial jet aircraft history

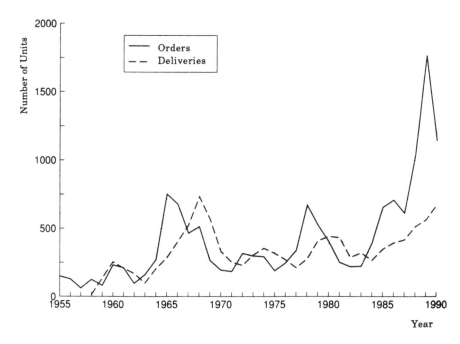

Figure 5.1   Source: Airbus

economy, but it has been due equally to the volatility of the airline
business itself.   During periods of traffic growth, the airline
industry tended to overestimate capacity requirements; they have
then often over-reacted as the down-turn arrived with deferments,
cancellations and a stubborn reluctance to order new aircraft in
anticipation of the next upward cycle.   The immediate post-war
years saw both a rapid recovery and expansion of civil aviation.
This period was dominated by US manufacturers benefiting from
technological leadership and the largest home market in the world.
The 1950s saw the introduction of jet-powered aircraft with a huge
increase in speed and productivity. Despite a British challenge, the
first jet age was again a victory for the US aircraft industry. By the
end of the 1960s, the US had established a stranglehold over most of
the market sectors - certainly for airliners larger than 100 seats.
The Europeans were stronger in the smaller categories.   US
dominance continued into the 1970s with the introduction of long
range wide-bodied aircraft.   Between 1947 and 1991, the US
supplied over three quarters of the total market for large

commercial aircraft (see Table 5.1). For the period up to the mid 1970s, the US share was nearer 90 per cent. Within this general picture, the success of Boeing in pulling ahead of all other civil manufacturers was also marked; by the mid 1970s, Boeing controlled over half of the world market for large civil aircraft and had a monopoly of long-range wide-bodied airliners.[7]

A number of factors contributed to Europe's poor commercial record. Even when narrowly drawn specifications aimed at domestic carriers did not hinder European airliners, superior marketing, customer liaison and support tended to give American manufacturers an important edge. The sheer size and natural preferences of the US home market led to larger guaranteed launch orders, a sustained production run and lower prices on the world market. American producers, especially Boeing, were better able to develop 'families' of aircraft, offering customers different types to suit different route and capacity demands, but with high degrees of commonality in terms of basic structures, cockpit layout and equipment fits. This reduced both customer and manufacturer costs, as well as allowing the manufacturer to offer attractive package deals between different

Historical Civil Airliner Market Share: 1947-91

Boeing	57%
MDC	20%
Airbus	16%
Other	7%

Table 5.1   Source: Boeing

members of the 'family'. US firms had a better level of productivity even when offset against lower European wage costs. In the 1950s and 1960s, the US government also provided substantial sales assistance through the provision of export credits.[8] As we have discussed above, in most cases, the European industry remained a contender in the market only as a result of direct state aid.

European aero-engine industry has been more successful. Rolls-Royce in particular has had a strong presence in the world market, supplying half the world's turbine engines up to 1955. Although Rolls found the launch of its large turbo fan in the early 1970s hard going, since then Rolls has maintained a respectable position in world markets. The French company Snecma, through its links with GE, has further helped to reduce the imbalance (see Fig 5.2). But the competition for business has been fierce and ruthless. Most of the large civil aircraft have three engine options and airline orders

The World Aerospace Industry

Civil set engine market shares (units shipped)

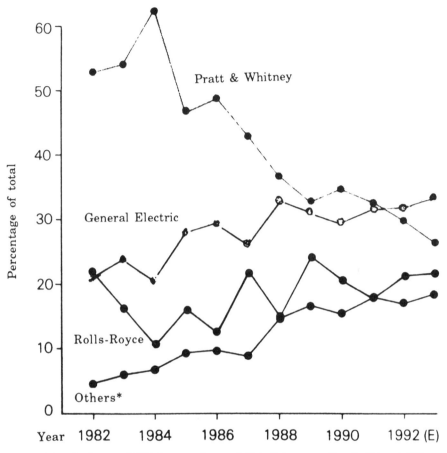

*Primarily Snecma, MTU, Japanese Aero and Fiat. Data source: County Natwest USA

Figure 5.2   Source: Interavia

have usually been subject to often bitter struggles between the 'Big Three'. Even by the standards of the civil aircraft industry generally, the engine business is very long term. Much of the profit in engine sales lies in the spares and replacement engine market over the lifetime of an airframe. This can be over thirty years and may generate business worth three times the value of the initial sale. However, thanks to the reliability of modern jets engines, revenue from spares has been declining. The air transport recession of the early 1990s also led to a drop in sales of spares; as aircraft flew less, the need to replace engine parts at regular intervals declined. Rolls-Royce, for example, reported a 20 per cent fall in revenue from spares during 1991.[9]

US equipment manufacturers have also benefited from the dominant position of American airliners in the market. Companies such as Honeywell-Sperry, Rockwell-Collins and Garret have all become market leaders in their respective fields. In recent years, European companies such as Smiths, Dowty and GEC have made considerable headway, in the US market and the French avionics industry has also been helped by the emergence of the Airbus family. Consequently, the world avionics and equipment market has become a truly global affair, with a high degree of interdependence between the US and Europe. In general, the world civil aerospace industry is based on a wide range of collaborative and international subcontracting which has tended to obscure the national origins and content of most civil aeroplanes.

Although the US advantage in export credit has disappeared and the Europeans continued to benefit from high levels of state aid in development, the US industry has retained a powerful edge as result of the key role played by the dollar in airline transactions and other aspects of aerospace pricing. Fluctuations in the exchange rate, especially over the life-time of aerospace contracts, have increased the risk for European companies. In the 1970s, even with the advice of the Bank of England, Rolls-Royce made an expensive mistake on exchange rate calculations.[10] In the late 1980s and early 1990s, the low relative value of the dollar made life very difficult for European firms who received revenues in dollars and whose costs were mainly in their stronger national currencies.

Both the EC Commission and the European aerospace trade association, AECMA, now regard the exchange rate risk as the single most problematic issue facing the European civil aerospace industry in challenging the US As a Commission source observed, '*since 1986, the European aircraft industry has permanently been penalised by the weakness of the dollar*'. (original emphasis). There are three areas of impact:

- The European aircraft industry may have to launch a new programme at a time when the dollar rate is insufficient to guarantee its long-term viability.

- If a programme is launched on the assumption of a viable dollar rate, subsequent changes in that rate may undermine a programme's viability when orders are made.

- Even if the aircraft are ordered at a viable rate, deliveries paid for in still lower dollar-values will lead to losses on sales.

The Commission concluded that the 'impact of the volatility of the dollar constitutes an excessive handicap for the European aircraft industry'. The Commission has also observed that the relocation of activity by companies towards the dollar zone for purely monetary reasons was not a satisfactory solution for the European aerospace sector as a whole. This would lose EC employment and would jeopardise the viability of the European equipment and sub-contracting industry.[11]

The Europeans have made a number of attempts to convince the airlines that aircraft could be priced according to a basket of currencies or in European Currency Units (ECU). However, the airline industry resisted the introduction of a second currency - especially as much of their overall business was done in dollars. Even Air France, which might have been expected to have been loyal to the interests of the French national aircraft industry, preferred to stay with the US currency. Manufacturers have been able cover forward some of their currency risk, but not to the extent required by the amounts of money involved and the time needed to bring a new product into service or to show a return on their investment.[12]

In short, civil aerospace is a risky enough business without the additional hazard of foreign currency speculation. the Europeans found that a boom could be a mixed blessing when it brought in low-value dollars. The dollar 'crisis' was seen by some Europeans as a deliberate ploy engineered by the US government to undermine European export industries and the Airbus in particular.[13] Conspiracy theories of this kind are easier to formulate than to prove, but there is no doubting that US firms have obtained a significant competitive edge as a result of dollar pricing. As a result, the Commission is looking at the possibility of introducing some form of guarantee scheme. However, the Commission recognises that it may prove difficult to reconcile any guarantee scheme with obligations under GATT, or to remain consistent with the agreement reached with the US over civil aircraft subsidies.[14]

Airline market dynamics in the 1980s and 1990s.

In the early 1970s, uncertainty in the airliner market was increased by the oil crisis of 1973 and the following period of generalised economic 'stagflation'. During this period, Lockheed finally abandoned civil aerospace to concentrate on the 'safer' defence market, leaving just three manufacturers of large airliners - Boeing, MDC and Airbus Industrie. By the end of the decade, with airlines looking for fuel efficient and quieter aircraft to meet increasingly stringent airport noise standards, the market began to recover. However, general recession returned more rapidly than expected, and its effect on the civil aircraft industry was intensified by the financial vulnerability of many airlines.   In 1983, the cumulative debt of US airlines had reached $10 billion, with a comparable figure of $9.4 billion for IATA members.   Under circumstances where a 13 per cent return on capital was regarded as the sign of a healthy enterprise, the world's airlines were averaging only 1.7 per cent.   As a result, another wave of cancellations swept through the aircraft industry.   During this period, the airline industry also lost much of its protective mystique and willingness to invest in new technology without due regard for total life-cycle costs.   On the other hand, the need to replace a whole generation of old and environmentally unacceptable aircraft, combined with predictions of strong traffic growth to the end of the century, triggered a new round of orders.

However, this time the US was confronted by a powerful technological and commercial challenge from the European Airbus Industrie consortium.   Backed by three European governments and some imaginative sales campaigns, the Airbus began to eat into US sales.   Helped by the development of a 'family' of products, by the end of the 1980s the Airbus team had captured over a third of the market for large airliners.   This success, of course, fuelled the strong US opposition to European government subsidies for civil aerospace.[15] The dispute over Airbus funding should not obscure the fact that in many respects the Europeans have become the technological leaders in civil aerospace, especially in the areas of 'fly-by-wire', glass cockpits and the use of composite materials. Structural changes in the world market helped European and other non-US manufacturers.   In the decade and a half since 1975, the fastest rate of expansion in civil aviation occurred outside the US market.   This allowed European firms to compete more effectively amongst customers without a strong tradition of buying American (and, it should be added, from countries with a greater propensity to be influenced by commercial and political inducements).   The Asian market in particular, remains one of the most dynamic areas of air traffic growth and will be a key battle ground for airliner and aero-engine sales over the next decade.

In the second place, de-regulation in the US undermined the solidity of the American market as a base for US civil manufacturers. Although the largest US carriers such as United and Delta were still important launch customers, the overall weakness of the US airline industry and its increased permeability reduced its value as a base for US airliner development.   In the first instance, de-regulation increased the demand for smaller aircraft mainly produced by European and South American manufacturers. Moreover, the general weakness of American (and other international) carriers - partly the result of increased competition following deregulation - severed some of the long term preferences for US equipment and triggered fierce competition on price and delivery conditions.[16] Equally, the presence of Airbus enabled airlines to drive hard bargains on price and delivery, which, from a US manufacturer's perspective, further highlighted the advantages of government support for civil development in facilitating a sustained attack on important airline customers. Lastly, the rise of the leasing companies, offering airlines alternatives to outright purchasing, also reduced the power of US producers to dominate the market. The result has been to erode the historic domination of the market by US firms and by the early 1990s, Airbus had driven MDC into a clear and vulnerable third place position (see Figs. 5.3 - 5.5).

World Market Share, 1970-92
Large Commercial Transpart Airplane by Value of Deliveries

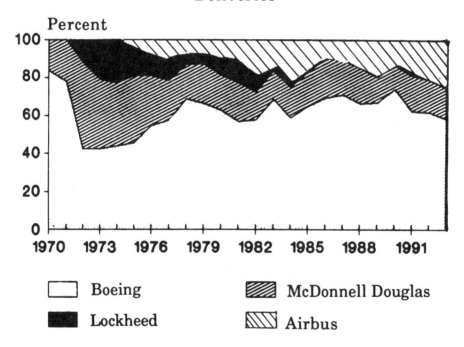

Source: Boeing, World Jet Airplane Inventory, '1989 and Bear Stearns,' *Aerospace Industry Review*, 9 May 1991

Figure 5.3

Announced New Orders

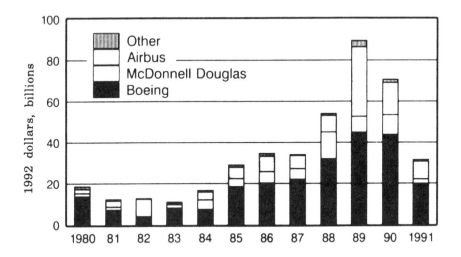

Figure 5.4   Source: Boeing

Confidence in a continually expanding market received a setback from the Gulf War and the subsequent dramatic decline in airline traffic.   Up to the summer of 1991, traffic fell by 25 per cent, costing the airline industry over $4 billion in six months.   This came on top of a general slowdown in growth due to the onset of economic recession in the US and Europe.   Although the aircraft manufacturers reported relatively few cancellations,   there were several postponements and deferrals.[17]   Equipment and engine manufacturers were also hit by the downturn and makers of executive jets and regional airliners also faced a rough time.   Many members of the civil aerospace industry still believe that the cyclical nature of the civil market will be less pronounced in the future.   All the major manufacturers   have predicted continuous growth well into the next century.   Boeing, for instance, estimated that the demand for new airliners between 1991 and 2005 will be worth over $650 billion, of which nearly two-thirds would be bought by non-American carriers.   The market should also be sustained by the retirement rate of old aircraft: between 3,300 and

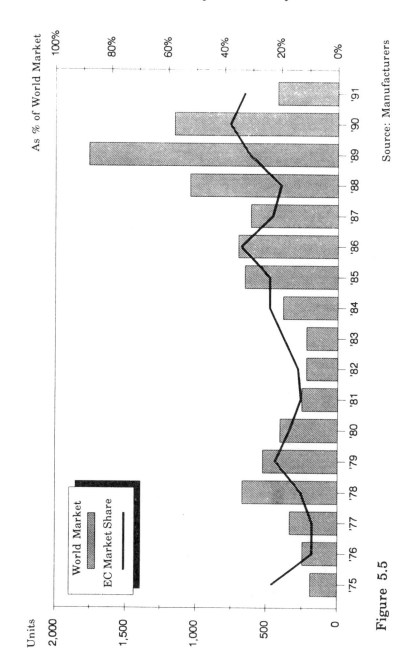

Civil Jet Aircraft Orders

Figure 5.5

Source: Manufacturers

6,500 airliners will have to be replaced up to 2005, which translates into a realistic average of about 350 new aircraft needed each year.[18] All the forecasts indicated that the fastest growth in the market for air travel would be in the Far East and that high-capacity, long-range airliners with commensurately high thrust engines would be the products most in demand. Boeing, for example, predicted that over half of the forecast demand would be for aircraft over 350 seats. These would be high-value, high margined products which would help to sustain profitability for the winners. The market for smaller, regional aircraft was, however, expected to be less buoyant. The prospects for more 'exotic' types, including a second generation supersonic transport (ASST) to replace the Concorde, were more doubtful.[19]

Projections like these led the manufacturers to take a sanguine view of the Gulf-induced recession. Although several airlines did go out of business, and a number of important orders were deferred or postponed, the future still looked buoyant. Boeing, for example, lowered its traffic growth forecast by only 0.3 per cent, but most of this was attributed to the adoption of a more conservative view of general economic conditions.[20] Nevertheless, this 'blip' in the market led manufacturers to delay some planned increases in production rates and dented many of the hopes held by defence contractors of picking up new business from the civil sector. More worrying, according to the more pessimistic forecasts, the blip might last until 1996, with a very damaging effect on several civil manufacturers.

Throughout the early 1990s the airline industry remained in a fragile state and the collapse of several important carriers such as Eastern and the vulnerability of others like Pan Am and TWA, forced several manufacturers to reclaim aircraft. Others, such as United, deferred orders forcing Boeing, Airbus Industrie and MDC to cut production. Up to May 1991, there were 150 cancellations and deferrals, but most were re-scheduling of delivery times rather than outright lost orders. But figures for 1991 showed a 36 per cent fall in orders compared with 1990 levels (MDC, in fact, recorded a net loss due to cancellations) and with a total of 138 cancellations, the industry had suffered its sharpest rebuff for a decade. As a result, the 'Big Three' civil manufacturers were forced to reduce production rates and to lay-off workers - Boeing alone cut 10,000 jobs in 1992 and planned to reduce its overall labour force by another 28,000 by 1994.[21]

Moreover, the vision of continuing future growth seems to depend upon a number of confident, if not heroic, assumptions about the world economy. There was a tendency during the 1980s to base market predictions on the basis of a simplistic picture of the airline market derived from generalised econometric variables. Little attention appears to have been given to more qualitative factors. High levels of debt in the airline industry and a slow recovery from the trough of 1989-91 have continued to cast doubts over the solidity of much of the backlog of orders held by the three major civil manufacturers. Equally, growing problems associated with airport and airway congestion, the uncertainties of wider environmental questions and uneven world economic growth might invalidate the more optimistic market projections cast in the late 1980s. One estimate suggested that total deliveries in 1994, might be as low as 500, down from the 850 made in 1991. More ominously, there were growing doubts about the capability of the world financial system to sustain the growth in demand, even at a reduced level. In particular, grave doubts were being expressed about the health of the airliner leasing sector, which held 19 per cent of all civil aircraft orders in 1991.[22]

The leasing market

Over the last two decades, other customers for civil aircraft appeared, changing the market and introducing both new opportunities and risks. These were companies, such as Guiness Peat Aviation (GPA) or ILFC, which bought and owned airliners, leasing them to airline customers. The advantage to the airline of leasing is that it can change its fleet to match the rise and fall of capacity and to respond to new patterns of traffic. Equally, if not more important, a leasing agreement is not included in the airline's debt. For example, up to the end of 1989, American Airlines had been able to avoid $3.47 billion in long term debt and British Airways $0.8 billion. Although the airline does not retain the aircraft equity, leasing has proved especially valuable to increasingly cash-strapped and impoverished airlines. The leasing company, because it owns the aircraft, retains the security of the airliner and is thus prepared to take on airlines which carry a high level of risk, or who are short of hard currency, such as Third World and East European airlines. Aircraft at the end of a lease can be re-leased or sold on the second hand market.[23]

Leasing deals have been part of the industry for several decades, and began with financial packages arranged by the aircraft manufacturers. MDC was one of the first to pioneer this form of airline financing in the early 1970s. Boeing and Airbus Industrie followed soon after, although of the three majors, Boeing has been the most conservative in its attitudes towards 'innovatory financing'. Airbus, on the other hand, used leasing to secure some of its most important early sales including a landmark deal with Pan Am.[24] The emergence and rapid expansion of the independent leasing companies has introduced a new commercial force in the market. In 1981, six per cent of the world airliner fleet was leased; by the end of 1989, it had risen to over 16 per cent and was predicted to rise to 22 per cent by the early 1990s. In 1991, following deregulation, between 40 per cent and 50 per cent of the US airline fleet was in the hands of lessors. The leasing business could also be very profitable; GPA's profits grew from $17 million in 1984 to $242 million in 1990.[25]

The leasing companies were able to thrive during the 1980s on an expanding market for airliners backed by cheap finance. The move into airliner leasing was fuelled by ambitious Japanese banks, but US and European banks and other lending institutions flocked to advance money for what seemed to be a relatively risk-free investment.[26] However, the 1990 recession, followed by the Gulf War and its impact on airline traffic, raised questions about the long term stability of a market so dependent on credit and the residual value of its airliner assets. There were also growing doubts about some of the dubious mechanics of the leasing schemes and the over-extension of financial institutions which rendered them vulnerable to external pressures.[27]

The recession which accompanied the Gulf crisis saw several small leasing organisations collapse as airlines terminated their leases or, worse, when the airline itself went out of business leaving the lessor with unplaceable aircraft. The problem was exacerbated by a reluctance on the part of the world's banks to support airline financing with the necessary credits. This was due in part to the general problems affecting the banking industry, but it was also a reflection of the greater caution with which the banks viewed the airline business. As one commentator put it, the crisis and its aftermath focused the attention of the financial community on the 'ridiculously inadequate capital base of its airline customers'.[28] These problems were exacerbated by contemporaneous moves to close various tax shelters which had helped to maintain lessor profitability and to support higher risk leases. Many of these had been financed by Japanese banks whose position was worsened by the Tokyo stockmarket slump of 1990 which accounted for 40 per cent of the world's airline investment capital.[29]

Moreover, the prospect of lower than expected growth rates for air travel and a reduced demand for new aircraft held the threat of unwanted fleets of lease-owned aircraft. In the early 1990s, the second hand price of airliners also softened, lowering the value of the assets held by the lessors - a particular problem for those owning older aircraft increasingly constrained by noise regulation. Between 1989 and 1991, $27 billion was wiped off the second-hand values of civil aircraft. The smaller leasing companies without large financial reserves and which had speculated excessively on new aircraft delivery positions were especially vulnerable to changes of this magnitude in aircraft values. Even the largest leasing organisations, such as GPA, found the future increasingly uncertain. GPA, in particular, suffered a major setback in the summer of 1992 when a share floatation failed. Over the next six months, GPA's financial position steadily deteriorated. It was forced to re-negotiate its debts and commitments with its banks and with the aircraft manufacturers, cutting its $12 billion order book by nearly a half. GPA was eventually taken over by the GE finance house, giving rise to concern on the part of GE's engine competitors that its financial leverage could give it a powerful edge in winning future orders.[30]

All three of the major airliner manufacturers tried to limit their degree of exposure to the leasing market. Although the lessors were prepared to make huge bulk orders, the manufacturers recognised the risks of allowing so much of their business to depend on the short term horizons of leasing companies. In particular, in times of slump, the lessors would try to place their aircraft at a large discount, thereby depressing the market for new orders. As a deliberate policy, Boeing endeavoured to keep its leasing business to below 25 per cent of its total orders; with a 20 per cent total, MDC was even more conservative. Airbus Industrie also kept its exposure below 25 per cent, but its order book was more dependent on the more vulnerable US carriers such as Pan Am. Nevertheless, with over a fifth of the world's 1990 order backlog dependent on the leasing business, the civil aircraft industry was increasingly affected by the oscillations and unpredictable actions of financial markets.

By the early 1990s, there were growing doubts about the capacity of the international financial system to support the projected rate of airliner sales, whether leased or sold directly to airlines. According to some analyses, the projected rate of airliner replacement could be too great to be sustained by the financial community. Even the best run and most solvent airlines had to pay more for their credit, others struggled to obtain the necessary funding. Market conditions generally were such that some airlines were too risky even with aircraft as assets. Moreover, the whole 'climate' of financial risk was beginning to turn against airliner financing. The total capital requirement for deliveries scheduled through 1992-2002 has been estimated to be over $700 billion. Airlines will need something like five per cent margins to pay for their new equipment. This has to be set against an average annual return over twenty years of one per cent. In monetary terms, this translates into $45 billion per year in interest charges alone at a time when the total cumulative cash-flow for the airline industry was only $22 billion. Most airlines have long had a 'ridiculously inadequate financial base' and have depended upon the apparent willingness of banks to assume long term risks on their behalf. But the environment of the early 1990s was less conducive for airline financing. As a result, lending organisations abruptly raised their rates even for financially solid airlines such as United, Delta and BA. As one banker put it 'some airlines and some transactions will be unfinanceable at any price'.[31]

As these problems grew, export credits provided by governments re-emerged as a key element in sales. The greater availability of export credit should bring confidence back to the market and could reduce the risk for commercial sources of capital, but it might also increase the role of other, less legitimate forms of inducement. Airbus Industrie has already complained that European national export credit facilities cannont match those offered by the US Eximbank.[32] Similarly, manufacturers may also have to assume greater responsibility for raising finance for their orders; for example, by offering residual value insurance. But with agreements such as the 1989 GATT 'Commonline' in place, and with the US on the offensive over subsidies, unless there is a return to a free-for-all in the area of airliner financing, export credits will only supplement other sources of finance. As a result, the civil aerospace industry will have little insulation from the vicissitudes of the financial market.[33]

Changes in the civil market - green issues

The civil market will not escape the effects of increasingly stringent environmental constraints. The industry has already felt the impact of some green issues - notably attempts to curb noise pollution through the prohibition of simple jet engined aircraft. The unacceptability of sonic booms forced the Concorde SST to over-water supersonic operation, and noise issues nearly blocked the aircraft's access to the United States. Through the 1970s, with the advent of the high by-pass turbo-fan, aircraft became quieter and Stage 1 aircraft - first generation turbo-jets - were phased out. Europe and the US and the International Civil Aviation Organisation (ICAO) agreed to an even more stringent Stage 2 for full implementation by 2002. Some of these mainly, but not exclusively narrow-bodied aircraft dating from the late 1960s, could be retrofitted with 'hush kits' or new engines. But the cost of retrofitting would be between $2 and $11 million depending on the aircraft. Many others will be replaced by the latest generation of quiet aircraft and as such, will add to the demand for new airliners. Increasing airport congestion and barriers also suggested an increased market share for higher capacity aircraft.[34]

But the effects of wider environmental issues on the evolution of the market for civil aircraft will be harder to predict. In particular, international responses to the problem which high altitude pollution represents will be a key issue over the next decade. Although civil aircraft cause only a small proportion of airborne pollution, the height at which civil aircraft operate makes them particularly significant in terms of 'greenhouse gasses'. The introduction of a fleet of ASSTs would be especially threatening, carrying risks of a direct attack on the ozone layer as they would fly at a very high altitude. The main culprits are nitrogen oxides (NOx), unburned hydrocarbons and carbon dioxide. Water vapour may also be a significant pollutant at high altitudes. The extent of the problem posed by civil aviation is still unknown, and extensive research programmes are in hand to clarify the situation and to define standards. The ICAO is working towards the establishment of standards for airborne emission. Clearly, the implementation of stringent environmental requirements would have an unpredictable effect on the civil market. It could mean new business, especially for engine manufacturers who claim that they are already close to meeting 40 per cent reductions in emissions. On the other hand, an over restrictive regime, or a too rapid introduction of new standards, could lead to restraints on operations or impose impossible financial burdens on the airline industry which could depress demand. With very high stakes involved, the issue will be the subject of high-level bargaining between governments on a world-wide basis.[35]

The civil market - final observations

The environmental issue notwithstanding, the long term prospects for the civil market appear to be healthy. The demand for air travel, especially in the Far East, should continue to grow along with the world economy. As *per capita* incomes increase, more people will want foreign holidays, and business travel should provide the basis of airline profitability. Although there will be inevitable downturns the prognosis is one of steady growth. We should, however, be seriously concerned about the financial stability of the airline industry and of the ability and willingness of the international banking system to finance the production planned for the next decade. The perennial optimism of the market forecaster tends to ignore more qualitative aspects of market development such as the effects of airport congestion and alternatives to business travel.[36] Boeing, for example, baldly stated that the money needed to support demand would eventually appear, expecting the appearance of 'innovations' in the field of aircraft financing to cover any major deficiencies.[37]

The worst scenario is that the promised bonanza will prove illusory. There are fears that the airline industry will be unable to find the money (around $350 billion between 1993 and 2000) to support its fleet replacement plans. Airlines will need average return of between four and five per cent to fund their own aircraft - the world average rate in 1992 was one per cent. The leasing companies will also have to fight hard to maintain their credibility and credit ratings.[38] Deliveries could peak in the late 1990s and *production rates* would then fall dramatically. There would still be a steady demand for new aircraft, but the aircraft manufacturers might only have had the benefits of a short term boom, leaving a massive over-capacity by the end of the 1990s. A more efficient operational use of their aircraft by the airlines could knock two per cent off industry forecasts.[39] This analysis would have several implications: the competition between the 'Big Three' airframe and engine manufacturers would be even more intense, with the third placed company looking increasingly vulnerable. There would be even more pressure on the civil aerospace majors to reduce their input costs by using more advanced process technologies and to off-load production to lower cost countries. The manufacturers would be under even more pressure to finance sales. This was already becoming an important feature of the market by the late 1980s, but airframe and engine companies may have to increase their exposure still further - especially difficult for firms such as BAe and Rolls-Royce with limited capital resources. Indeed, the availability of leasing finance to support aircraft sales was one of the major attractions for BAe's deal with Taiwan.[40]

A final consideration is the likely impact of continued rationalisation and de-regulation of the world airline industry. As we noted above, change in the US market during the 1980s had serious consequences for the US civil aerospace industry. The creation of 'mega-carriers' in the US and, increasingly in Europe and the Far East, will reduce the number of key customers and, by implication, the importance of winning their orders for either airframe or engine manufacturers. This is likely to increase airline leverage over price and conditions of sale. More 'winner take all' competitions would clearly threaten that a succession of lost sales could drive firms out of the market. The prospect, therefore, of a global market which would resemble military procurement systems - with a limited number of buyers and sellers - is likely to grow over the next ten years. This would take the industry into unkown territory and may again place a premium on access to state funding or financial guarantees. On the other hand, a more sensibly structured airline industry, charging realistic ticket prices, would ease the airliner financing problem and, perhaps, counteract any tendency towards a 'negotiated' market structure.

The space market

The space market can be divided broadly into two functional areas - launchers and applications satellites. These can be further broken-down into manned and unmanned missions. The bulk of world space activity is absorbed by the military - generally for remote sensing, reconnaissance, navigation and communications. The civil sector is also dominated by public or quasi-public customers; national and regional space agencies such as NASA and ESA; the national and international communications satellite users such as Intelsat, the Japanese NTT and the European Eutelsat; remote sensing organisations such as Landsat and Spot Image; and publicly-funded scientific bodies. There are, of course, private satellite users such as BSB-Sky TV and the US Comsat organisation. NASA also acts as an agent for some US defence-space activity, primarily through residual commitments to launch military satellites on the Shuttle and to perform a number of Strategic Defence Initiative (SDI) experiments during manned missions.

Accurate data for the total world space market are difficult to estimate. The US-based AIAA puts the figure at around $80 billion a year. The US accounts for 42 per cent, the former USSR 45 per cent and 13 per cent by the rest of the world. Of the latter, Europe spends 40 per cent, China 30 per cent and Japan 15 per cent. With 60 per cent of the European total, France has the largest investment in space programmes, followed by Germany with 21 per cent and Italy at 15 per cent. Of the major aerospace powers, the UK is amongst the smallest space nations.[41]

Launch services

The main players in the world market for launch services are the US and Arianespace, the organisation responsible for the commercial exploitation of the European Ariane family of launchers. During the late 1970s and the early 1980s, US expendable launchers (for most medium to heavy payloads) were phased out in favour of the Shuttle. However, the *Challenger* disaster and the hiatus which followed in US launch capability led both the US military and major private customers to swing back to expendable launchers such as the Titan. By the early 1990s, the main US expendable launchers were beginning to show their age and a series of expensive failures led the US to consider replacement systems. The main beneficiary of the Shuttle failure and subsequent US dithering over alternatives was the European Ariane.[42] The Ariane, now in its fourth generation, is built and marketed by the Arianespace organisation. Originally developed by a French-led international team for ESA, Ariane has come to dominate the world market for commercial launches (its military business has been very small compared to US systems which have also launched most of the European-NATO satellites). In 1991, Ariane had orders for 38 launches worth nearly $3 billion - about 60 per cent of the world market and in 1992 signed its 100th contract.[43]

The former Soviet Union attempted to sell its Proton launcher to western and other users. However, sales to the west were then constrained by COCOM and other US restrictions on satellites transported to the USSR for launch. The Chinese have also entered the market and have made some inroads into the US/European dominance. The Japanese targeted space systems and services as a key element in future technological and industrial policy and Japanese customers were expected to chose a Japanese launcher. This led to a clash with the US which eventually forced the Japanese to open their satellite market. Nevertheless, in the early 1990s, Japanese customers were still paying a premium to use the national launcher (the 1991 launch of the BS-3b TV-sat cost NASDA, the Japanese space agency, $204 million, three times as much as competing US or European launch services).[44]

As in the case of civil aircraft, the satellite launch business has been affected by disputes over subsidisation and political interference in supposedly 'free markets' - although how any market so closely involved with government agencies and other public customers could ever be thought to be a genuine market is a little difficult to understand. The primary issue has been the question of pricing. The US has accused the European Space Agency of subsidising Ariane launches to buy its position and both have charged the Soviet Union and Chinese of systematically underpricing launches in return for hard currency. The issue was first raised in 1986 following a complaint brought by Transpace, the marketing arm of MDC Space, that ESA was giving Ariane a 20-30 per cent subsidy as well as providing low-cost insurance to customers to cover rocket failure. However, following the revelation that NASA was subsidising Shuttle launches, the US government had to reject MDC's complaint. Attempts to establish an international agreement covering launcher pricing proved as frustrating as the US-EC dispute over civil aircraft subsidies. The US grudgingly accepted that an Arianespace rate for ESA's own satellite launches was not a subsidy. The Europeans, in their turn, continually accused the US of preventing access to its public markets, mainly in defence, which constituted over 80 per cent of US launcher sales.[45] The US government also paid the full fixed costs of launch with commercial users carrying a percentage; as European governments only paid per launch, the US commercial operators had a distinct advantage over Arianespace.   In practice, therefore, the three main US launchers were able to sustain operations on a much lower proportion of 'commercial' business (between a half and one third) than Ariane.[46]

Soviet Union and Chinese prices, although reflecting a lower cost of production and operation, were even harder to justify by western commercial criteria.   The entry of both in to the launcher market was motivated by the need to acquire hard currency. The Chinese, for instance, have offered launches for between $25 and $40 million which compared to Arianespace's $45-50 million and over $50 million for an MDC Delta 2 launch. The Russians offered a similar range of low-price launch services.   Until 1991, the US could restrict Soviet penetration by forbidding the transportation of US satellites to the USSR for launch. With the end of the Cold War, such prohibitions were harder to sustain. President Bush, for foreign policy reasons, had already granted licences for US satellites to be launched by China. Although President Clinton was, in turn, keen to police the 'fair price' regime, the need to bolster Russia's economy was further reason to allow Russian launchers access to world markets.   The growing chaos in the former Soviet space programme may deter western customers and despite some initial orders, China has yet to make significant headway against the US and Europe.   But both they and the ex-Soviet space services industry could offer a highly competitive challenge in an increasingly tight market.[47]

Applications satellites

The only proven commercial market for space systems (as opposed to launch services) is in telecommunications, accounting for about 90 per cent of the total commercial satellite market. Space-based equipment accounts for about one per cent of the world's telecommunications infrastructure. In 1991, nearly a third of this business was from US-owned customers and a quarter from Europe. The future value of this market is expected to be $12 billion by the Year 2000; equivalent to around 20 launches per year through to the mid 1990s. Although space-based telecommunications will face increased competition from terrestrial technology such as fibre-optics, this should be balanced to some extent by the expansion of mobile communications. The modernisation of the East European telecommunications system, and the need to provide dedicated weather satellite coverage for the region, will add to the demand for satellites. Similarly, the deregulation of national and regional PTTs will increase the need for competing systems.   Finally, the expansion of TV-Sat services, including high-definition television, will add another factor to the market for satellite systems.   But overall, telecommunications is a mature market: indeed, the increasing reliability and capacity of the latest types of satellites (now 14 years compared to seven years in the 1970s) will also limit the rate of growth in demand.[48]

The bulk of this market has been absorbed by US manufacturers such as Hughes, GE, Ford and TRW (see Table 5.2). European manufacturers, although often able to achieve preferential treatment from national users, have had a hard and increasingly difficult time competing in open commercial markets against the Americans.   US satellite companies derived considerable benefit of scale from their larger home market and technical and commercial advantages of a huge defence space programme (several US commercial satellite platforms were first developed for military applications) closed to outsiders.   As a result, US firms have often

Civil Geo-Stationary Communication Satellites Market Shares (%)

Country	1980-9	1990-5
United States	69.7	69.6
Hughes	27.7	21.4
GE/ RCA	16.8	21.3
Ford	18.9	9.6
TRW	6.3	7.3
Europe	23.5	36.0
Matra	4.4	13.9
Aerospatiale	5.2	9.9
BAe	8.2	5.6
Alenia	0.9	4.3
DASA	4.8	2.3
Canada	3.8	2.4
Japan	3.0	2.0

Table 5.2   Source: *Economist*   15 June 1991

had a 40 per cent price advantage and have usually been able to offer faster delivery times. As European telecoms markets are de-regulated, the pressure on European satellite manufacturers could be overwhelming; indeed, in 1991, only two out of 27 comsats ordered internationally went to European firms. The rationalisation of European space industry should improve the capital mass of firms: and sub contract work and strategic alliances with US companies will also help. But without a substantial improvement in the support given to the European satellite industry, it is likely to be doomed to a secondary role in world markets.[49]

The growth of other commercial markets, such as remote earth sensing services offered by organisations like Spot Image - a French-based European company, has been disappointing. There is a wide range of potential uses for earth sensing, but customers have been slow to see the advantages and the availability of data already presents a formidable task for interpretation and dissemination. An interesting side application of Spot has been the provision of 'intelligence' photographs for news media of suspected chemical and nuclear facilities.

In practice, the most lucrative market for applications satellites has come from military users (the US for example, spends between $15 billion and $20 billion a year on military space). Both the US and the former Soviet Union have deployed large numbers of reconnaissance and other intelligence satellites systems. These were amongst the heaviest and most complex satellites put into space, and by their nature, must be replaced at regular intervals. The US also developed a highly accurate navigation technology, Global Positioning System (GPS), which also has civil uses, including *en route* air traffic control and airliner navigation. Military satellites communication systems have been employed in tactical and strategic modes, forming a key element in nuclear command and control.

Indeed, the end of the Cold War is likely bring new opportunities generally for the space industry. In particular, the need for verification of arms control agreements is bound to increase requirements for space based surveillance systems. Rockwell, for example, has already seen its space business double in two years. Some of this was related to NASA contracts, but the greater part was from defence-related contracts. The Gulf War, for example, confirmed French determination to develop independent (national or European) intelligence gathering systems. As a result, the Helios (a French-led European programme) and other systems were afforded an increased national priority. The 1991-2 French defence budget contained an 18 per cent increase for space systems; planned spending of Fr3.5 billion was about the same as the French annual contribution to ESA.[50]   As the idea of a more overtly European regional security system began to evolve in the early 1990s, even the British government, hitherto strongly Atlanticist in terms of satellite systems commitments, was prepared to consider collaborative projects with the French.   In 1991, France and Britain agreed to begin consideration of a joint communications satellite which could cost up to $4 billion to develop. Similarly, the WEU has proposed the development of a European multi-sensor satellite recognisance system.[51]

In general, the space industry was one of the clear winners from the Gulf War - a conflict which one Pentagon spokesman called the 'First space war'.   The impact of observation, communication and other satellite-based systems was readily apparent.   One immediate effect was to stabilise defence budgetary allocations to space technology.   Combat testing also led to demands for more 'user friendly' ground elements and to the provision of real-time data for tactical command.   Even civil operations, such as the French Spot Image, reported increased business from military and political users looking for mapping data.   Increased military traffic eventually outpaced capacity of dedicated comsats, again leading to emergency leasing of civil transponders.   The experience also underlined the need for a new and greater range of military comsats. A major beneficiary was the Lockheed Milstar programme which had been under some threat from Congressional critics.   Finally, the huge success of GPS led to a massive increase in orders of ground receivers (including 10,000 civil sets bought for individual and small group use).   Generally, the critical role of space-based systems could encourage other states to seek access to this kind of capability; it will certainly underline growing European interest in developing autonomous systems.[52]

The Strategic Defence Initiative (SDI)

The SDI programme, launched by President Reagan in 1983, although regarded as an electoral ploy, rapidly acquired a powerful political and institutional momentum.   Participation was also invited from the US's allied partners.   In many respects, SDI served to unite several independent programmes investigating various aspects of ballistic missile defence, advanced sensor technology, communications and data processing.   With a budget of over $30 billion covering the period 1986-90 and an operational system cost estimated at between $100 and $800 billion, SDI was the focus of a major R&D effort throughout the US defence/aerospace industry.[53] From the high point of the Reagan years, the technical scope and budgetary allocation of SDI narrowed substantially.   Throughout

1991-2, the SDI budget was subject to Congressional erosion. The SDI budget for FY92 was \$4.6 billion with Congress inevitably looking to cut the allocation further. More than a third of these cuts were made in the space-based elements, and by 1993 most of the remainder had been lost as the focus of the programme shifted to point defence against lower level missile threats.[54]

Manned space programmes

To date, there are only two nations with operational manned space programmes - the US and the former Soviet Union. The European Space Agency is developing an independent capability for early next century; ESA and a number of other countries are also working with the US on the International Space Station *Freedom*. By their nature, manned programmes are highly specialised and very costly. The ESA Hermes shuttle, Ariane 5 heavy-lift launcher and the Columbus module will cost over \$9 billion. *Freedom* itself will cost over \$30 billion, and has already been reduced in scale and scope.

Generally, manned space is viewed by the space industry and space agencies as the most prestigious and technologically most stimulating aspects of space research. Even the former Soviet programme, with the most experience of routine and long term manned space exploration, was in crisis, starved of funds, its space-based infrastructure decaying and morale amongst its personnel plummeting. In the US, the Challenger disaster was a major setback to the whole industry and called into question the effectiveness and efficiency of NASA. Subsequently, US space policy has tried to focus attention on new targets, including a mission to Mars, but this tended to clash with other, more earth-related programmes which have attracted broader political support. The European manned space programme, despite being pushed hard by the French, also faced technical problems and cost escalation.

In general, although proponents of manned space programmes have often pointed to the commercial potential of space-based industrial processing, the value of man-in-space remains primarily a closed technological cycle with a dubious cost-effectiveness.[55] Nevertheless, most of the major aerospace nations have begun to investigate advanced manned systems. Most have taken the form of hypersonic 'spaceplanes', single-stage, earth-to-orbit fully reusable concepts. The main examples are the National Aerospace Plane (NASP) programme in the US and the German Saenger. The Japanese and the British have also shown interest in similar ideas. The French, as the leading European space nation, were initially hesitant because of the threat such systems might pose to the Hermes, but they too have begun to express interest in a

European-wide programme. These projects are important not only because of the break-through promised in launch costs, but because they are also seen as technology drivers for aerospace in general. However, the huge cost of developing operational 'spaceplanes' may yet prove prohibitive, or at least force the adoption of inter-regional cooperation.

Space markets - final observations

Space is already an important part of the world aerospace market - for example, civil and military space accounts for just over a fifth of US aerospace output, more than civil aerospace. As general military spending declines and defence-related production and R&D contracts dry-up, space has been seen as a growth area. But like civil aerospace, the space sector has its own pitfalls and problems. It is also an area where the established player clearly has an edge. Similarly, although work on space systems is a very high-value activity, it is a low volume business. The old Soviet space programme was perhaps the nearest in turning space-launcher construction into mass-production, but very few others have reached this position. On the strength of its order book, Arianespace has been able to order rockets in quantity which will reduce unit costs. The US GPS system, with Rockwell as prime contractor, and Hughes' family of commercial satellites have also been able to benefit from a limited form of mass production. In the main, however, space projects are complex, long lead-time, one-off products. The returns may therefore be substantial in financial and technical terms, but space work does not fill factories nor generate long term, repeat revenue.

In 1991, the US Congressional Budget Office reported on the commercialisation of space; it concluded that this would be slow and difficult, 'requiring large sums of governmental seed money if its to happen at all'. The CBO predicted a glut in the supply of launcher services as the Soviet Union, China and Japan emerged to take on the US and Europe. Nor was there any sign of a breakthrough for commercial remote earth sensing. In both cases, government subsidisation would remain a major feature of pricing and even survival. Above all, space-based processing remains a very high risk activity with no obvious growth of a strong customer base.[56] The space market will continue to be dominated by government customers with well over 90 per cent of the world's investment in space systems coming from the state.[57] As a result, the health of the space industry will continue to be dependent on national budget priorities and the oscillation of public policy. However, the future of large, publicly-funded space programmes in the US, the former

Soviet Union and Western Europe looks increasingly uncertain. The cost-benefit of high-cost space projects has been under steady pressure for some time. The privileged and politically well supported Soviet space industry faced the full force of *perestroika* for several years before the break-up of the USSR. From the outset of the Gorbachov reforms, the space sector had to meet a 40 per cent conversion target. Since the abortive coup of 1991, and the formation of the CIS, the manned space programme has been wound down and in 1991-2, the space industry was hit by extensive cuts in its civil and military programmes.[58]   The ex-Soviet space programme's major asset may yet prove to be its expertise - a resource which has already attracted interest in Western Europe, Japan and the United States.[59]

Similar demands for a re-orientation of spending priorities affected NASA during the late 1980s. After the *Challenger* disaster, NASA had a further run of embarrassing failures, including the faulty Hubble space telescope, and continuing difficulties in meeting Shuttle launch schedules. The space-station was steadily pared back in terms of scale and scope and often barely scraped through Congressional budget reviews. The steady reduction in the scope of the space station programme led to lay-offs in the US space industry and cancellation would be a severe blow to major contractors such as MDC and Grumman.[60]   Although NASA received strong political support from the Bush Administration, this was not translated into extra money and NASA space programmes lost money in the 1992 budgetary round, a trend continued by President Clinton.

Finally, ESA's plans for an ambitious expansion of its activities, including an independent manned capability, have also been cut back. By 1991, the $47 billion programme authorised in 1985 to develop the Hermes shuttle, the Ariane 5 heavy-lift launcher and the Columbus module for the space station by the Year 2000, was in difficulties. Although the French still backed the programme unreservedly, the Germans, under pressure to finance re-unification, wanted a review and a stretch-out. Matters were not helped by a 30 per cent cost escalation in the Hermes project and growth in its design weight which necessitated costly changes to the Ariane 5. The Germans wanted a 20 per cent cut in ESA long term space spending and were already nearly $1 billion short in funds needed to support the Columbus and Hermes. However, with the French still heavily committed to Hermes and the Germans preferring the Columbus, the future of the ESA programme hung on a complex political bargain between the French and the Germans. In November 1991, the ESA Ministerial Council decided to roll-over funds for the Hermes and Columbus for twelve months. It was also decided to tighten political control over expenditure by moving towards an annual review of costs - a move which could severely hamper long term planning.[61] In December, 1992, the ESA Council decided on a further round of cuts, including the relegation of Hermes to technology demonstrator status.   This meant that European hopes of a manned space programme would rest largely on the future of the Space Station - or links with the Russians, which the December Council sought to encourage. More ominously for the future cohesion of ESA, the French warned that the cuts made in the Hermes might lead to a major review of their commitment to the Columbus programme.[62]

ESA's long term role in the development of the European space industry has been   questioned.   ESA undoubtedly accelerated European progress in the space sector. The Ariane and several pioneering applications satellites helped European firms take on the might of US manufacturers. But its industry policy of rigid *juste retour* and the scattering of European space capabilities in a wide spread of politically protected centres of excellence, may have fatally delayed the evolution of a fully commercial space industry. ESA's military restrictions also placed European space at a disadvantage compared to the US. While several European states, notably France, have produced military applications satellites, ESA's prohibitions might have blocked some of the dual usage which has aided the US space industry.[63]

The civil aerospace and space - problematic markets

In general, if aerospace companies 'threatened' by the 'peace dividend' were expecting readily to increase their space and civil aerospace business in order to compensate for falling defence sales, neither promises to be an easy nor entirely satisfactory alternative. Although both are growth areas, capitalising on that growth will still require heavy and risky investment with no guarantees of success. Indeed, in the case of the space market it may even be a case of jumping from one problematic government customer to another, with high profile budgets under as much pressure as in the defence sector. In short, few national aerospace industries will be able to avoid major structural reform by simply shifting to civil aerospace markets or to the space sector.

6

Diversification,
Teaming and Rationalisation

Introduction

The last two chapters have shown that the market and general
commercial position of the world's major aerospace companies have
become more difficult, and for some, the outlook for the next decade
looks bleak. In the face of these pressures, several strategies are
open to aerospace firms. The most dramatic is simply to get out of
the business; indeed, several US companies have sold
defence/aerospace subsidiaries or have given up defence contracting.
Others may have no choice, being forced out by bankruptcy or
financial collapse. However, this chapter and the next will examine
the response of aerospace firms and their government sponsors to
fundamental changes in the market environment. These are not
necessarily novel - many of these developments have been evolving
for much of period since 1945 - but events of the last half decade
have accelerated many of these trends. This chapter will consider
domestic responses - diversification, and domestic teaming and
rationalisation - while the next will examine international
approaches.

Diversification and conversion: general issues

In the past, when times were bad, aircraft companies have tried to
find alternative areas of business or to apply their skills to other
areas of manufacturing. In the demobilisation that followed the two
World Wars, aircraft companies were prepared to take on work
ranging from caravan production to the manufacture of milk churns.
Others returned to automobile manufacturing whence they came;
while a number tried their skills at developing civil airliners. In
some cases, aircraft development was protected by a broader
corporate context, particularly in the US, where the aircraft-
engineering conglomerate with the possibility of cross-subsidy and

interchange of skills and personnel emerged early. In Europe, this was somewhat rarer, but diversified arms manufacturers such as Vickers produced a range of goods from battleships to Spitfires. Up to the late 1950s - certainly during the early 1950s - the range of skills and technologies required of aerospace, and especially defence aerospace, were readily transferable to civil aircraft development; nor was the distance between aerospace and general manufacturing too wide to make diversification a relatively straight forward exercise. Since then, diversification has been more problematic and fraught with difficulties.

In the years since 1945, because the bulk of the industry's business has been with government, the main concern has been to provide a hedge against contract termination and/or a general, but usually temporary downturn in defence procurement. The problem could be worse for aerospace than for a normal commercial enterprise because cyclical 'recession' could be sudden and total. Equally, given the complexity of modern aerospace technology and production, design skills once lost and production teams dispersed were difficult to rebuild - certainly not cheaply.   Niche manufacturing and subcontracting were possible options but, over time, this could lead to dependence and permanent relegation. The more sophisticated, but often riskier strategy was to diversify - to create alternative business opportunities which could either maintain technological and industrial skills, or supply alternative sources of revenue on a scale sufficient to keep the enterprise in being.   Ideally, a successful diversification campaign should bring both.

Bright has identified six forms of diversification which have been open to aerospace companies since 1945: (1) diversify within the aerospace industry by making aircraft plus missiles or space vehicles or all three; (2) enlarge a company's defence interests generally; (3) acquire a more varied range of aircraft production; (4) use aerospace technology or systems integrating skills in other related aerospace sectors such as avionics and electronics; (5) develop parallel manufacturing areas to aircraft construction; and (6) to acquire totally unrelated sectors which can offer counter-cyclical business sectors.[1] The last three forms, if directed at defence aerospace firms looking to enter the civil market, could also be described as 'conversion' activity. It might also encompass the development or expansion of civil aerospace interests.[2] As we shall see below, at various times over the last half century, aerospace firms have adopted one, several or all of these strategies. With the 'end of the Cold War', the fifth option has become particularly attractive, but in practice, one of the hardest to achieve successfully.

There have been several waves of diversification in the post-Second World War US industry. The first was in the years immediately after the war. Rapid demobilisation left the aircraft industry desperate for work. Nearly all of the US companies tried to enter the civil sector; but only Lockheed, Convair and Douglas had the capital to build airliners. Others burnt their fingers in general aviation. Convair made consumer items; Grumman aluminium canoes and Lockheed did well out of consumer finance. However, few of these examples of diversification out of aerospace were successful and most were abandoned by the late 1940s. The European, and especially British experience had some similarities with the US experience; at the end of the Second World War, aircraft companies diversified into other areas of engineering and sheet metal work including the construction of pre-fabricated housing. With the opening of Cold War 'hostilities', confirmed by the Korean War rearmament programme, the industry on both sides of the Atlantic returned to business as usual.

A second wave of diversification came during the 1950s, but centred on the growth of missile and electronics work, novel, but clearly aerospace-related activities. Further diversification opportunities opened up with the upsurge in space contracts for the DoD and NASA in the 1960s. North American moved towards missile, avionics and space technology, but by retaining the necessary airframe design skills, it successfully bid for the B-1 bomber in 1970 and the Shuttle prime contract in 1972. Grumman and Douglas also benefited from this new business.[3] A number of European firms, De Havilland, English Electric and Dassault also entered the missile business, but the demand was never as high as in the US. In general, the US market offered more diverse opportunties to American companies than was the case in Europe. For example, with the exception of France, few European companies have had the stimulus of a large strategic missile programme; certainly until the establishment of ESA in the early 1970s, the European space sector was small compared to the NASA and DoD funded programmes.

The growing importance of electronics and guided weapons from the mid 1950s also brought specialist electronics firms such as Westinghouse, Hughes and Raytheon into aerospace. Similar trends were discernible in Europe, where firms such as Ferranti and Thomson entered the missile business from their electronics base. Indeed, during the 1950s and increasingly into the 1960s, the growing importance of electronics in aerospace acted generally to blur the boundaries between aerospace and other industrial activities. Similarly, aerospace firms could broaden their market base by moving into other defence-related sectors. The formation of General Dynamics, for example, spanned aerospace to submarines.

Some European firms, notably BAe, also expanded their general defence interests.   For BAe, this has included training and infrastructure development.   In 1987, BAe bought Ballast Nedam which reinforced BAe's ability to offer 'turnkey' airfield and air defence packages.   The purchase of Royal Ordnance (RO) from the government in 1987 for £190 million gave BAe access to an even wider range of defence activities.[4]

Generally, as the most promising opportunities were again in electronics and related fields,   some companies expanded existing capabilities or bought into these sectors.   The trend towards more electronically dependent aircraft had been pushing systems integrators in this direction since the late 1950s, but the rising proportion of electronics in defence and aerospace contracts made this an important source of diversification in its own right.   In the US, electronics tended to be one of the most profitable areas of aerospace and defence activity, with rates over twice those earned through prime contracting.   Even under current depressed circumstances, the fall in overall demand for defence products will be to some extent balanced by their rising electronic content.[5]

Fewer large defence programmes, however, have meant fewer large systems awards and, as a result competition in the elctronics sector, became particularly fierce and increasingly international. Even in the US, where the defence market was more tightly protected, several foreign firms won important contracts.   The tendency to 'buy into' defence contracts through merger and acquisition followed the reduction in the number of contracts awarded.   Specialist electronics firms came under pressure from vertically integrated conglomerate prime contractors who began to do more work in-house.[6] While this strategy has been especially well-developed in the US, the trend was also discernible in Europe, with Aerospatiale, BAe and Dassault all developing interests in electronics and systems applications. BAe, for example, steadily increased its presence in the defence/avionics market to become the sixth-ranked defence electronics firm in Europe and the third largest in the UK.[7]

Another potential source of business has been in extending the life of existing military aircraft by giving proven platforms new engines and advanced avionics (upgrading). The market for aircraft retrofits and upgrades could be worth $44 billion up to the year 2000.   Upgrading also provides the military customer with an alternative to buying expensive new systems and could, under certain circumstances, offer increased flexibility in the face of rapid technological change. In some cases, the cost saving on a new aircraft can be between 40 per cent and 60 per cent of their original price.   This has presented a tempting option for procurement agencies facing a substantial drop in purchasing power, particularly as other defence costs such as wages and pensions rise in line with inflation. In the case of the B-52, continual improvements have extended its lifetime to 39 years in USAF service and, as the Gulf War showed, still provides a unique addition to American airpower.[8]

An upgrading programme is not necessarily a cheap option - the Harrier 11 Plus could cost the US and UK $110 million, with a further $40 million investment coming from the major contractors. But this would still be quicker and far less expensive to develop than an all-new A/STOVL. The US Army has considered similar programmes for some of its helicopters, including an all-weather version of the AH-64 Apache. This, however, was tantamount to a new development programme costing $761 million. A more conventional updating programme was the re-building of its CH-47C Chinook fleet - at a third of the cost of a new aeroplane. In the 1990s, several other airforces were looking at upgrade programmes, including giving the multinational F-16s built by Belgium, Norway, Holland and Denmark new radar, central computer and other updated nav-attack systems. With unit costs of $3 million compared to $16 million for a new F-16, this would offer very good value for money.[9]

In business terms, upgrading is a double-edged sword. On the one hand, it promises new sales and continued cash-flow for a modest additional development cost. Of course, most of the value-added would be spent in the avionics sector; but a company like Dassault was happy to offer updates of the Mirage 3 and 5 as a way of maintaining links with customers until they could afford to buy new aircraft. On the other hand upgrading could divert arms budgets away from investment in new systems. In the US, for example, several options were presented as cheaper alternatives to major programmes such as the F-22. In most cases they were presented by firms which had lost or stayed out of the original competitions. Upgrading also provides opportunities for new firms, particularly in the Far East, to break into world defence markets.

In most of these cases, however, the diversification was within the defence/aerospace sector; with very few exceptions, the basis of the business remained delivering a highly specialised, pre-defined, high-cost product to a single government or public agency. The development of space technology, for example, was a variation on this theme. In general, by the late 1980s, the search for new markets presented defence/aerospace firms with a daunting prospect. Increased competition in both domestic and international markets depressed margins and increased risks. In the longer term, the major companies had to consider alternatives to defence work.

Civil aerospace as a hedge

In many respects, a mixed civil and military aerospace capability has been one of the most obvious diversification strategies. For most of the early history of aviation, there was a continual interplay between civil and military aviation technology. Strong links, particularly in the propulsion field lasted well into the post-1945 period. There are still important synergies between the two sectors, especially in terms of basic technological and engineering concepts. While the technological linkages have become steadily less direct - certainly in the airframe sector - the counter cyclical nature of civil business has been much valued.[10] The rationalisation process in both the US and the UK saw several examples of military-orientated companies acquiring civil interests; HSA's purchase of De Havilland and McDonnell's acquisition of Douglas were particularly important examples. Other US defence firms, such as General Dynamics (Convair) and Northrop, became specialist large structure subcontractors for MDC and Boeing.

As we have noted earlier, European civil aerospace has been helped by state aid justified on strategic grounds. In general, European firms were less hampered by government restrictions on technology transfer between civil and military divisions, the use of plant for both civil and military work and have had a tradition of civil-military, state-industry R&D activity.[11] For this reason, perhaps, large scale diversification outside aerospace and related technologies has been less urgent in Europe than in the US. In other cases, Korea and Japan for example, aerospace firms were subsidiaries of large, already diversified industrial conglomerates where aerospace has been supported by the state for industry-policy reasons.

Diversification even within the civil aerospace industry can be a testing exercise. As Dassault discovered, despite its skills as a manufacturer of fighter aircraft, its foray into civil airliners during the 1970s was a commercial disaster. Further attempts to break into the large civil airliner market through collaboration with MDC were also nugatory. However, state aid protected Dassault from the cost of this failure and the company has had more success in developing a range of executive jets.[12] As competition grew during the 1970s and as the costs and risks of civil aerospace increased, civil production became more rather than less concentrated. But with the defence down-turn of the late 1980s, the promise of a boom in civil orders was increasingly attractive. Despite internal problems and a persistent struggle to achieve profitability, MDC's civil division was seen as one of the main hopes for stemming the threat of bankruptcy. As the market leader, Boeing was rather better placed, and losses on defence business were more than matched by profits from airliner sales.   Several other defence aerospace firms such as Northrop, Rockwell and Lockheed looked to civil subcontracting either with MDC or Boeing, or with European firms. The Europeans, as we have noted above, found it harder to produce civil aircraft profitably; nevertheless, for BAe, Aerospatiale and DASA, the Airbus is regarded as vital to their future.   Similarly, all the major engine companies sought to increase the proportion of their civilian output. But civil aerospace remains an unforgiving business.   The costs and risks of development and the fierce nature of competition has made sustained profitability hard to achieve.

The synergistic merger

Industrial conglomerates have been part of the aerospace industry since the 1930s. In the post 1945 period, firms such as United Technologies and General Electric developed a wide range of interests from aero-engines and helicopters to consumer electronics and nuclear power.   On a more modest scale, Saab has built cars, trucks and aircraft since the 1940s.   Until 1971, Rolls-Royce produced both aero-engines and luxury autos, and in 1989, bought the British firm of NEI in order to expand its power-engineering interests.[13]   Industrial and technological benefits have frequently crossed the boundaries between different engineering interests. During the Second World War, for example, the mass-production techniques of the automobile sector were applied beneficially to aircraft construction.   Saab has certainly claimed a useful interchange between its various divisions in areas such as ergonomics, materials and structures.   But as the aerospace industry has become more specialised and its technologies more exotic, some of the linkages have disappeared or have shifted into the electronics and systems areas.   In recent years, Saab's most successful synergy appears to have been an advertising campaign which tried to create an image association between high performance fighters and upmarket cars.[14]

Since the 1960s, there have been several new cases of synergistic mergers which have tried to marry general engineering (largely in the automobile sector) with aerospace. The first major example of the genre was the merger of North American and Rockwell Standard, an automotive and engineering group. As Bright observes, the merger came at a very fortuitous time for North American, which was beset by several problems in its defence and space business. Rockwell had a varied range of automobile and other commercial interests which were counter-cyclical to North American's activities with a shorter pay-back time. The two firms also believed there would be mutually beneficial linkages between a technologically aggressive aerospace company and the cost and marketing conscious Rockwell. In the event, the creation of a much larger capital base to support high-technology development was probably more important than any specific exchange of technology.[15]

General Motors' (GM) $5.2 billion bid for Hughes Aircraft in 1985 was a calculated attempt to reduce the company's dependence on the auto industry. GM also believed that the future of automobile development would require more electronics, and GM wanted access to this technology. Hughes was regarded as an 'R&D powerhouse' and the Detroit company paid a substantial premium for its acquisition. Hughes joined Delco Electronics, GM's automobile electronics subsidiary which also had some defence work on SDI and missile guidance systems.[16] Since acquiring Hughes, GM has made a considerable effort to forge synergistic links between the two cultures of automobiles and aerospace. A joint project office was created to manage technology transfer and a separate budget was allocated to avoid conflicts with established divisions. Hughes has always had to 'pay its way' within the GM conglomerate, by delivering both financial and technological returns as an autonomous business. In recent years, like the rest of the US defence/aerospace industry, Hughes has been hit by declining markets and by more stringent procurement practices. GM, however, kept faith with the synergy concept and claimed to have discovered numerous linkages between the two sectors. This has including work on advanced instrumentation, cellular telephones, high definition television. Hughes' experience of stringent quality control demands has been deployed to help improve GM's production processes and in turn GM's low-cost manufacturing expertise and commercially-orientated culture has benefited Hughes.[17] But in the final analysis, Hughes, representing only six per cent of GM's total revenues, has acted as an in-house R&D centre which also happened to make money selling missiles, radars and satellites.

The two European cases, BAe-Rover and Daimler-MBB, represent more comprehensive attempts to forge broad industrial linkages, albeit from different directions. In both instances, while commercial judgement was the dominant factor in corporate decision-making, there was also a powerful political element. BAe's 1988 bid for the nationalised Rover company, the last UK-owned volume car manufacturer, helped the Conservative government to privatise Rover while keeping ownership in British hands. For a £150 million price tag, BAe obtained a hugely favourable deal. Not only was Rover on the verge of profitability, but the government wrote-off £1.6 billion in accumulated debt and gave a cash injection of £800 million. Later revelations showed that BAe had received some £44.4. million in additional 'sweetners' to seal the deal.[18]

The immediate value of the merger to BAe was more financial than industrial or technological. Overnight, BAe considerably increased its capital base to become the nation's seventh largest company, the twenty-fourth largest company in Europe and one of the world's top hundred manufacturers. Although the car division would place additional demands on the group for investment capital, the payback was expected to be shorter than most of BAe's other programmes and, of course, was less vulnerable to arbitrary shifts in public markets. In short, buying Rover provided BAe with counter-cyclical business. Although the car market was itself highly volatile and, on past experience, Rover a weak player in the European automobile industry, the development and production agreement with Honda reduced BAe's risk.

The BAe management team made much of the likely synergies between the two companies which included a pooling of knowledge in systems engineering; the transfer of advanced automated manufacturing techniques from Rover to BAe; and increasing Rover's access to high technologies such as advanced electronics and materials from the aerospace sector. Later, BAe set up a central R&D facility at Sowerby near Bristol to improve technology transfer throughout the company. Some of its early programmes included research into the application of composite materials in automobiles and the ergonomics of cockpit and dashboard design. Rover's expertise in Japanese production technology has been used to increase the productivity and efficiency of BAe's aerospace divisions.[19] These synergies have proved significant, but the major benefit of BAe's expansion was to bolster BAe's place in British and European industrial policy. BAe's larger 'capital mass' increased its bargaining power within European industry and its ability to influence the future pattern of developments in several key European manufacturing sectors. The general programme of diversification both within the aerospace core and through acquisitions also served to reduce the company's defence dependence from 70 per cent to 40 per cent of turnover. But as we will consider, below, the price of synergy was to increase the managerial complexity of BAe's operations and a loss of focus on the firm's core operations.[20]

The Daimler-MBB merger was also a highly political exercise. The rationalisation of the German aerospace industry had left MBB as the dominant actor in the German aircraft industry. A series of internal reforms had improved its efficiency but there were still serious problems; MBB was still a relatively small actor in the aerospace business with some very heavy commitments and it was heavily dependent on the state for capital and R&D funding.

Moreover, the cost of Airbus production, the depressed condition of the helicopter market and the uncertainty affecting key programmes including the European Fighter and the Tiger helicopter, cast a cloud over MBB's future workload and financial outlook. In 1986, the company lost over DM104 million and, although it returned to profitability the following year, the German government, looking to cap its commitment to expensive programmes such as Airbus, felt that radical measures were necessary. The obvious solution was for MBB to come under the wing of a more powerful German company. A number of prospective suitors, including BMW and Siemens, considered a take-over, but only Daimler was prepared to take-on the problematic MBB.[21]

Daimler's 1987 bid for MBB was strongly supported by the German government which made several important concessions including placing a limit to Daimler's Airbus risk until 1999. The government also agreed to finance new MBB projects and to write-off debts and credits to the tune of DM 4.9 billion. The merger and its terms were highly controversial. Many Germans feared the creation of a 'military industrial complex' based on Daimler's dominance of German defence markets. The merger left Daimler in control of 36 per cent of German defence production. The sheer size of the new company - with 400,000 employees and sales of DM75 million, Daimler-MBB was one of the largest companies in Europe, certainly in Germany - raised the spectre of a 'state within a state'. The junior members of the ruling coalition were unhappy with the terms of the merger and forced some modifications to the terms of the deal. The *Länder* were also unhappy at the loss of influence over 'their' aerospace interests. In the event, while some changes were made to the terms of the merger, the German government had to overrule Federal Cartel Office objections, an unusual step in German industrial politics.[22]

Although it received highly attractive terms to buy MBB, the merger had been actively sought by Daimler. Its chairman, Edzard Reuter, was fully committed to the concept of 'industrial synergy'. As a senior executive of Daimler he had chaired its 'synergy committee' which had been remitted to look for new, high technology business opportunities. This had already led Daimler to acquire MTU, Dornier and AEG, the consumer/defence electronics firm. The take-over of MBB and the creation of Deutsche Aerospace (DASA) was seen as a logical continuation of this policy. The strategy left several of Reuter's more conservative associates uneasy, but his view was that Daimler needed to enter higher value, higher technology sectors to ensure future profitability.   He too believed that the commercial disciplines and cost-conscious nature of automobile production would be beneficial to the aerospace sector. Reuter also had a wider vision of German industry in general, and for the aerospace sector in particular, believing that the German aerospace industry had to acquire a larger capital and industrial mass in order to have more influence over the evolution of European aerospace policy.[23]

Both Daimler and BAe encountered post-merger problems. In both cases, most centred on the increase in managerial complexity and the need to rationalise a scattered set of defence and aerospace interests. Handling Rover was less of a problem than turning Royal Ordnance into a commercially senstive organisation; its own trauma of contraction and reform had been largely overcome by the time BAe bought the company. Earlier investment had created one of the most efficient auto operations in Europe, and while sales volumes were still low, its assets added to BAe's corporate strength. Yet the doubt remained over BAe's overall direction. In the autumn of 1991, BAe's strategy (or lack of) was severely tested. A sharp fall in earnings, a mishandled rights issue and the resulting boardroom struggle raised doubts about BAe's ability to control such a diverse range of interests. The crisis led to a general questioning of BAe's 'deal based' strategy and left the firm vulnerable to take-over. From 1992, BAe began to resolve some of its problems by divestment and by re-focusing on its defence and large civil aircraft core.   This entailed another round of re-organisation and rationalisation as well as the search for international partners in some of its loss-making operations. The option of selling all, or part of Rover, was also open.[24]

Daimler faced similar problems in fusing the various elements within DASA and in melding the aerospace elements with the rest of the company. Merging the old rivals of MBB and Dornier was, perhaps, trickier than the larger units of BAe. The aerospace divisions resented the influx of automobile managers and attitudes. They also feared the impact of plant rationalisation. In 1991, DASA was re-organised into functional, autonomous profit centres which may have been necessary to increase long term efficiency, but further threatened to undermine morale. The need for some focus of identity helped to fuel DASA's determination to launch its own programme, or at least to lead a collaborative venture. According to Johann Schaeffler, DASA's deputy chairman, 'we need a DASA aircraft that the workforce can identify with'.[25] Daimler's position was also exacerbated by the downturn in defence spending and a more critical attitude on the part of the German government towards civil aircraft and space programmes. This raised the prospect of having to help DASA's own conversion and diversification into civil aerospace and a wider range of commercial products. The re-organisation of AEG, especially the loss of lucrative defence and aerospace work to DASA, was much resented. Although it is still too early to evaluate the technological gains which Daimler has won from synergy, the automobile sector was certainly disenchanted by the money being absorbed by DASA in the early 1990s, at a time when Daimler was under pressure in its traditional truck and luxury vehicle markets. Other observers pointed out that the aerospace industry taken over by Daimler was, with a few exceptions, not of the highest technological standing. Association with weapons sales - covert or open - also proved a source of embarrassment and unaccustomed controversy. But on balance, German aerospace has benefitted from the increased capital and political weight provided by Daimler, as was evident in the campaign to assemble the A321 in Hamburg.[26]

On balance, the synergistic merger has tended to generate more problems than obvious advantages. Both Daimler and BAe, especially the latter, have discovered that business cycles might not always be synchronised; a depression in automobile sales combined with the fall in demand for both military and civil aerospace had a serious impact on corporate results at both BAe and Daimler. BAe's particular poor interim results in 1991 were, according to some analysts, a product of the disparate range of interests the firm had collected over the years.[27] In the US, other automobile companies, such as Ford and Chrysler, sold their defence/aerospace subsidiaries. In both the Ford and Chrysler cases, their aerospace divisions were well established, but neither had expanded into aerospace/defence electronics with a clear strategic view of the technological synergies to be obtained through these combinations. Although Ford Aerospace was consistently profitable and had been well-financed by the parent company, cultural differences between the two elements were never fully bridged. But both Ford and Chrysler had found it increasingly hard to make headway in a harsher defence environment and in the event decided to re-focus on their core businesses.

The true value of synergy remains unproven and perhaps unquantifiable. All three major examples offer anecdotal evidence of useful linkages. However, the main value of the exercise, certainly in Europe, seems to have been related to the political and commercial benefits of sheer size. Neither BAe nor Daimler (despite complaints to the contrary) can be ignored by their respective governments and both can afford to assume more of the risk in an increasingly competitive defence market - a major advantage for BAe in the UK defence sector where capital reserves have become an important criteria for the MoD in awarding contracts.[28] DASA's confidence in making a bid for the leadership of new European programmes and to be more assertive within the Airbus consortium was linked to the muscle and credibility provided by Daimler.

On balance, synergy was perhaps a fashionable concept which helped to justify some old fashioned mergers and acquisitions activity.   However, GM and Daimler had at least given some conscious thought to the direction in which they should go; both came to the conclusion that aerospace, or at least aerospace/electronics offered important opportunities.   Daimler also tried to learn from the Hughes experience, with Hughes' chief executive, Malcolm Currie, briefing DASA officials on the American experience.[29] However, Daimler's decision was clearly influenced by the wider politics of German industrial life and GM was attracted by the apparent profits to be won from defence.   Of the three examples, however, industrial synergies were the least significant part of the BAe-Rover merger and seem to have been an *ex post facto* rationalisation of a classic industrial deal.

Diversification strategies and the end of the Cold War

The end of the Cold War has led to another surge of interest in diversification as well as in the more radical option of defence industrial conversion, especially important in the former Soviet Union, where the defence sector had absorbed such a huge proportion of scarce national resources.[30]   Throughout the world aerospace industry, firms stated their intention of expanding their civil business.   Even before the collapse of Soviet power in Europe, a 1989 US industry poll of the top 100 DoD contractors suggested that 41 would be looking to reduce the proportion of turnover devoted to defence work.   This was compared to only five who had considered such a move during the previous 15 years.[31]   Similar sentiments were expressed by all the European major aerospace companies.   Dassault hoped to reduce its military activities to less than half total turnover by the mid 1990s.   Much of this effort would focus on expanding Dassault's subcontract work, civil avionics and industrial software services.   The company also looked to increasing its work on space systems, although in the area of manned space, this only substituted one form of uncertain public funding for another.[32]   Others, such as Snecma and Saab had already shifted away from being predominantly military companies. As we noted above, throughout the 1980s BAe expanded the range of its core businesses in defence and aerospace, as well as diversifying into other manufacturing and service sectors.

However, the main problem for the defence-orientated aerospace company was to shift from a public market, with its set procedures and often comforting relationship with the customer, to the more aggressive context of commercial operations.   Equally important, firms had to adapt to an environment which stressed reliability and cost control over sheer performance. Even in the parallel areas of civil aerospace, the different corporate culture needed for commercial as opposed to defence contracting made it difficult for some defence aerospace firms to meet the sector's more stringent commercial requirements.

Diversification in the US and European aerospace industries

As we have noted above, aircraft firms have found diversification into non aerospace business sectors far from easy. In the late 1960s, Boeing tried its hand at rapid transit systems and hydrofoil construction and Grumman built a range of buses for New York. Neither were particularly successful, and, after recording a $250 million loss, the Grumman bus achieved some notoriety as a case study in failed diversification. MDC had similarly unhappy experiences with an over-complex fire-fighting platform and an excursion into the information systems business. Even where an aerospace firm has experience of the commercial aerospace sector, this is not necessarily valid for other, less focused business sectors. As one MDC executive put it, 'we are sadder and wiser' and, since the early 1990s, the company has adopted a 'back to basics' strategy.[33] This entailed concentration on aerospace, albeit with a broad commitment to the full range of aerospace technologies from defence to space. GD adopted a similar strategy by concentrating on core defence work, even divesting profitable commercial divisions and its missile business in order to 'de-conglomerate'.[34]

In practice, the most attractive targets for diversification remained in parallel, or dual technological sectors such as simulators and air traffic control radars. Hughes' diversification strategy was particularly well developed. Having opted out of several 'self-destructive' US defence contracts, the company sought to deploy its radar and avionic technologies as broadly as possible. However, Hughes could build on established civil radar and satellite activities. Nevertheless, tackling new markets required careful thought. In the spring of 1991, Hughes established a new commercial Radar Systems Group with a brief to apply existing technologies, developed for military programmes, to new civil ventures. From the outset the company recognised the difficulties of 'conversion'; as Malcolm Currie put it 'the history of defence aerospace companies expanding into commercial areas and industrial areas is not a happy one. The road is full of the dried-out old bones and skeletons of chief executive officers who have tried...'.[35]

Other ideas for diversification focused on sectors where the large scale systems integration skills of aerospace firms could be used to advantage. The key here was to break down defence activities into functional areas such as sensors, transport, monitoring and control and to apply these technologies to other equally complex systems. For example, DASA applied this approach to areas like environmental control and traffic management; Martin Marietta tendered for US Mail processing systems contracts; and Alenia was able to use its defence electronics capabilities to devise a pollution control system. Several US defence-aerospace firms considered bidding for US government contracts to clean up hazardous waste and plant left by the Cold War - a 'market' estimated to be worth $1.5 billion a year. Lockheed, for example, suggested that its management skills and technology base were particularly suited to environmental systems and equipment development.[36] However, most of these prospects were insufficient to replace lost defence contracts, and in many cases there has not been a lot to show for all the effort involved.[37]

Significantly, with the problematic history of diversification and conversion in mind, companies looking for new business in the 1980s took more care to match their existing expertise to new markets and to re-organise corporate structures to make best use of the opportunities. Lockheed, for example, re-grouped its military C^3I divisions into a civil communications systems integration unit. Similarly, in 1990 Raytheon formed a new business unit to explore civil ATC activities which would utilise its overseas companies to tap new markets. Other companies have elected to sell process technology rather than products. Dassault, for example, has sold its Catia CAD/CAM system to other aerospace companies and to firms in other industrial sectors, including leading automobile manufacturers.

However, successful diversification often takes time. Together with IBM, Dassault began work on the Catia system in 1976 and did not have a marketable product until the mid 1980s. Since then, the Catia package has captured 70 per cent of the world market and 80 per cent of the US market for such systems.[38] Similarly, GEC-Marconi took five years to increase its non-defence sales to 20 per cent of turn-over despite well-established civil interests.[39] Conversion and large scale diversification is not cheap, and usually requires extensive re-training, investment in new plant and market research.[40] Moreover, the problems facing firms seeking to diversify during the early 1990s were compounded by the depression in the defence industry; poor business prospects reduced credit ratings and the high levels of debt incurred by US firms as a result of unprofitable defence contracts made it very difficult to attract investment in new ventures.

In the final analysis, the most daunting problem for defence-aerospace firms seeking to diversify was the need to adjust to a different corporate culture. As Bill Anders, chairman of General

Dynamics observed, looking to give his firm a more commercial orientation, he found a company with 'a major cultural problem'.[41] Even in a firm such as MDC, which had an existing commercial division, there could be a cultural problem in changing the balance of work from military to civil operations.   According to John McDonnell 'the shift from military to commercial in our product mix does not favour our traditional strength as a builder of high-performance fighter aircraft.' Paradoxically, in this case, MDC tried to improve output and productivity in its civil division by applying the tighter management systems it had developed for some of its military programmes.[42] Significantly, many of the 'new' markets are structurally similar to the defence sector; single, monolithic customers who help to define the nature of their requirement. The idea of developing and selling a product to a more anarchic consumer - the essence of the risk-taking entrepreneur - is still alien to large parts of the defence/aerospace industry.[43]

There are signs that the aerospace industry is beginning to adjust to a new cost-driven environment. The rapid spread of 'Total Quality Management' (TQM) is evidence that the industry, especially in the US, is trying to learn from Japanese production and management concepts. Aerospace has been a pioneer in using CAD/CAM to cope with design and manufacturing complexity; the emphasis is now on commercial levels of productivity, quality and cost-control and customer satisfaction. The adoption of TQM was in part the result of a US DoD initiative in the late 1980s, but it has also been triggered by pressure from overseas competition. There have been problems - MDC's experience with an over-rapid imposition of TQM combined with job cuts stands as an object lesson in how not to manage the transition to a 'people-orientated' management system.[44] Positive gains are now being reported throughout the US defence/aerospace industry. Rockwell, for example, claims that TQM saved its Tactical Missile Division from extinction. European firms, such as Fokker and BAe, have also re-evaluated their approach to management and production and have discovered significant improvements in productivity.[45] In 1992, BAe announced a radical re-think of its production organisation; by combining its civil and military assembly operations, BAe intends to use new flexible process technology to generate higher levels of productivity.[46] Internal reform, and shrinkage, would seem to be the most effective approach to 'conversion'. State aid might help to MITIgate some of the transitionary effects, but huge sums would be needed to stave off the lost employment or corporate casualties implied by the transformation of a 'Cold War' structure into a 'peacetime' industry.

Conversion in the former USSR.

In the west, conversion and diversification issues have had a relatively narrow focus, based on individual firms, or at worst, regions where there are significant concentrations of defence-aerospace activity - the British south-west or southern California for example.   There are macro-economic implications of defence industrial retrenchment, especially for a state like the UK where defence manufacturing and defence R&D have played a more important role in overall industrial life and trading activity.   But the problem affecting the former Soviet Union is a fundamental question affecting the whole structure of the economy.[47]   The defence sector - especially aerospace - was hitherto an island of quality in an obsolete manufacturing system.   The historic priority attached to defence and the prestige goals of space exploration gave it a privileged position in terms of access to resources and skilled manpower.   *Glasnost* and *pererestroika* exposed the aerospace sector to a wave of reform and re-orientation.   Even before the end of the Cold War, the Soviet defence and aerospace industries were expected to achieve a 40 per cent conversion factor.   All aerospace plants had a quota of civil goods; the manufacturers of the Buran space shuttle, for example, turned out artificial feet.

In this context, conversion was in part a panacea for the long term ills of a command economy, and a necessary catalyst to release skills and technology for use in the wider Soviet economy.   For Soviet aerospace, this entailed the search for alternative uses of its technical and production skills outside aerospace.   The industry was also expected to sell its products and services for hard currency.   The problem of cultural adaptation seen in western defence companies was accentuated in the former Soviet Union by the absence of a broader experience of free-market values.   The separation of design bureaux and production units and the centralised allocation of funding and scheduling created an inflexible and monolithic structure ill-suited to the demands of an international market.   Even the privileged defence sector had to overcome decades of under-investment in capital equipment and to cope with huge social overheads associated with running the production 'cities' at the heart of the ex-Soviet aerospace industry.   Defence managers 'converting' to the civil sector also faced problems of lost prestige and lower salaries.   This led to a 'brain drain' from defence/aerospace towards the new private sector and employment with western joint venture companies. The industry also had to cope for the first time with shortages and inefficiencies in the supplier chain and   legally-backed complaints from its civil and military customers.[48]

Following the collapse of the USSR, funding cuts accelerated with long term implications for the technical development of the aerospace sector. The political back-lash against the military-industrial bureaucrats associated with the 1991 coup and fragmentation of the Soviet state speeded up the creation of decentralised industrial structures similar to those in the west which might better facilitate the development of a commercial orientation. However, the claims of the respective republics on 'their' aerospace facilities and the demands by the Russian federation to 'charge' for R&D activities (which were largely concentrated in Russia) added to the problems of transition to the free market. The turmoil also acted to deter western firms from launching joint ventures. On the other hand, the end of the Soviet threat held out the prospect of a relaxation in controls over technology transfer.[49]

The situation facing the ex-Soviet civil aerospace sector is only a little better. Although the Soviet civil aerospace sector had benefited from a closed domestic and east European market, their products were uneconomic and unreliable. With the breakdown of Soviet control over Eastern Europe and the break-up of the USSR, those airlines have moved quickly to seek western replacements. A new generation of Soviet airliners is appearing, but in the short term the new Russian and Ukranian firms will have to look for help from the US and Europe to improve propulsion and avionics technology. Even so, aerospace managers, with no real concept of marketing or sales activities, will have a hard job coping with the new environment.[50] In the final analysis, the conversion of the Soviet defence-aerospace complex must be seen as part of a massive socio-economic change - a problem which is outside the terms of this book. However, the depth of the difficulties facing Soviet aerospace managers should put the problems of western firms into some perspective.

Domestic teaming

Domestic teaming refers to development cooperation between companies within the same national industry. Teaming excludes conventional sub-contracting, but the partnership may entail a defined leader or prime contractor. In many respects, the motives - particularly where government actors are concerned - may be similar to those of international collaboration. Against a background of rising development costs and falling defence budgets, teaming is a way of increasing or maintaining the technological and industrial base needed to support increasingly costly and complex aerospace programmes, particularly in the defence sector. From a corporate perspective, it gives a company at least a share of business which it might otherwise not have had.   Under certain conditions, domestic teaming might be a step towards industrial consolidation (as it was in the UK and Germany) but it could also serve as an alternative to either rationalisation or international cooperation.

In Germany, teaming was an important stage in the re-birth of the national aerospace industry after the Second World War. In the late 1950s, a number of development consortia were formed to work on international and domestic projects. The most important example of the former was Deutsche Airbus formed in 1966 to facilitate German participation in the European Airbus programme and comprised every German airframe company except Dornier. The Federal Government played a major role in the creation and continuation of these groups, and in time, most were absorbed into a rationalised German industry.[51]

For Japanese firms, teamwork reflects both a strong cultural imperative and a well established national strategy used to lift industrial or technological capabities to world level. Characteristically, the Japanese formed domestic teams, or Development Consortia (JDCs), to develop national aerospace projects or to participate in international ventures. As we noted in Chapter Two, the JDCs are non-profit making organisations designed to reduce duplication of resources and to expand Japanese capabilities. Members contribute cash and personnel to various projects in rough proportion to the workshare they desire. The system ensures that work, development experience and revenues are distributed around the industry and prevents smaller manufacturers from being squeezed out by the giant conglomerates. The Japanese government, through MITI, acts as a sponsor and facilitator. MITI ensures that all of the relevant Heavy Industry companies with aerospace subsidiaries are represented in a defined 'national programme', regardless of which among them has been chosen as prime contractor or commercial consortium leader.[52] The JDCs, in turn, are remitted to identify other possible projects for development or participation. Currently, Japan's civil aerospace activities are channelled through the JADC (airframes) and the JAEC (engines). The JADC is responsible for all the major sub-contracting and risk-sharing agreements with Boeing and the JEDC represents Japan in the International Aero-Engines group.   The JADC is also coordinating work on second generation SSTs and hypersonic transports.[53] Other coalitions are engaged on domestic projects, including the FSX and the H-2 rocket. In the Japanese case, the primary aim of teaming is not to reduce costs or even to encourage rationalisation, but is a deliberate, government-sponsored industrial strategy to extend Japanese industrial capabilities over the long term.

In Britain during the 1950s, teaming was not only used to facilitate the development of the TSR-2 strike aircraft, but also formed part of a government-inspired rationalisation strategy. The government 'mixed and matched' the technical characteristics of several design proposals, and used its contract power to force companies into larger, permanent groups.[54] More recently, the demands of 'value-for-money' in procurement has led to the formation of domestic teams to manage complex, fixed-price programmes (for example, the IBM/Westland EH-101 team). Similarly, the French government has pooled the efforts of several firms to manage the Rafale programme. Here, however, domestic 'teaming' was a second best option to an international joint venture under French leadership. Having failed to attract foreign partners, the French government required Dassault to surrender formal leadership to a domestic consortium.

In recent years, the most significant use of domestic teaming has been in the US. During the 1980s, the US government requested bids for, amongst others, a new fighter for the USAF and USN (ATF), a carrier attack aircraft (ATA) and an advanced light helicopter (LH). All were expected push the boundaries of technology - especially in the degree of integration that would be required between airframe and electronics. The need for Low Observability (stealth) further complicated many of the specifications. Most important of all, it was evident that production runs would be shorter than before and that the Pentagon would insist on more stringent contract terms even for development. Similarly, much of the development and production work would be on a fixed price basis and few companies were prepared to assume that level of risk alone.[55] The Pentagon, as a matter of policy, also wanted to preserve as many design and production centres as possible and a single 'winner-take-all' would have led to a significant loss of industrial capability. Although in the initial stages individual designs were solicited and presented, development work was based on groups led by a designated team leader.

In the case of the ATF, seven firms submitted initial bids for the 'Dem-Val' programme; all were well qualified, with recent experience of managing a large, complex weapons programme. But in the summer of 1986, Lockheed, General Dynamics and Boeing announced that they would act as a team if one of their proposals was selected for the Dem-Val phase. This triggered a counter-response from Northrop and MDC. In the event, Lockheed was chosen to lead one team and Northrop the other, with the Lockheed team's F-22 eventually winning the development contract. GD and Lockheed were the more experienced in fighter and stealth technology, but as overall management competence proved decisive in the final choice of teams, Boeing's huge resources and general knowledge of advanced manufacturing technology, large-scale programme management and systems integration was vital.[56] F-22 development responsibilities were shared between three companies; Lockheed, as the prime contractor, was awarded overall design leadership and responsibility for the forward fuselage; Boeing has designed and built the wings and the aircraft's avionics suite; and GD was to develop the aft-fuselage, landing gear and tail surfaces. In order to create a coherent group, design and engineering teams from the three companies have been integrated and other links were established through secure data transmission systems. F-22 final assembly will be at a government-owned plant managed by Lockheed.[57]

A similar example of competitive teaming was employed by the US Army in the LH helicopter programme. One team comprised Boeing and Sikorsky (UTC), the eventual winners while another linked Bell (Textron) with MDC. The contest was again a 'winner-take-all' match with similar pressures on the firms to invest in preliminary R&D and to pool technology in order to meet the Army's testing requirements. As in the case of the ATF/ATA, two of the LH competitors were also cooperating in the development of another project - in this case the Bell-Boeing V-22 tilt-rotor aircraft. But all were potential competitors, especially in the use of advanced helicopter technology in civil applications.

Preliminary work on the X-30 National Aerospace Plane (NASP) was an even more extensive use of the team concept. The NASP was envisaged as a major R&D programme to enhance US *national* aerospace technology. The advantage of teaming was seen in terms of the elimination of duplication and effort. It was also recognised that even with a NASA contract, a single contractor could not afford to do all the research alone. Four US firms, GD, MDC, UTC and the team leader, Rockwell, were awarded a $2 billion NASA contract which pooled the best features of several independent designs. The NASP was regarded as a way to maintain US leadership in aerospace technology into the 21st century. Significantly, US anti-trust law was circumvented by reference to the 1990-1 National Defence Authorisation Act which designated the X-30 as a research vehicle with design requirements entirely 'related to the exclusive research mission'. As such, it was not a commercial product built for profit in a competitive market and subject to the anti-trust laws.[58] By the end of 1991, US industry had also adopted teaming strategies to support basic research in areas such as composite materials.[59]

For US firms accustomed to a competitive environment, the experience of working in development teams for the first time on such important programmes was not easy, certainly in their early stages. There were, for example, fears of 'technology leakage' to current and future rivals. The position was eased to some extent by the fact that the two leading fighter companies, GD and MDC, were on opposite sides for the ATF. But on the other hand, as members of the parallel ATA (A-12) group, 'Chinese Walls' had to be erected between the various design teams. There was a danger that cooperation could be affected by fear that participants might abuse the partnership to gain an edge in other programmes. But in the final analysis, as in the F-22, the partners felt constrained to channel their collective efforts into a 'relatively secure, $95 billion programme rather than risk holding back for the remote possibility of future business'.[60]

Indeed, in most cases the companies had to cooperate to an 'unprecedented extent to win the prized contract'. According to the winning ATF team, for example, the generation of collective 'camaraderie and collective capabilities' were a crucial part of their success. In this respect, external pressure - the 'winner take all' nature of the contract - and the importance of the programme to their future as major defence aerospace contractors clearly motivated the contestants. On an individual level, people who were unable to make the transition to a cooperative environment 'were filtered out ... Most people now think of themselves [as not] working for just Lockheed or General Dynamics or Boeing. They work for the ATF'.[61] In effect, US firms involved in teaming, like Europeans facing international collaboration in the 1960s, had to 'learn' how to collaborate in the development process. They had to face the loss of some elements of independence; accept some cost and efficiency penalties; and above all, they had to explore how to handle more diffused authority in programme management.

Teaming has been criticised in the US as an over complex solution to procurement problems. The continued proliferation of teaming threatened more 'overlapping and convoluted arrangements'.[62] For example, initial bids for the A-12 successor, the AX, came from six teams, often with overlapping membership and exhibiting clear conflicts of interest. This can create complex management problems; MDC, for example, had to establish two separate design units. According to MDC officials, 'they will work as if they were competing companies'. Both have had to work under strict rules governing information exchange. This required physical separation, different management chains and led to a complete absence of cross-clearance. Given the need to prevent 'leakage' and collusion, it was often the case that new ideas and concepts within the same company could not be used in different projects. As a result of some of these requirements, costs have risen and important technological opportunities might have been lost. For example, GD and MDC were denied access to government-owned data concerning stealth technology developed by Northrop for the B-2 for use on the A-12. The F-22 team faced similar constraints on the use of technology developed for the F-117 and the B-2, although Boeing was able to apply some of its B-2 production experience to F-22 work. As Bill Anders of General Dynamics put it 'teaming has no redeeming value and entangles everybody, spreading profits as well as risks.'.[63]

On the other hand, domestic teaming was a way of coping with the dilemma of developing expensive and sensitive projects which, in a European context, would have been internationalised. Although several of these examples of teaming will have foreign components or use overseas systems (such as the GEC head-up display on the F-22), they are clearly US programmes where the technology, while shared, will remain within the US aerospace industry. Teaming on the NASP was also an application of the principles which motivate Japan's use of domestic consortia to promote a *national* presence in aerospace. Indeed, other critics of teaming have seen it as a dubious form of implicit government intervention in the market. From this perspective, the pooling of design ideas and technology threatens to promote mediocrity and to hamper entrepreneurial initiative in the US aerospace industry.[64]

Domestic rationalisation

For the US, the use of domestic teaming might have been seen as an alternative to either rationalisation or internationalisation. The losers in major contract competitions could fall by the wayside, but the remainder would hopefully retain independent design and development capability in order to compete for future domestic and international business. Where there have been cases of rationalisation, they have reflected market forces and the actions of individual firms; the US government has not intervened in the process. Nor has the US had much need to internationalise core defence programmes, although as has been noted, the civil sector has adopted collaborative strategies. In short, up to the early 1990s, the US aerospace industry and domestic demand for its products was still large enough to sustain competition between companies or domestic teams.

No such luxury was possible (nor perhaps, politically acceptable) where major European combat aircraft were concerned. Throughout the 1950s and 1960s, domestic rationalisation followed rapidly by international collaboration became the norm for European industries. As was noted in earlier chapters, the current European national aerospace industries have seen successive waves of domestic consolidation, leaving, by and large, single national champions in engines, airframes and major systems. In contrast to the US, national governments were also often active participants in the rationalisation process. There is still some scope for further national rationalisation. In the UK throughout the late 1980s and early 1990s, GEC steadily increased its dominance of the avionics and electronic equipment sector.[65] And there are a relatively large number of medium-sized firms whose independence may be increasingly under threat. The French aerospace industry seems finally to be moving towards the creation of a single national airframe champion by uniting Aerospatiale and Dassault within the state holding company Sogema. However, Dassault has argued strongly that this is not, and not likely to be, a full merger. Nevertheless, as defence markets continue to shrink, Dassault's position will become less viable and a merger by stealth is almost certainly to occur. For Europe, however, the next stage - and one in many respects already underway - is rationalisation at a regional level, entailing the creation of more permanent transnational industrial structures and perhaps the emergence of genuine international companies. This issue will be explored in more detail in the last two chapters.

Across the Atlantic, the pace of domestic rationalisation sharply increased in 1992. The earlier shake-out in the US defence industry during the late 1980s had seen a large number of mergers and acquisitions in the second and third tiers. But in the early 1990s, more substantial changes began to occur near, or at the top of the industrial pyramid. In November 1992, GE sold its aerospace subsidiary to Martin Marietta for $3.05 billion, turning Martin overnight into one of the largest US defence contractors.[66] In December, General Dynamics triggered an even more fundamental re-alignment of US industrial capacity. In short order, GD sold its tactical missile business to Hughes and its fighter division to Lockheed. Many analysts felt that GD's actions had broken a log-jam at the top of the US industry - removing a psychological barrier to the exit of a prime contractor. Lockheed certainly felt that it made sense to consolidate two elements of the F-22 Team and to rationalise design and development activities in the tactical fighter sector. As Norman Augustine of Martin Marietta put it, ' We may be at the start of a similar process to that which occurred in post World War Two France and England, so that we look more like what we see in Europe today'.[67] Unlike European governments under such circumstances, the US government again stood aside from the process of rationalisation. Defence officials expressed some concern at the possible loss of design capacity; but they conceded that rationalisation made economic sense and that it was not their place to shape the exact features of the US defence-aerospace industry. The prospect of still deeper rationalisation - possibly precipitated by the bankruptcy of a major contractor - may yet lead to a change in policy, with some form of interventionism to protect key national assets.[68] Should the worst happen to a company such as MDC, the US government - with President Clinton moving towards a more interventionist industrial policy generally - might assume a more direct role in saving or otherwise re-structuring such a major element of the US defence industrial base. But for the moment, the US government appears to be content to allow commercial decisions to re-shape the US aerospace industry.[69] Commenting on the Aspin review of September 1993, Pentagon officials specifically ruled out 'bail-out' as an option, re-affirming the primacy of market forces in driving rationalisation in the US defence/aerospace industry.[70] Indeed, without direct state aid or interference, the US has already moved faster and with more apparent effect than the European industry to cope with reduced and more competitive markets.

The significance of the end of Cold War certainties and the pressure of new conditions throughout the world aerospace industry cannot be underestimated. The re-orientation of a whole industry world-wide requires long term thinking and, ideally, investment at the top of a market cycle. The comforting security of the 'permanent' arms race dulled too many companies into believing that this was a fixed condition. Realisation that this is not to be has left the industry in a desperate crisis. For the first time since the mid-1930s, managers must cope with structural over-capacity and the need imaginatively to seek new markets and new approaches to industrial development. The industry has for decades now talked of international markets and the importance of international cooperation. Europe has long admitted the inadequacy of national solutions to complex and expensive aerospace programmes; if, in the final shake-out, the US aerospace industry does end up with a limited number of national champions, would the same pressures for internationalisation apply? There have been significant changes in the attitude of US industrialists towards joint ventures and other forms of collaboration; but as will be explored in the next chapter, the US still has some way to go before it embraces the degree of internationalisation that has been forced on the Europeans.

7

International Collaboration

Introduction

Since the late 1950s, international cooperation has become a significant, and for some national industries, a dominant industrial strategy. In several cases, collaboration remains the only realistic way for firms to participate in major programmes. Even for those with a complete range of technical resources, financial and market pressures have often forced the adoption of an international approach to development and production. Collaboration is also likely to be a highly political issue; it may be a condition imposed by government on companies wishing to do business in a country; or it may form part of a broader national strategy for technological development. In the past, international cooperation was predominantly a tactic adopted by the Europeans and others in the face of US dominance; but as development costs rise and world markets become more competitive, US firms have begun to follow similar routes. In the longer term, the establishment of collaborative links could lead to the evolution of a more interdependent world aerospace industry - if not on a global, certainly on a regional scale.

Definitions and forms of collaboration

Collaboration can take many forms and the term is sometimes used, especially in the US, to describe all forms of international links between companies.[1] At one end of the spectrum is the supplier/subcontractor relationship, where equipment, components, and structures are bought on the international market. This has been a well-established part of international aerospace since well before the Second World War. More commonly, however, collaboration relates to international development and manufacturing. Again this can vary in complexity and in the degree of interdependence between the partners. The simplest forms are

151

licensing and/or international co-production of a foreign design.[2] In most cases, the recipient's interests are in obtaining employment, technology and trade balance benefits. For the source, the hope is to extend production lines and/or to obtain further revenue from amortised R&D. Governments on both side of the equation may hope to obtain political influence or to reinforce security commitments.

Licensing and co-production, while cost-effective ways of building-up or maintaining a basic aerospace capability, have clear disadvantages for the more ambitious firm or nation. Unless, as in the case of the Japanese FSX, the intention is to use the foreign design as a platform for more advanced domestic development, licensing or co-production activity will rarely lead to a place on the leading edge of aerospace technology. There may also be severe restrictions placed by the source company or its government on subsequent commercial exploitation. That being said, the British helicopter firm of Westland improved substantially on Sikorsky-licenced products to achieve an impressive technical standing in the European helicopter industry.

In recent years, subcontractors have begun to take on some of the financial risk of developing structures and components for new aircraft and engines - especially in the civil sector. All the major civil primes - Boeing, MDC, Airbus and Fokker have a network of subcontractors and risk-sharing partners, especially in the Far East. A risk-sharing partnership is likely to provide a more rewarding technical and industrial experience. In this form of cooperation, a subcontractor invests in some aspect of development in return for a share of the profits and specified privileges in respect of project management and possibly some access to other aspects of technical and commercial exploitation. This is a considerable advance on licence/co-production activity and may lead to a long term partnership. In many respects, this is an ideal form of relationship for a firm which is happy to remain a junior or niche player in the world aerospace industry. The prime contractor, on the other hand, can spread the cost and risks of development without losing control of the programme and transferring too much technology or expertise to a potential competitor.

In Europe aerospace collaboration has come to mean much more than even a risk-sharing partnership - although the format is used extensively by European primes. Collaboration is defined as 'two or more nations agreeing to share the development and production costs of a new project'.[3] Moreover, such collaboration has usually implied comprehensive work and technology-sharing agreements proportionate to the level of a nation's or company's contribution to the costs of development. The specific form of collaboration can vary considerably and has changed over the years in the light of experience and new requirements. Most of the current European programmes are (or started out) as international project-based consortia where industrial leadership and direction are vested in a trans-national holding company.

All forms of development collaboration have a balance of advantages and disadvantages. Collaboration is more costly, especially if there is duplication of development and production activity. The exact premium is difficult to calculate but estimates of between ten per cent and 50 per cent have been typical; but it is difficult to reach firm conclusions about the 'cost of collaboration' because of the limited number of directly comparable examples. One authoritative study concluded that European collaborative ventures have been no more expensive than national programmes.[4] Similarly, the IEPG concluded that the Tornado cost more to develop than a comparable national programme, but that this was 'more or less balanced by the benefits in terms of reduced unit price through increased production runs'.[5] The belief that collaboration would inevitably drive up costs has been one of the strongest counter arguments deployed by American firms against full-scope development cooperation.

Evidence given to the British House of Commons Defence Committee investigating the European Fighter, suggested that 'a national programme would be more costly than a collaborative programme ... in terms of procurement cost we would be talking of an increment in excess of 20 per cent'. However, other data suggested that the UK's requirements over the life-time of the project could have been met by a national project for only five per cent more than the collaborative programme. According to the UK National Audit Office, collaboration has tended to reduce the net development costs to contributing states but the 'unit production costs of a collaborative programme might be higher than a national equivalent'. The Parliamentary Comptroller and Auditor General concluded from an analysis of ten international defence programmes that it was hard to identify the extent of 'financial and other benefits actually accruing from collaboration'.[6] In general, however, any assessment of the costs and benefits of collaboration will be based on subjective judgements or will face the problem of 'counter factual' arguments - the 'what ifs' of a hypothetical national alternative or a foreign purchase which itself may be deliberately underpriced in order to undermine long term competition

The work sharing agreements associated with collaborative programmes, especially if based on the principle of *le juste retour,* can affect efficiency and increase costs, especially if one of the partners is technically less advanced or industrially less experienced than the others. This has become less of a problem for

European airframe and engine manufacturers as standards have levelled up - mainly due to collaboration. However, work sharing issues can still cause problems in the equipment sector where national capabilities can still vary. In the case of the European Fighter, the differences in competence between British and Spanish equipment firms have caused problems in adjusting the balance of work between the two countries.[7] Equally, as the Airbus example will illustrate, disputes over work sharing can re-occur even in a mature programme such as the Airbus. While politically difficult to avoid in major European programmes, the impact of *le juste retour* is rarely economically beneficial. The existence of several production lines for the EFA and the fact that each wing is built in two countries inevitably reduces industrial efficiency. Under pressure to reduce costs to meet German targets, the EFA team have been able to find savings of 13 per cent, but any further improvement could only come from either simplifying the specification or the work sharing agreements.[8]

The extent to which work shares and equipment sub contracting can be subjected to the financial rigours of competition is an increasingly sensitive aspect of collaboration. But its application to international programmes could increase industrial efficiency and considerably improve cost control.[9] An improvement in the day-to-day management of cooperative programmes might help to reduce costs. In the view of the UK National Audit Office, ideally this would mean that programmes would be led by 'real companies' rather than trans-national consortia brought together for a particular programme. This would sharpen efficiency and establish clear lines of responsibility. However, the Audit Office recognised that this would not be possible for large projects; in this case 'the consortium company had to be vested with sufficient authority by its parent companies to run the collaborative programme effectively'.[10]

A major benefit of collaboration is, of course, its role in maintaining and improving national and corporate technological standing. Collaboration has been the main vehicle for the re-birth of the German and Italian aerospace industries. Spain is using participation in projects like EFA to build up expertise in electronics, materials and engine technology. Similar interests are integral to Japanese work with Boeing and in the International Aero-Engines V2500 project, in China's participation in MDC programmes and in Taiwan's deal with BAe Regional. On the other hand, where companies have held leading positions in the European industry, such as in the case of Rolls-Royce and much of the UK equipment sector, they can lose technically as a result of collaboration. This fear has certainly overlain US attitudes towards the FSX. However, the reality of European aerospace is that there would have been few opportunities to maintain a national capability without collaboration. On the other hand, collaboration alone cannot ensure a complete capability. The Germans, for example, have felt that their lack of independent, systems integrating skills is a serious handicap in obtaining the full industrial and commercial benefits of aerospace.[11]

One of the main problems associated with collaboration is the reconciliation of national requirements and fluctuations in political support for a project. These can be especially difficult if, as in the case of military projects, genuine differences in tactical need are complicated by divergent national industrial and technological interests. Even in civil projects, the need to obtain national government funding has often caused additional delay and uncertainty. At worst, these problems can lead to the breakdown of collaboration or the defection of a major partner. Collaboration also implies some degree of compromise over design and performance characteristics. This is now less of a problem for civil projects which are shaped by a wider commercial environment; but military programmes can still suffer from the reconciliation process and national armed forces may obtain less than optimal equipment. On the other hand, once launched and into production, the stability afforded by collaborative development is much welcomed by national firms used to a history of crippling, budget-driven cancellations. Even before final commitments are made, the fear of diplomatic repercussions from withdrawal and the risk of losing credibility as a partner acts as a stabilising factor in securing support for development.

The European experience

The European aerospace industry has perhaps the most extensive experience of collaborative development, which began in the mid to late 1950s with co-production of the US F-104 and Hawk missile, as well as the NATO-sponsored Fiat G-91 and Breguet Atlantic. Collaboration came of age, however, with the Franco-German Transall military transport, the Anglo-French Concorde and Jaguar fighter programmes launched in the early 1960s. These were followed by the Airbus and Tornado, several missile and helicopter joint ventures and the beginnings of a European space programme. The initial experience of collaboration was neither easy nor harmonious, with national and corporate rivalries, disputes over work shares and project leadership, and problems stemming from fluctuating political support providing a continuous backdrop to development.[12]

By the 1970s, however, collaboration was accepted as a routine strategy for European aerospace programmes and some of the early problems had been eased by the experience of successfully working together. Practice, and some expensive lessons, had also led to the evolution of more efficient and equitable forms of managing international projects. In particular, the emergence of trans-national project-based consortia such as Panavia and Airbus Industrie, was viewed as a major advance in international programme management. In the case of civil programmes, the growth of industry-led rather than government-inspired collaboration was regarded as an even more significant improvement.[13] The experience of the 1960s and early 1970s was not always positive. The problems associated with Anglo-French collaboration in military aircraft and helicopters during this period had a long term impact on the structure of European aerospace development. Similar difficulties in civil aero-engines encouraged the evolution of trans-Atlantic collaboration.[14] Overall, the result of European collaboration up to the late 1980s was to bind European firms in a network of agreements and joint projects which did not, at the same time, entail the surrender of national control over aerospace. Airbus Industrie and Arianespace have successfully challenged US dominance in commercial aircraft and satellite launchers, and Europeans can hold their own in a range of defence products from advanced strike fighters to missiles and helicopters. Even the Americans have had to concede that the effect of collaboration has been to narrow, if not to close, the technical and industrial gap between Europe and the US. This, in turn, has forced the US to view Europe as a more equal partner in a trans-Atlantic industrial system.

Although Europe has an impressive and unprecedented experience of collaboration, the present position falls short of full interdependence. There is, of course, no reason why competitive elements should not exist in European aerospace - indeed in some respects this may be highly desirable. Equally, the concept of a 'Fortress Europe' in aerospace is absurd and runs counter to the globalisation of aerospace development and production. However, there is a case for suggesting that there could be better ways still of organising European aerospace which would not only strengthen the region's ability both to compete against and to work with the US as an equal, but also to maintain its position in respect of the emerging aerospace nations in the Far East.

Commercial and political pressures are already at work pushing companies and established transnational partnerships beyond the format created in the 1960s and which matured during the 1970s. European aerospace may be at a point where a collaborative process which has achieved so much may have reached the limits of its ability to respond effectively and efficiently to rapidly changing market conditions. European defence equipment budgets will have to stretch further and governments want more value for money from their defence contractors. Global competition is also increasing as Europe, the US, the Soviet Union and new entrants vie for defence export sales. Although the commercial sector is experiencing a boom, European civil aerospace is also being forced by American competition to reach even more stringent levels of efficiency and productivity.

European aerospace collaboration in practice

By the early 1990s, a large number of European collaborative programmes were either in service or in the course of development. There were over a dozen industrial consortia producing a range of aircraft, engines, missiles and space vehicles, several of which dated from the late 1960s and early 1970s. As we will discuss in the final chapter, a number of these comprised actual or embryonic transnational companies or subsidiaries of groups of European firms. Despite a substantial record of cooperation, political and industrial interests could still divide or threaten to divide European companies and governments. These problems could be clearly seen in three of the more important European programmes, the European Fighter Aircraft (EFA), the Tiger helicopter and the Airbus.

(i) The European Fighter Aircraft

The origins of the EFA programme, and the manoeuvring which led to its launch, underline the fact that the politics of collaboration could still be highly complex and bitterly fought. Yet when the need for a new fighter aircraft emerged in several European states in the late 1970s, there was little doubt that it would be a collaborative venture: ever-higher development costs and the acceptance of collaboration as a routine strategy on the part of those governments and most of the companies likely to be involved in the programme, combined to press the case for a joint programme. The difficulty was in defining a project and establishing a collaborative structure acceptable to all. In the event, the problem boiled down to the impossibility of accommodating French interests with those of the 'Panavia' states, Britain, Germany and Italy.[15] There were also differences over design characteristics and requirements, but these could have been resolved if there had been greater congruity between industrial and technological concerns. The EFA negotiations also confirmed the emergence of Germany as a key actor and arbiter in European aerospace politics.[16] Nevertheless, the division between Rafale and EFA has left Europe with two competing fighter aircraft - a luxury which both sides might yet come to regret.

Although the 'Panavia' grouping (with the addition of Spain) settled quickly into a partnership based on two international consortia, Eurofighter and Eurojet, there were serious Anglo-German conflicts, over work-sharing and the balance of design leadership.   In theory, political intervention in the award of sub-contracts was to be confined to the most expensive and politically sensitive items such as radar, engines and control systems.   In practice,   potential   sub-contractors   usually   anticipated worksharing requirements by forming international consortia drawn from the participating countries.   Indeed, Eurofighter was required to monitor the balance of contract awards and to 'encourage greater participation in a consortium where a country is   lagging'.   French firms or European subsidiaries of US companies were not to be excluded provided they met Eurofighter standards and that contracts were worded so that an EFA sale could not be blocked by US government intervention.[17]

Even so, a dispute over the choice of a radar system revealed serious divisions between the British and the Germans. Although there were important technical aspects involved, it also reflected significant national industrial/technology policy concerns.   There were two alternatives, each backed by international consortia, but the German-led group proposed a design based on American (Hughes) technology. This was matched by a British-led team with an all-European concept.   The British contended that despite agreements with the US, dependence on American technology would render EFA vulnerable to a US export veto. It was also evident, however, that German preferences were reinforced by the fact that the German-led programme would in some degree match British 'leadership' of airframe integration and engine development.[18] The issue was not resolved until January 1990, seriously threatening the EFA timetable. In the event, an agreement in favour of the British system was reached with the British government undertaking to guarantee technical performance and with a cost ceiling for the German contribution.[19] The contest between the two radars was also complicated by US pressure. The US government already felt that the Europeans had not given the MDC Hornet 2000 (a proposed F-18 update) a fair chance to compete against EFA in the original design competition. The negative reaction to the Hughes radar (predominantly from Britain) again left US officials very angry and helped to fuel fears of a 'Fortress Europe' in some American official and industrial circles. The radar dispute showed that despite a long tradition of working together, and general agreement to go ahead with a particular programme notwithstanding, political factors, driven by industrial and technological interests, could still divide apparently close partners. From the German side, the determination not to be taken for granted and their concern to achieve parity in high-level systems integration tasks belied the advances made by consortia such as Panavia in burying concepts such as 'design leadership'.

For their part, the British were consistently disturbed about the reliability of their German partners. Always a controversial project inside Germany, from the late 1980s, the collapse of Communism, the cost of unification and growing domestic opposition to an increasingly expensive and irrelevant programme began to call into question German commitment to EFA. By the spring of 1992, a majority of the German Cabinet appeared to be against producing the aircraft. This would not necessarily mean an end to EFA; the British and Italians were prepared to consider production without the Germans. Although costs would rise with a smaller production run (by about seven per cent, or by 12 per cent if the Spanish followed the German example) some of these would be offset by lower wage costs in Britain and Italy. The German government also faced strong pressure from its national aerospace industry and from the Bavaria-based CSU. Withdrawal would threaten the loss of 20,000 jobs at DASA and amongst other German suppliers, and would save little money if the Luftwaffe was to have a replacement for its aging Phantoms.[20]

The German government was also well aware of the impact their withdrawal would have on their reputation as a reliable partner in international programmes: according to Erich Riedl, the Federal Aerospace Coordinator, 'the constant questioning of, and above all a unilateral withdrawal from a contractually agreed programme, would lead to a clear loss of confidence in our reliability as a cooperative partner and would have adverse affects on European cooperation in all sectors'. The British Prime Minister John Major made this clear at a meeting with Chancellor Kohl in June, noting how cancellation would be 'very damaging to Germany's credibility as a reliable partner'.[21] Nevertheless, the crisis rumbled on through the autumn and winter of 1992 and was still largely unresolved by the spring of 1993. The German Defence Minister Volker Rühe, in part motivated by his own political ambitions, continued to press for substantial price cuts in the EFA and hinted strongly of cancellation. The British took a tough but conciliatory line; they were prepared to discuss cost reduction, but were not prepared to countenance cancellation. If the Germans pulled out, they would still be required to pay for development and the British implied that a three nation or even a UK-only production programme would go ahead.[22]

In October, Eurofighter revealed that the cost reduction exercise had achieved a 13 per cent saving, but this was still short of Rühe's

DM100 million fly-away price. Rühe was unable to detach the Spanish or the Italians (despite the latter's own financial problems) and was under growing criticism from German industrialists who feared loss of business and technology. However, Rühe clearly believed that he had domestic public opinion on his side and that his opposition to EFA was bolstering his own standing as a possible successor to Kohl. The Luftwaffe still needed a fighter and the alternatives were felt to be less cost effective than EFA. In the event, Ruehe agreed to a compromise whereby the Germans would have a less sophisticated version which should in theory, meet his cost targets. This was officially designated as the New EFA (NEFA).[23] This, however, was still not the end of the saga. In March 1993, Rühe stated that the German defence budget could not afford to pay for development that year. Germany's partners wanted payment and DASA could face paying for its share of current costs out of its own resources. Further problems have arisen stemming from the reduction in the German specification. GEC laid claim to design leadership of the EFA flight control system, hitherto a DASA responsibility. DASA was hardly happy to contemplate being reduced to 'metal bashing' and resisted GEC's demands.[24] At the time of writing, the future of the EFA programme is still far from assured, despite the clear need for a fighter replacement on the part of three airforces. The industrial consequences for a large part of the European aerospace industry of not proceding with EFA would be very serious and would damage much of the collaborative spirit and infrastructure painfully built over two decades or more.

Even before the crisis of 1992-3, there were signs that BAe was increasingly disillusioned with German reliability and would not necessarily be bound to seek a European solution to future military aircraft development. In 1991, John Weston, head of BAe Military Aircraft, warned that due to the 'confusing messages' from Germany over EFA, they might not be a suitable partner for future military programmes. 'Partners,' he said, 'need to be reliable'. Even if these problems were overcome, he also doubted whether the German government would be able to bring a big enough market to justify a large German share of another major programme.[25] To back its words with actions, in 1992 BAe announced talks with Dassault over a next generation fighter and in 1993, joined Rolls-Royce in a US-led advanced STOVL research programme.

As a final word on the EFA, the initial delays as well as the uncertainty which continues to hang over the programme, underline the problematic nature of *ad hoc* collaboration, even in its most sophisticated forms. As Trevor Taylor put it, 'nothing could have demonstrated more clearly the tendency of collaborative projects to move at the speed of the slowest member'.[26] If European aerospace, and especially its military sector, is to flourish in the next decade, a rapprochement between the three most important military aircraft manufacturing centres - Britain, France and Germany - will be essential. In this respect, the talks between BAe and Dassault on a post EFA/Rafale generation could prove highly significant, especially following agreement between Thomson and GEC on advanced military radar systems for the twenty-first century.[27]

(ii) Tiger

Although the events surrounding the launch of the Tiger helicopter were not as complicated as the EFA/Rafale, its development and final configuration owed at least as much as to political interests as to the military needs of France and Germany. The prospect of renewing Franco-German military aerospace cooperation, largely dormant since the early 1970s, attracted high level political support. Nevertheless, the two countries were divided over the aircraft's exact requirements and the technological solutions needed to meet key mission needs. In the first instance, this led to what was effectively three distinct aircraft, each with different equipment fits. Inevitably costs rose and the programme fell seriously behind schedule.[28]

A serious dispute arose over the question of the aircraft's primary offensive system. The German army wanted to use modified US equipment whereas the French were determined to develop equipment based on a Thomson-CSF design. As the two sides could not agree between the two alternatives, there was a strong possibility that wholly separate systems with different cockpit layouts would have to be developed. The commensurate increases in cost caused by this duplication threatened the future of the entire programme. This debate bears comparison with the fight over EFA radar - a US-licence based technology preferred by the Germans pitted against an all European solution proposed by their partners.[29] With a less advanced and less technically autonomous equipment industry, they also had less to lose as a result of depending on the US. The French, on the other hand, had more industrial/technical interests at stake and were more concerned than the Germans at the threat of a potential US veto over export sales.

In the end, political and broader industrial considerations were again sufficiently important for the two sides to find a compromise. The programme was consistent with growing military cooperation between the two countries. French and German industrialists regarded the Tiger as a potential core for a European industrial re-alignment capable of sustaining a competitive challenge to the Americans. In July 1986, following the joint intervention of President Mitterand and Chancellor Kohl, the national armaments directors reached a compromise over the use of French systems technology. Continued cost escalation forced a further review of the programme. Early in 1987, the two governments agreed on a simpler, dual-use design; as one French official admitted, for the first time since the initial agreement, the two countries really had got a 'common helicopter' rather than four different designs with 'some similarities'. Even so, the Tiger will not be in service before 1997, a slippage of nearly five years on the 1984 target, and the total programme costs of DM9 billion were double the 1984 estimate.[30] Like the struggle to get EFA airborne, it was a rather poor advertisement for the virtues of collaboration.

However, the Tiger programme helped to trigger an important re-alignment in the European helicopter industry. The two prime contractors, MBB and Aerospatiale already had close links as a result of working together on other joint aircraft, missile and space programmes. More important, unlike Dassault in the EFA case, Aerospatiale had 'learnt' how to cooperate and relations between the two firms were generally cordial. In order to facilitate programme development, the two companies formed Eurocopter based on the French GIE formula pioneered by Airbus Industrie and also used by Euromissile. However, both companies felt that a more sophisticated approach was needed to meet the challenges of a rapidly changing European and world defence/aerospace market. As a result of these considerations, Eurocopter was transformed in 1990 into a jointly-owned subsidiary of Aerospatiale and DASA-MBB, pooling their assets across a range of helicopter programme. The change was designed to put the two firms in a better position to compete effectively in world military and civil helicopter markets.

Eurocopter had a combined workforce of 12,000 and turnover of $2.3 billion, the largest helicopter group in Europe and was a size comparable to Sikorsky. Both firms were involved in a number of different collaborative and national programmes, but in the long term the aim was to produce a common range of products. Eurocopter had a world market share of just over 37 per cent and was quickly recognised by US helicopter manufacturers as their major potential competitor. As Aerospatiale's Henri Matre put it 'I think this kind of organisation corresponds to Europe of today - it combines two operations from separate countries while allowing the two divisions to keep their own individualities'. According to another Aerospatiale executive, Eurocopter was not 'a cooperative agreement that we can dismantle when the original goals are complete'. Although Eurocopter was structured so as to leave both sides with a 'complete manufacturing capability', its formation marked an important innovation in transnational aerospace production and was the first involving a major airframe type - a 'platform' in military parlance.[31]

(iii) Airbus Industrie

The Airbus is one of the most important, and in many respects, the most successful example of European aerospace collaboration. It unites the three largest aerospace European nations - France, Germany and Britain[32]; the programme has been an overwhelming technical success; it has successfully challenged US dominance of the civil aerospace market; and the Airbus Industrie (AI) organisation is one of the most sophisticated forms of conventional consortia-based cooperation. Martin Bangemann, the EC Industry Commissioner, has described AI as *the* model of European Industrial Cooperation and its success a symbol of European technological enterprise.[33] This confident assertion contains more than an element of truth: AI has been able successfully to focus the industrial efforts of four European countries, but it faces, nevertheless, a number of difficult medium to long term problems

The Airbus consortium is no stranger to crisis and difficulty. Born in the mid 'sixties, it nearly came to grief in 1969 and was threatened by defection on several occasions over the following decade.[34] Since then, AI has assembled a complex and impressive transnational production system, launched five distinct types of airliner and several derivatives and has pioneered major advances in civil aerospace technology. The creation of an interlocking family of aircraft was, perhaps, the most important strategic achievement of the Airbus consortium and its industrial members. Each launch was accompanied by a long drawn-out fight to secure funding - particularly in the UK. But AI now matches Boeing, the market leader, in all but the largest class of current civil airliners. Since its conception in the mid 1960s, the basic partnership has remained the same with the later addition of CASA of Spain. For most of this period, the overall pattern of development and worksharing remained constant, bringing benefits in terms of industrial efficiency and learning curve advantages.

The market penetration made by AI since 1971 has been, for a European civil airliner programme, quite spectacular (see Figure 7.1). By the early 1990s, AI had achieved its long established target of 30 per cent of the world market for large airliners - mainly at the expense of McDonnell Douglas. Over the next decade, AI hopes to claim a share of the estimated $815 billion worth of business up to 2010.[35] Should MDC fail to survive the current recession and the effects of its other internal problem's, AI's 30 per cent target may turn out to be an underestimate. Although products from the ex-USSR might provide some additional competition, the huge entry costs of civil aerospace implies a long term oligopoly in the supply of large civil airliners and Europe's expensive search for a viable civil aerospace industry stake may end in financial as well as technological success.

The most difficult problem for AI in the short term is coping with the current recession in airliner sales. Along with its US competitors, AI has seen a net loss of orders over the last two years as airlines have sought to cancel purchases or to defer delivery. AI itself has begun to show a modest annual profit ($250 million in 1992), but its members have yet to show consistent return for their, or for their government sponsors' investment. The main difficulty in recent years has been the weakness of the dollar, which during the late 1980s and early 1990s led to heavy losses on Airbus work for the four partners. This has put more pressure on AI and its partners to deliver higher productivity and efficiency. However, the search for greater efficiency and effectiveness has been constrained by the nature of the consortium and final resolution of this problem might require a transformation of AI into a fully autonomous and accountable enterprise. This would mean a significant shift of authority and decision-making in a core element of the European aerospace industry and, inevitably, would represent a major step towards the creation of a more integrated European industrial structure.

Industrial decision-making within AI is based on consensus and is conducted within a complex and often opaque structure where AI's shareholders are also sub contractors responsible to the consortium for the quality and efficiency with which they deliver work. AI is formally a holding company provided with legal identity under the French GIE[36] formula which allows firms to concert specified activities without entailing any generalised commitment of assets or capital. The GIE formula demands unlimited liability in respect of operations, but the accounts involving the partners are fully transparent, known in detail only to each member. AI has some key planning and production coordination functions, but its main role is to sell aeroplanes and to act as the focus for Airbus customers. There have been some disputes between the partners as shareholders and the AI management (primarily over AI's pricing policies in the early 1980s). But the nostrum of hanging together, or being separately hanged in the face of overwhelming competitive pressure from the US has tended to minimise conflict over strategic questions.

However, this structure always contained the potential for tension between the partners simultaneously acting both as shareholders and manufacturing subcontractors. This has had an impact on routine managerial functions. For example, the system for negotiating transfer prices which each partner charges the consortium, and the impossibility of calculating a partner's real costs, has made it difficult, if not impossible to obtain significant increases in productivity and efficiency for the programme as a whole. The temptation has always been present to end-load partner costs on the programme as a whole and to let several sets of European tax-payers carry the load. While this might deliver gains for the partners as individuals, it served to undermine the economic viability of the consortium over the longer term. It certainly tended to justify outside criticism of the programme as a 'black' hole for public money.

With both European governments and US trade officials beginning to look harder at the subsidies supporting Airbus, the consortium came under pressure to reform the worst of its opaque and uncommercial practices. The most commercially driven member, BAe, had long wanted to increase programme efficiency, but with the the falling value of the dollar affecting all the partners' accounts, the need for organisation reform increased dramatically. In 1988 a 'wisemen' report into the Airbus system produced some improvements, with the AI management team being given more autonomy and responsibility for taking routine decisions. More competitive tendering, including a proportion of major structural work, was introduced. Some attempts, albeit largely nugatory, were also made to make the partners' Airbus accounts more transparent. However, a British proposal for a rapid translation to independent company status - the 'Airbus Industrie Plc' solution - was rejected. In short, over twenty years of operation, the Airbus consortium had made considerable progress towards becoming a commercially-driven enterprise, that it remained at heart a traditional consortium of autonomous national actors. As a BAe-CASA report on the Airbus system noted: 'it may well be that a fully commercial operation will only be possible when the activities of Airbus are 'ring-fenced' and identify with, and are accountable totally to, AI'.[37]

However, the pressure for reform in the Airbus system did not go away: indeed, it increased markedly during the early 1990s. At one level, the sheer scale of the programme implied a more radical approach to cost control and managerial responsibilities. More important, the continued weakness of the dollar underlined the need for major improvements in programme efficiency. The 1992 GATT agreement on civil airliner development financing and a more aggressive US view on long term subsidisation re-inforced the need for commercial rigour. The general context of European aerospace had also changed since the 1988 wisemen report. Proposals for cross-border shareholdings and transnational subsidiaries in the aerospace sector were emerging in response to changes in the defence market and as a result of the Single Market. In short, by the early 1990s, the idea of an autonomous Airbus company, or some other form of major organisational reform, was again under active consideration.[38]

Even in its simplest form, an 'Airbus Plc' would have to be capitalised, with designated assets. An autonomous AI would want full commercial freedom in respect of project and production financing. It would have to have an untrammelled ability to control costs and to direct changes in work practices in order to maximise industrial efficiency.[39] A major problem would be the extent to which AI could take full control of plant and facilities used to produce its aircraft but which are currently owned by the partners. These are often used to produce other aircraft and, within limits, companies might want to retain the ability to adjust work-loads and plant utilisation in the light of their own business requirements and changing commercial conditions.[40] An AI 'Plc' would want the freedom to extend its range of civil aircraft - a requirement which could bring it into conflict with the plans of its erstwhile partners who would retain control over other civil aircraft manufacturing capacity.

In practice, any major change to AI would have to have the full support of all four partners and their respective governments; as Schaeffler put it, 'there must be consensus'.[41] In particular, the nationalised status of Aerospatiale raises some problems. Although the French government has conceded that a more autonomous Airbus organisation might be necessary, it reiterated the right to retain some form of public control over national aerospace assets and would insist on a veto over industrial decisions which might be inimical to French industrial interests. No one, in fact, had any illusions that reforming Airbus so radically would be an easy process. In May 1990, Jean Pierson, AI's managing director, declared that while the Airbus partners would begin to look more closely at the possibility of changing AI's GIE status, he accepted that it would be 'long and complex'.

Financial pressures were, however, forcing the Airbus consortium to adopt a stricter commercial regime - pressures which might in time lead to a fundamental change in AI's status. With revenues from military work in sharp decline, the partners had to capitalise on their investment in Airbus and this meant achieving consistent profitability. As Pierson put it, there had to be a 'move to create an integrated company like Boeing with its own industrial and labour system'.[42] This makes economic and industrial sense; however, there is a major political-industrial qualification attached to the economic rationality of reform - Airbus has become more than an aircraft programme, it is at the heart of three European aerospace national industrial strategies. For much of the last two decades, the potential for conflict between these three sets of interests has been muted by the contest to secure a place in the world market and to mount a credible challenge to the likes of Boeing and MDC. In recent years, there has been resurgence of national competition for influence and control within the consortium. It would be too strong to suggest that these tensions could unravel the deep and fundamental industrial linkages forged over 20 years of cooperation. But they may undermine to a degree the consortium's stability and damage the prospects for a necessary reform of the Airbus system.

The Airbus has always been a politically important programme; without government support and sponsorship it would never have survived. This has involved a close governmental involvement in the affairs of Airbus. For most of the first decade of the Airbus development the three governments actively participatied in industrial decision-making. But from the mid 1970s, AI steadily became more independent of government, with the industrial partners taking the intitiative in all commercial and technical issues. However, political factors could still impinge on AI decisions, especially when they involved explicit national industrial interests and ambitions - for example in the mid to late 1970s when Boeing and MDC tempted both the French and British with alternative strategies. But with this crisis resolved, major internal political problems seemed to have died away and Airbus could get on with building and selling airliners. These problems returned in 1989 with a fundamental clash between German and French interests.

The focus for conflict was the location of the final assembly of the Airbus family of narrow-bodied aircraft. German dissatisfaction with the quality of their work share, combined with a more generalised determination to increase national aerospace industrial capability, turned what might have been another temporary squabble into a longer term question about future evolution of the Airbus consortium and the leadership of European civil aerospace development. To 'de-nationalise' the organisation, Airbus was always careful to distribute its top managerial posts between the three main nationalities. Nor was technology transfer *per se* the issue: AI has always had a reasonably open regime on technology developed under its remit - although there have been some national proprietary restraints on technology brought into the programme. But the real benefits of technological innovation stem from hands-on experience and the specialisation to date inherited through successive generations of Airbus types has tended to work to the disadvantage of the Germans locked into the less advanced aspects of Airbus development. BAe and Aerospatiale were also less affected by specialisation because of participation in a broad range of other projects which filled key gaps in their expertise.[43]

In 1989, Deutsche Airbus, backed by the German government made a bid for a second A320 production line and responsibility for final assembly of its larger derivative, the A321. The German proposal was resisted by the French and the dispute rapidly became the subject of high-level political discussions. The affair took a bitter turn when the German Aerospace Minister, Erich Riedl, attacked French dominance of the programme - 'taking the best cuts' - and hinted of a possible German withdrawal or at least re-orientation of its civil aerospace partnerships.[44] The British and Spanish members of the consortium remained publicly reticent about taking sides, and were concerned only to protect the programme's external credibility. But they were both disturbed that industrial questions might be decided above their heads, and those of the Airbus management, bilaterally by the French and German governments. In an attempt to regain some control over events, the AI Supervisory Board concluded that a second A320 assembly line in Germany was uneconomic, but agreed that there were sufficient orders for the A321 at the time to justify a separate assembly line in Hamburg.[45]

From a French perspective, the question was a mixture of prestige and economic efficiency. Toulouse was *the* centre for Airbus and the centre of gravity for programme management. It also made sense to locate all narrow-body assembly on the same site. Boeing, for example, has separate assembly plants for different members of its family; but not for derivatives. By separating A320 from A321 production, the consortium had to hope that volumes would indeed come up to expectations, but the downturn in demand experienced in the early 1990s, meant that two assembly lines rather than one had to operate below-capacity. However, industrial efficiency was not the key issue; the decisive factor was German determination to assert its position as a leading European aerospace nation. One way to resolve the efficiency issue would be to locate all narrow-body final assembly at Hamburg - a view which the Germans have continued to press in the case of the proposed 120 seat A319. Although plans to launch the A319 were postponed pending an up turn in the market, DASA's take-over of Fokker, with its range of small and medium sized airliners, has strengthened its claim to a leading role in the design and final assembly of any new small airliner project. According to DASA's chairman, Jürgen Schremp, 'we will be the narrow-body centre for Airbus in Europe', with the A319 forming the basis for a new generation of advanced technology aircraft.[46]

BAe also harboured fears about German ambitions, although these were less immediate than Aerospatiale's loss of some final assembly work. BAe, with some cause, believed that Deutsche Airbus would like at some future stage to challenge British control of wing box development and production. With very high learning and capital investment costs, the Germans would find it difficult to break BAe's monopoly of the current Airbus family of wings. Over the longer term, however, BAe was concerned that DASA could use the proposed European military transport, Euroflag, as a means of acquiring the necessary competence to challenge BAe for future Airbus wing work. These fears may well have contributed to BAe backing off from its commitment to transforming AI into an autonomous company. As matters stand now, BAe would be in a strong position to fight a DASA bid for wing-box work; it might not be so well placed as a 'mere' shareholder.[47] The German stance on Airbus was part of a wider national and corporate strategy. Despite some setbacks, German ambitions, shared by both industry (Daimler-DASA) and the government, to increase the technical standing of German aerospace and its ability to lead rather than follow in collaborative structures, were consistent throughout the 1980s.[48] The Germans wanted an aerospace industry capable of taking on the highest value-added aspects of the business which implies systems integration and design leadership capabilities. Taking a more central role in Airbus development and production was an important element in this campaign.

Airbus Industrie was very sensitive about the potential effects of national aspirations on the consortium's stability. Suggestions early in 1993 that DASA was 'leading' European negotiations with Boeing about a joint programme to build a 700 seat Ultra-High Capacity Airliner were rapidly played down by Airbus chairman Jean Pierson.[49] Yet there is a feeling that if a programme should be launched, Europe's contribution might be better made from outside AI - Boeing's primary commercial competitor. In this respect, the Airbus partners could use their dual status in respect of AI as buffer in their dealings with Boeing.[50] There is certainly life outside AI for the European civil aircraft industry. BAe, Aerospatiale, DASA-Fokker and Alenia all have interests in regional and commuter airliner production. Indeed, some of these projects could compete with the A319. There is little doubt that AI will carry the flag for Europe in the central commercial struggle for 120-350 seat airliners; but one should not allow the rhetoric and symbolism which often surrounds Airbus to obscure the fact that AI remains at heart an industrial coalition and not a true transnational company and that its partners may have conflicts of interest which may compromise the efficiency and effectiveness of the Airbus operation.

In general, the problems facing Airbus have tended to mirror the dilemmas confronting the European aerospace industry. Collaborative structures and practices which have served the industry well for the past twenty years have come under pressure from a rapidly changing market and political context. European aerospace trans-nationals are gradually emerging out of what is still essentially a collection of nationally-owned industries. Eurocopter may well have made the transition from *ad hoc* consortium to transnational enterprise. The DASA-Fokker deal of 1993 was the first trans-national aerospace undertaking involving the merger of two 'national champion' airframe companies since the VFW-Fokker merger of 1969-78. In addition, there have been a number of trans-national mergers and equity swaps in the missile, space and systems sectors.[51]

However, the 'strategic' nature of the industry - in both its strict defence and wider industrial meanings - could remain a barrier to extensive 'Europeanisation'. Aerospace funding - especially on the military side of the business - is still determined by national governments. Despite increasing intervention by EC institutions in the industry's affairs, the Community's role in sponsoring aerospace is very limited.[52] Firms and governments, while accepting the need for some coordination of research efforts, are still loathe to share 'crown jewels' technology. However, with the new US administration confirming its determination to support its aerospace industry through an increase in Federally-funded and directed research and technology acquisition, a fragmented Europe could yet fall behind the competitiveness race. To maintain the position won by consortia such as Airbus, the European aerospace industry and its various political sponsors may have to accept an even more fundamental restructuring of both industry and markets.

The US experience of collaboration

The European aerospace industry has had little option but to cooperate. Alone, the various national industries could never have sustained a major competitive challenge to the US. The pressure to submerge individual national and corporate interests in a common cause has rarely affected US firms. Of course, American companies have collaborated with foreigners, and since the 1950s, many have been involved in international programmes.[53] These were mainly co-production agreements to build American designs for particular domestic needs.[54] The trend towards offset and co-production agreements associated with major export deals also encouraged off-shore collaboration. But US firms have regarded full scope collaboration (defined in terms of shared design and development as well as production) with considerable suspicion. There have, of course, been important examples of full-scope cooperation involving US firm, most notably the BAe-MDD AV-8 and the GE-Snecma CFM-56 engine programmes, where the partnership has lasted over twenty years. But these have been relatively rare, and have not involved 'core' programmes for US firms.[55] US companies, used to a single prime contractor approach to programme management, have regarded international collaboration, with politically determined worksharing and complex international management systems as being intrinsically less efficient than conventional programmes. Many US companies have felt that their technological and industrial strength entitled them to a leadership of cooperative projects as of right.

From the 1970s, several US firms, mainly in the civil sector began to look for overseas sub contractors to share the financial risk of launching programmes and to play some role in the design and development of new aircraft and engines. During this period, several smaller European and Japanese firms joined US civil programmes.[56] In the case of the 777, Boeing sought out potential suppliers and involved them in the design process from the outset. Major structural partners, such as the Japanese were fully integrated into Boeing's computerised design system. Under even greater commercial and financial pressure, MDC was prepared to embrace an 'Airbus' style of cooperation in order to attract investment in its MD-12X programme. Although these programmes marked a more expansive view of collaboration the part of both MDC and Boeing, they still shared the general US disinclination to compromise control over design leadership and programme management.[57] These attitudes were increasingly at variance with contemporary developments in the world aerospace industry, particularly in Europe. As the US industry trade association, the AIAA, observed: 'the US is no longer the undisputed leader across the technology spectrum. European companies are proud of their technological capabilities, believing them to be as good as, and in some cases better than those of their American counterparts'.[58] In short, the US has had to re-evaluate the form of collaboration acceptable to potential partners and the transition has not been easy.

Within NATO, US governments have extolled the virtures of allied industrial cooperation in order to improve standardisation and to encourage closer links between the US and Europe. But over the last twenty years, the US has faced an increasingly difficult task in reconciling the benefits of encouraging NATO industrial cooperation with national and regional industrial ambitions. The 'two-way-street' in arms supply has always looked too much like a one way highway in an west east direction. During the 1980s, the relationship was increasingly affected by mutual concern over trade balances and the loss of technological leadership. As early as 1982, the Currie report underlined the basic dilemma for the US in encouraging allied industrial cooperation - 'increased technological sharing might establish and inevitably bolster competition for US industry'.[59]

The initiative sponsored by Senator Sam Nunn in 1986 appeared to offer a way of sharing the costs and the industrial and technical benefits of weapons development without involving substantial transfers of US technology. Under the Nunn formula, R&D was jointly financed and therefore jointly owned. The Nunn programme was complemented by a number of procedural changes within NATO and in the US weapons acquisition process aimed at improving the joint formulation of weapons requirements and to encourage the 'two-way-street' in arms purchasing.[60] But by the early 1990s, the collaborative foundations laid by Nunn and earlier joint programmes were being undermined by fears and actions on both sides of the Atlantic.

The problem stemmed partly from differing political systems and administrative attitudes towards international programmes. The Europeans regarded the US as an 'unreliable partner' largely because the annual battle with Congress to secure budgetary authorisation for all weapons or Federally-funded aerospace programmes affected several joint ventures. But according to DoD procurement officials, international projects have fared no worse, and in many respects done rather better in fending off Congressional 'zeroing'.[61] Nevertheless, Europeans used to binding MoUs and long term funding, found the instability and uncertainty associated with trans-Atlantic cooperation unsettling. Equally, the greater pluralism and adversarialism of US government-industry relations was a problem for Europeans accustomed to working in a context of close government-industry partnerships and 'national champions'.[62]

A good example of US 'unreliability', or at least American insensitivity to its partners' interests and concerns, was the international space station *Freedom*. Together with Canada and Japan, Europe resented US moves to militarise the space station (especially its potential use in SDI research), the unilateral imposition of design changes in response to US domestic financial pressures and the general assumption that the US, through the weight of its contribution to the programme, should determine access rights, research priorities and the day-to-day administration of this ostensibly international facility. The US's partners also suspected that American commitment to the Space Station would be undermined by changing national space priorities. Again, however, the major problem was the lack of multi-year funding on the American side. Congress clearly had legitimate worries about Freedom's viability, but the interests of the international partners appeared to have had little importance in the eyes of American politicians.[63] Although the June 1991 decision to authorise payment for the first phase of full development ended some of the uncertainty, the damage had already been done. As Reinhard Loosch of the German R&D Ministry observed, 'partners do not make unilateral decisions that will damage the investment of the other partners, neither do they simply shift their own difficulties on to their partner's shoulders.' These problems had a wider impact on perceptions of the US as a collaborator. If they continued, Loosch argued, 'the international partners would probably decide not to cooperate with the US in major science and technology projects for some time to come.'[64]

'Unreliability' is an accusation that can work both ways. US officials noted with some asperity that, between 1986 and 1991, whereas they pulled out of two NATO programmes, the Europeans withdrew in twelve cases - the British being the worst offenders. Problems in other programmes, such as the ASRAAM/AMRAAM family of airborne missiles, were caused by difficulties and suspicions on both sides, as well as by mis-management and technical failure.[65] However, Congress had the unhappy knack of hitting especially high profile programmes such as the Advanced Precision Guided Missile (APGM) and the Modular Stand-off Weapon (MSOW). As the APGM was one of the first Nunn programmes, one DoD official conceded that 'this does not bode well for the US. We're seen as untrustworthy'.[66]

The symbolic and industrial value of initiatives such as the Nunn programme and similar initiatives - as well as the substantive achievements of 'mature' collaborative projects such as the CFM56 and the AV-8 - should not be understated. However, cooperative programmes have been, and still are, a small proportion of the overall US defence equipment budget and their value has often been undermined by other disputes which exposed deeper clashes of interests. This was well illustrated by to what many Europeans thought was an attempt by the US to undermine the EFA and Rafale European fighter programmes in the name of cost-effectiveness and allied stardardisation.[67] For their part, US industrialists and Pentagon officials believed that they were deliberately frozen out of European programmes for political-industrial reasons.[68] US apprehension about the Single European Market and other European technology programmes such as Eureka and Euclid only made matters worse. Even though the much vaunted 'Fortress Europe' has still to emerge, the fact that so many measures adopted by the Europeans seemed specifically targeted against the US fuelled US unease.[69]

By the early 1990s, the Nunn initiatives and other collaborative schemes, as well as the goodwill which existed on both sides of the Atlantic towards collaboration were in danger of being swept aside by events. Just as US-European collaboration in civil aerospace was hampered by competitive rivalries and bitter exchanges over trade policy, cooperation in the military sector became entangled in a web of mutual fear about technological dependence and the need to defend, or to improve industrial competitiveness. While some Pentagon officials still believed that, on balance, the flow of technology through collaboration aided the US and the common Allied defence effort, the intervention and the growing influence of other US government agencies, most notably the Department of Commerce, introduced a sharper edge into US policy towards defence and aerospace cooperation. The mood in Congress also became decidedly more protectionist about foreign access to US markets and more hostile to the free movement of US technology. In practice, the urge to protect US jobs and technology began to act as a counterpoint to collaboration. As one Congressman put it, 'most members favour the concept of cooperation, but when in practice cooperation threatens jobs in their own districts, they oppose it.'[70]

In turn, Europeans pointed to the 'Buy American' legislation and the natural preferences of the US military for domestic equipment. Indeed, as even one senior US official recognised, the teaming requirement for any major foreign purchase could be regarded as a form of 100 per cent offset. According to European officials, under the Single European Act, US firms would still have far greater freedom to trade in Europe than European firms had in the US. European firms have made steady progress in the US defence aerospace market, especially in the equipment sector, and several have holdings in US firms; but overseas penetration of the US defence market has been relatively small - in 1987, about two percent of the US equipment budget. European companies which acquired US subsidiaries also had to accept restrictions on ownership and operation imposed by the DoD.[71]

US ambivalence towards collaboration was even more marked where the Far East was concerned. US firms have had several long standing partnerships with Japanese, Korean and other aerospace industries in the region and the area has been a major market for American civil and military products. Asian aerospace companies were also increasingly highly-regarded for their productivity as sub contractors and for their access to risk sharing capital. US firms were not slow to capitalise on Asian preferences to work with the market leader. They were also careful to limit technology transfer and the extent to which Asian firms would gain access to programme management. In particular, Boeing has handled its relationship with the Japanese in a typically hard-nosed fashion.[72] But as governments and companies began to set more ambitious targets for aerospace development, US worries about the nature of long term competion from Japan and elsewhere in Asia began to grow. Political sensitivity over aerospace was further heightened by general concern in the US about its deteriorating trade and technology balances with the Pacific Rim states. These tensions were especially evident in US reaction to the Japanese FSX fighter programme.

Japanese frustrations with the technological return from their investment in civil collaborative programmes and tighter US controls on licence-built military programmes led the government to propose the development of an independent advanced fighter aircraft, the FSX.[73] Under pressure from the US and as a conciliatory gesture on the trade issue, the Japanese government decided in favour of a collaborative project based on the General Dynamics F-16. Japan's primary objective was still the improvement of its national aerospace capabilities and the F-16 was selected as the best suited to 'Japanisation'.[74] Despite the adoption of a collaborative programme, the FSX touched a sensitive nerve in Congress and in the US Commerce Department, increasingly worried about the long term health of the US aerospace industry. The dispute revolved round the extent to which US technology would be transferred to Japan and the potential damage this might cause to US industrial and commercial interests. Set against these were the possible, but much disputed, benefits to US security of accessing Japanese technology, especially miniaturised phased array radar and the general desirability of maintaining friendly relations with Japan. According to Clyde Prestowitz, a stringent critic of the whole affair, the 'collaborative' FSX was not even a co-development programme, but an exercise in self-development, with the Japanese buying in only those elements they could not build themselves.[75] After long and increasingly bitter negotiations, several close Congressional votes and a last minute intervention from the newly elected President George Bush, the US and Japan finally reached an agreement. The US would have 40 per cent of FSX production and full use of any technology developed by Japan but the transfer of US data relating to the F-16's fly-by-wire flight control system and advanced engine technology was strictly limited.[76]

US industrial reaction to the FSX affair was mixed. General Dynamics felt that it had got a good deal, but some equipment manufacturers felt that the interests of the avionics industry had not been sufficiently protected. However, although the FSX should clearly help to raise Japan's overall technical competence, its direct contribution to Japan's civil ambitions was questionable. For all the protection which controls over the FSX might afford for US civil aerospace, the civil manufacturers themselves were keen to find risk-sharing partners. Private commercial contracts were not subject to Congressional approval; even so, in signing up Japanese

participation in the 777 programme, Boeing came under some
pressure to find alternative partners.[77]

The fight over the FSX signalled that economics and industrial
competitiveness questions were supplanting the Cold War as a
central policy issue in Washington. The FSX affair underlined the
growing strength of 'techno-nationalist' sentiment within the US. It
forced the US government into defining a position on collaboration
and technology transfer which reflected concern to protect American
leadership in aerospace. The Commerce Department used the FSX to
increase generally its role in aerospace and defence technology
questions - a 'power grab' as one DoD official put it. Passed in the
aftermath of the FSX agreement, the 1988 Defence Authorisation
Act, required the Department of Commerce to assess cooperative
agreements for their impact on US trade and industrial
competitiveness and, for example, insisted on strict controls over
the export of US technology for use in South Korea's much more
modest KFP programme.[78]

The future of aerospace collaboration

The globalisation of aerospace development and production is an
accomplished fact. US, European and other national industries are
linked in a complex network of collaborative agreements, joint
ventures, and strategic alliances. The distinction between a
'European' or an 'American' product is often hard to defend, as
production systems and sub contractor relationships span the world.
Several US defence/aerospace firms have an established presence in
Europe and many European companies have entered the US market
by acquiring a US manufacturing base. Nevertheless, the record to
date suggests that any extensive increase in that trans-Atlantic
cooperation was unlikely, with about half of the US-European
'strategic alliances' forged between 1986 and 1991 defined as
failures.[79] There is a global network of subcontractors and
equipment; at this level the industry has achieved a high degree of
interdependence between the US, Europe and the Pacific Rim. But as
far as major civil and military platforms are concerned, there has
been a definite clustering of collaboration around the two main
aerospace regions, the US and Western Europe. Numerically, these
may not be the greater part of the industry's activities, but they
are *the* focus for corporate activity at the peak of the industrial
pyramid. These 'core' programmes are those which attract the most
political attention and, potentially, are most likely to be the subject
of 'techno-nationalist' sentiments.

Increasing degrees of 'techno-nationalism' are in direct conflict
with the logic of a globalised, interdependent defence and aerospace
industry. Now that the Europeans and, to some extent the Japanese,

have achieved (or may achieve) parity with the US in aerospace and related technologies, technology transfer is no longer one-way. There are also distinct commercial and industrial advantages in international sub-contracting and collaborative development. As the American industry trade association pointed out, the US 'could lose out substantially on technical feedback - unless it remains open to technology sharing through cooperative endeavours'.[80] It is also evident that some US firms would like to use their technological leadership as leverage to gain greater access to European markets by leading joint ventures, but this may be blocked by US government restrictions on technology transfer.[81] There are obvious policy dilemmas presented by 'egalitarian' cooperation: US industry recognises that if it is to be influential in joint programmes, or even to be welcomed as a partner, it must bring a technological dowry. In this respect, US policy towards technology transfer will have to change in order to create an effective climate for increased trans-Atlantic and trans-Pacific cooperation. But inevitably, in sharing that technology, it will contribute to the levelling up of world industrial capabilities and the erosion of its position as an aerospace leader.

Inevitably when dealing with the US, there are always several 'voices' in major policy issues (especially in the defence sector); the problems of assembling a coherent and consistent policy towards collaboration have increased with the proliferation of bureaucratic and legislative actors with interests in trade, defence, technology policy and industrial competitiveness. Any extension of collaboration would have to be set alongside other considerations and pressures, not the least of these being the maintenance of the long term competitiveness of US high-technology industry. A major obstacle to increased trans-Atlantic cooperation in defence and aerospace technology lies in the possible reaction of Congress and of US domestic lobbies seeking to defend sectoral or regional interests. The US generally has had difficulty in accepting that collaboration requires a subtle blend of technological give and take, capital investment and market investment, often with a balance of advantage spread across several programmes. The Congress has perhaps the most difficulty in appreciating, or even wanting to address this reality. As Haglund put it:

whether the Pentagon's current official predisposition toward greater economic interdependence will prevail over the Congress's tendency to envision a defence-industrial-base approach that concedes more to import restrictiveness must remain a matter of conjecture.[82]

Some US industrialists advocated an aggressive but positive response to the changes occurring in the world aerospace industry. If procurement decisions were going to be driven more by economic and technological than by military factors, US companies 'must change substantially the way they do business in Europe'.[83] Under these circumstances, traditional licensing and partnership practices would no longer be sufficient and US firms would have to to establish a presence inside the European market. At the very least, US firms had to look for strategic alliances with European companies. This might entail investment in European industry, as well as more conventional teaming exercises, consortia or joint ventures. The vital step was to establish a formal linkage based upon a genuine partnership. Ultimately, 'such a development could create a blending of American and European defence contractors operating in both markets'.[84]

The   direction of US thinking towards collaboration was expressed in a 1990 review of US relations with the Pacific Rim by a Defence Science Board task force: the report set out a 'prudent' view of how the US should work with its partners. In the past, defence industrial cooperation had been considered separately from trade and economic issues, but 'the time is way past for that and we had better adjust our policies accordingly. National security can no longer be viewed only in military terms, but must include economic well-being as a key component'. The task force recognised the legitimate interests of nations such as Japan and Korea in building up their defence and aerospace technologies and they conceded the utility of cooperation as a way of bolstering US national security. But the US also had to take a long term view of industrial and technological priorities with cooperation predicated on the maintenance of a strong national technology base.[85]

In this respect, Haglund may prove prescient when he argued that where high-technology weapons developments are concerned:

> the future will likely be marked by heightened tension between allies, all of whom can be expected, aspirations of inter-operability notwithstanding, to continue to vie amongst themselves for advantage at the crowded apex of the West's defence industrial base.[86]

More recently, President Clinton and some of his key economic advisers have identified aerospace as one of the key trade battle-grounds of the decade. Although ready to concede the principle of collaboration, the emphasis of US policy is already shifting on the need to defend US industrial and technological interests.[87]

In the longer term, the prospect of far less money for new weapons might also shake the most nationalistic of military managers into viewing collaboration as the lessor of two evils.   But budgetary famine will not necessarily eliminate concerns over technological standing; quite the reverse, it might accentuate pressure to obtain 'national' value for money.   This problem was nicely put in a 1990 report from the US Congress Office of Technology Assessment:

> the US will face some difficult choices over collaboration with partners and to what extent it is consistent with national interests. In the 1990s, some international collaboration will be unavoidable and probably desirable.   Ultimately Congress will have to decide how much interdependence in defence technology and industry is prudent and supportable; which allies should be favoured and to what extent; what the United States should expect or demand in return for its technology; how best to support domestic development of critical technologies; and what kind of defence industrial structure must be maintained to meet the future needs of the United States.   Leaving such decisions to the vagaries of international defence markets could place the Nation's security at risk with catastrophic consequences.   Moreover, Congressional approaches that place constituency interests ahead of the national interest are potentially dangerous, as the Nation confronts dynamic new relationships in economic, political, and strategic security around the world.[88]

'Techno-nationalism' is not confined to the US; as defence and civil aerospace markets get tighter, there will be a temptation to close off imports and to restrict access to national (or regional) technology.[89] Rather than looking for increased cooperation, French industrialists have called for Europe to defend its market as much as the US protects its domestic industry. The situation may be a little more promising in the civil sector, with several extant linkages and with preliminary contacts between US and European firms on Advanced Super Sonic airliner design and a 700 seat 'Super Jumbo'. Nevertheless, the trans-Atlantic axis is likely on balance to emphasise competition over cooperation. As European aerospace and defence industries consolidate during the 1990s, they too should be better placed to defend their 'home' market, with or without formal barriers.   US firms, subject to similar pressures, will be equally loathe to give up their domestic market without a struggle. This was evident in the opposition from both US firms and Congress to Thomson's bid for LTV's missile subsidiary where financial questions were rapidly swamped by criticism of the backdoor nationalisation of US industry by a foreign government. But to Europeans it was a clear test of US willingness to embrace aerospace industry globalisation.[90]

The European aerospace industry, fully accustomed to the compromises of collaboration, stands at a different fork in the road. There are many attractions in following the trans-Atlantic pathway. Senior British aerospace executives have already indicated that despite its problems, the US may offer a more attractive option to European cooperation.[91] The transnational option may also be useful for weaker firms in a particular region to by-pass more powerful neighbours and to achieve a higher profile in world markets.[92] The competition that an open 'North Atlantic' market would afford might also serve to keep defence costs under control. On the other hand, the prospect of even closer links between European firms, supported by a regional R&D strategy, is growing. This may entail a more trans-national structure; at the very least, *ad hoc* collaboration may have to give way to more efficient forms of development and production in order to maintain Europe's competitive position *vis à vis* the US. But the US will always be a vital market for European firms and existing and growing industrial partnerships cannot be ignored. This potential conflict of interest forms a difficult dilemma for European companies and a policy tight-rope along which European political authorities will have to walk.

On a wider front, the attractions of working with low cost, high productivity aerospace centres in the Far East - which would include Korea, Taiwan and Indonesia - have already been recognised by US and European firms. But those in the region are beginning to drive a harder bargain. For example, both MDC and BAe courted the Taiwanese, attracted by the prospect of improving market access in the Far East and winning a cash-rich partner. In the event, MDC's multi-billion dollar programme proved too risky for the Taiwanese whereas BAe's $186 million deal to develop, build and to market the RJ146 appeared to be more acceptable. But both companies had to make significant concessions on technology transfer and joint management.[93] While both MDC and BAe were negotiating from relatively weak positions it was, perhaps, a further sign that the balance of power in the world aerospace industry was less concentrated than it was in the 1970s and 1980s. There is also the enigma of collaboration with the former Soviet aerospace industry. European and US and UK firms have joined forces with Russian design bureaux to re-engine and re-equip existing airliner designs. The Russian space industry offers a much prized source of data and experience - especially for Europe and Japan. However, the fear of nurturing a powerful competitor on its doorstep has led European airframe companies to adopt a more cautious attitude towards cooperation with the Russians.

All of these opportuntities present the same dilemma to western industries - how far does collaboration and co-production fuel tomorrow's competitors? For firms worried about surviving the next half decade, the long term may have to look after itself. In any case, globalisation of the aerospace industry is an established fact and many governments, rightly or wrongly, have latched onto aerospace as a key development sector. They will not easily be turned back. For the established players, their advantage will remain tied to the sheer diversity and technical quality of their industrial capabilities. This can be a diminishing asset, and needs the protection of dynamic investment in new technology. At a different level, the same dilemma exists in the trans-Atlantic relationship and the means by which cooperation and technological leadership can be reconciled remains at the heart of the tension between the US and European aerospace industries. The final chapter continues this theme and will consider the prospects for, and implications of an interdependent world aerospace industry.

8

Concluding Remarks

Introduction: forces for change

The aerospace industry is having to learn to live and to cope with rapidly changing times. Although the industry, both civil and military, has gone through several cycles of peaks and troughs in demand since the end of the Second World War, the conditions expected in the 1990s are likely to be harsh and unyielding. In some respects, the defence side of business is undergoing a much delayed 'demobilisation' as the Cold War is finally buried. As Malcolm Currie of Hughes put it, 'the defence industry has always been cyclical since World War Two largely because of dumb things the Soviet Union has done. Now we are in retreat to a lower permanent plateau'.[1] Question marks, albeit for the short term, also hang over the hitherto buoyant civil market as orders must be turned into deliveries to customers who may not have the money to buy them. The space sector, while likely to grow, will not provide the volume needed to replace lost sales of military aircraft, engines and systems. Moreover, governments in the US, Europe and the former Soviet Union, have begun to cap the more extravagant manifestations of space technology.

With a longer historical perspective, and allowing for the differences in sheer industrial and market scale, the next ten years may begin to resemble the inter-war period. Although the technical momentum of the last forty years will continue for a while, the pace of technological change will no longer be forced by a competitive arms race between two near-equals. The impact of commercially-driven innovation, already felt in the area of systems and components, will be even more evident and technological 'spin-on' from outside aerospace will become even more important than in the past. The industry will still need a solid base of engineering, particularly in propulsion and structural design (although metal-bashing as such will be supplemented by more subtle construction techniques involving more exotic materials). There will also be a need for the rare skills of systems integration, but there is no

182

reason to suppose that these will be the unique prerogative of the traditional aircraft builder.

Nor can the aerospace industry escape broader changes in the technological 'environment'. Innovation in communications is offering ways of reducing the need for physical contact between people, especially in the business world and suggesting alternatives to the communication satellite. Other challenges to the staple market of civil aviation are emanating from improved terrestrial forms of transportation. Constraints on growth (and new technical challenges) are likely to be found in over-stressed aviation infrastructure and the prospect of 'green' limits on the industry, its products and its manufacturing processes. Yet the aircraft and satellite offer unique and indispensable forms of transportation and communication. By the same token, 'command of the air', or at least the ability to dispute a potential enemy's control of military airspace, still constitutes a vital element in national defence and international power projection. Even a peaceful world will need the monitoring and verification capability of aerial observation. Aerospace products will, therefore, remain at or near the peak of a value-added pyramid of industrial activity and, as such, an important source of high-technology employment. Although changes in the mode of production may drive down some of the costs associated with aerospace, the price of entry will remain high and characterised by extreme risk. Those countries (or regions) with the established skills of aerospace will have a powerful competitive advantage compared to any new entrant.

But taken as whole, as a result of these changes, the industry world-wide is suffering from over-capacity and is undergoing a profound structural change. In the aerospace 'core', the US and Europe, too many firms are seeking a share of diminishing business and a process of rationalisation is under way throughout the world aerospace industry. As Table 8.1 illustrates, most of the major aerospace firms 'down-sized' between 1991 and 1992, and this was on top of earlier cuts. The average was a 6.2 per cent reduction, but significantly, the rate of contraction was highest in the US and the UK: countries with governments more willing to allow market forces to dictate events. With other more subtle developments occurring in the mode of production, one commentary suggested that aerospace was in the middle of a change comparable to the transformation in the automobile industry over the last 15 years.[2] BAe's chief executive Dick Evans succinctly summed up the consequences of these changes, 'in the US as in Europe in the next five years, there will be fewer, bigger and better aerospace companies competing in the world market - and each one leaner and meaner than anything around today'.[3]

Personnel   Changes   1991-93

Company	Country	Personnel	% Change
Boeing	USA	142,000	(-10%)
McDonnell Douglas	USA	87,377	(-19.9%)
United Technologies	USA	178,000	(-3.8%)
Martin Marietta	USA	56,000	(-7.4%)
British Aerospace	UK	108,500	(-11.9)
Aerospatiale	France	46,110	(6.5%)
DASA	Germany	81,872	(-2.1%)
Lockheed *	USA	71,700	(-0.8%)
GM/Hughes	USA	90,000	(-3.1%)
General Electric	USA	268,000	(-5.6%)
Raytheon	USA	63,900	(-10.8%)
Rockwell	USA	78,685	(-9.6%)
General Dyn *	USA	29,600	(-10.8%)
Northrop	USA	33,600	(-7.2%)
Thomson CSF	France	42,357	(-4.8%)
Allied Signal	USA	89,300	(-9.2%)
GEC	UK	104,995	(-11.4%)
Snecma	France	26,374	(No change)
Rolls-Royce	UK	55,000	(-10.4%)
Alenia	Italy	29,471	(No Change)
MHI	Japan		n/a
Textron	USA	54,000	(3.8%)
Dassault	France	13,592	(-3.3%)

*   Prior to merger

Table 8.1   Data: *Flight* - OC&C; *Flight*   4 August 1993

In the US, and to a lesser extent in Europe, there is still scope for domestic rationalisation. We have described in Chapter Six the rapid re-structuring amongst the US primes. Most predictions suggest that the eight or so prime contractors of the 1970s will shrink to perhaps five, or even four by the end of the century. Only they will have the capital mass and customer base to sustain the highest level of development and production.[4] While there is still some scope for domestic consolidation in Europe particularly, rationalisation is taking on an international dimension. As Dick Evans again noted, rising costs and the complexity of major defence platforms and airliners will drive firms together into 'larger critical mass'.[5] BAe's ex-chairman, Professor Roland Smith, shared a similar perspective. In his view, transnational mergers would occur and the process could only be stopped if individual European governments took it on themselves to interfere with the action of market forces. The European industry, he said, might be reduced to only three or four 'major players' and that pan-European companies were the only answer to the problems of scale and investment costs set against declining markets.[6] On the other hand, John Weston, another senior BAe executive, cast doubt on the drift towards trans-nationalism. In his view *national* consolidation was still likely to be the norm, with a trend towards vertical integration of nationally-based conglomerates.[7]

Whichever specific route aerospace companies take towards rationalisation, whether domestically or internationally, market forces will not be the only source of influence over the process. Aerospace has historically depended on the state for the bulk of its sales and much of its R&D capital. No national industry and few individual companies can say that it and they have not been at least indirectly dependent. Aerospace is still a central element in the defence industrial base of the great powers. Others have sought to acquire an indigenous capability if only better to reduce dependence on outsiders. Although the adoption of international collaboration in weapons production implies a limit to full national autonomy, it still provides some degree of control over key areas of defence manufacturing. Equally, pressure to obtain value for money in procurement through competition has begun to prise open hitherto tightly controlled national markets in Europe and, to a lesser extent, in the US. But again, access to the core aerospace technologies has been protected. In such a highly politicised industry, and again especially in Europe, national governments may try to protect key national technological assets for security and general economic reasons.[8]

What is sure is that the world of aerospace, traditionally so firmly located on a national base, will not be the same. There are several discrete policy issues which follow from these changes. First and foremost is the question of how states (especially the US) might manage the transition to a lower level of demand for defence goods without losing technological leads which even in the post Cold War era 'add value' to a defence capability. The second question is how international restructuring might be accomplished and to what extent national governments will still remain control. This is especially important for Europe where the movement towards transnationalism is most strongly felt. Finally, we must look at trends which may be creating the truly global aerospace industry or, on the other hand, shaping competitive regional blocs.

Managing 'the peace dividend'

National governments have accepted that they cannot, nor need to procure the range of military products and in the numbers they have done in past years. Governments strapped for cash would also like to derive the maximum value from a given technological investment by extending the life-time of weapon systems. A reduction in orders has a direct impact on costs as expenditure on development has to be amortised on a shorter production run. It also has a deleterious impact on the profitability of programmes for the manufacturer. A slow-down in the rate of replacement will make it difficult to maintain a steady sequence of products and to sustain expensive design and development teams. Production facilities and personnel may also atrophy. On the other hand, even without the dynamic of competing with the 'old' Soviet Union, the Gulf War confirmed that there is a premium on maintaining a technology edge in the face of threats from less developed, but well armed states.

The rising costs of maintaining this edge, especially if generation upon generation of weapons is deployed without use in combat, are likely to be unsustainable without a permanent and omnipresent enemy. This problem has led some states, especially the US, to consider investment in new weapons technology 'as an investment'. This has been referred to in Chapter Four as a 'technology on the shelf' policy, that is to say R&D or prototyping activity without large scale production, but which could subsequently be brought into play if necessary. This does not imply the facility to pull a new weapon 'off the shelf' to meet sudden contingencies such as the Gulf, but to maintain sufficient development potential to keep ahead of future Saddam Husseins. A few selected items would be taken to engineering and manufacturing development stages. Some production 'surge capacity' may be implied for 'bread and butter' weapons - basic platforms and munitions, but the main emphasis would be to respond in the medium term to specific threats and requirements as they emerged. Such a process would demand a much closer relationship between industry and customer to define more readily changing threat scenarios and technological opportunities.[9]

This approach may obviate expensive commitments to generations of unused weapons. For example, few strategic missiles have ever been 'used' and several generations of US aircraft developed in the 1950s did not see active service (at least by US forces). However, even allowing for the greater predictability of modern CAD/CAM processes and the increasing power of simulation, there are operational risks in bringing new technology rapidly into use. The British had a terrible time in the early 1950s translating R&D programmes rapidly into fully effective weapons.[10] In the nearest analogy to 'surging' production of modern aerospace technology, Boeing experienced severe quality control problems when it tried to increase 757 and other airliner production rates in the late 1980s. In this case, the problem was the lack of a cadre of experienced foremen and older staff, the 'lost generation' of production workers caused by recession-driven redundancies of the 1970s. The problem is that a whole chain of design-development-assembly personnel and systems cannot be re-constituted in the short term.[11]

In general, defence aerospace design and production teams represent a long term investment in skills and processes. The dispersal, or even a reduction in the numbers of key personnel can spell trouble if a 'surge' capacity is required. As Germany discovered after the Second World War, development teams, once dispersed, are hard and expensive to re-build. Admittedly, an emergency situation may stimulate prodigies of improvisation, the cutting through layers of red tape and formal demands for accountability and reporting as the British demonstrated during both the Gulf and the earlier Falklands wars. However, where complex development programmes are concerned, problems may not always be so readily resolved; nor could one rely on successful improvisation in every crisis. Equally important, given the three to four year delay between engineering and manufacturing development and production, it would be difficult to keep a supplier and subcontract chain 'tagging along' in the event of production.[12] According to one senior US Pentagon official, 'capacity (in the defence industrial base) has already declined to the point where domestic capability to support rapid reconstruction may no longer exist'. Others fear that 'technology off the shelf' may not work, or work as well as predicted when brought rapidly into production. As Chairman of House Armed Services Committee, Les Aspin noted 'If we gamble everything on high-technology systems we don't have yet and then the technology hits snags, we could be in trouble'.[13] There may also be a false economy in divorcing development from production. One of the key sources of savings in complex weapons development is to 'design-for-production'. This was the weakness of the UK aircraft industry moving into the 1930s rearmament. The government had maintained a variety of design centres, but few had any experience of large scale production or of the skills needed to design aircraft for cheap and easier construction.[14]

On the other hand, the advent of advanced CAD/CAM and other flexible process technologies pioneered by the automobile industry (especially in Japan) may reduce the emphasis placed on the sheer volume of production needed to sustain an economically viable programme. (In Europe, such techniques may also have the effect of cutting the number of collaborative partners needed to provide a base market) This is a subtle revolution affecting civil and military aerospace alike. It involves changing both the organisation of aerospace production and the relationship between prime contractors and suppliers. Subcontractors, in return for accepting lower prices and tougher terms on delivery and quality, are absorbed into a vertically integrated design and development process with guaranteed repeat business. Such trends may encourage the adoption of internationalisation of design and production to access the best and the most efficient supplier/sub contractor; but the cost is likely to be further reductions in national employment and some degree of control over technology.[15]

Indeed, the most radical option is to abandon any pretence of national autonomy and to embrace a regional or even a global approach to the development and procurement of key aerospace systems. This has already been accepted to some extent in the European defence market, it is commonplace in the civil sector, but even the US may have to accept it as a more routine feature of maintaining a cost-effective, high-technology aerospace/defence industrial base. However, as we have noted, there are also limitations to *ad hoc* collaboration and that more complex forms of transnational industrial structures may be needed fully to meet the challenge of over-capacity. However, the US, even in its post Cold War mode, will still retain a market and industrial capacity of sufficient size to insulate it to some degree against the pressures of internationalisation. In this respect, European firms will remain at the centre of any trans-national restructuring in the world aerospace industry.

Beyond collaboration?

As we have noted in Chapter Six, the process of national consolidation in the European airframe and aero-engine industries is virtually complete.[16] The breadth and depth of intra-European collaboration and European involvement in other joint ventures is marked: in 1969, there were 11 joint ventures under way world-wide; 10 were intra European and one was US-European; in 1979, there were 17, with Europeans involved in all of them and US companies in three; in 1990, there were 36 and European companies were taking part in 33 with the US still only participating in nine.[17] As a 1991 AIAA report observed, 'compared to European international cooperative efforts, the number of US foreign business alliances is small'.[18]   More qualitatively, international collaboration has been a success in terms of helping to maintain a world class aerospace industry in Europe.   But a much closer integration still of European aerospace companies may be needed to sustain future development.   Thirty years of *ad hoc* collaboration on individual projects for companies such as BAe had left a 'mosaic around the world' of competition and cooperation which would have to be rationalised through company-to-company links.[19] There are problems, as BAe's Dick Evans recognised, in the process of creating transnational companies, including the long standing issue of the lack of a single European fiscal and legal regime.   He also conceded that the issues of national identity, and national and international funding will entail the resolution of complex public policy questions over national access to key technologies, arms sales regimes and, possibly, common procurement systems. Nor should the process be confined to Europe, even if the main focus of European corporate efforts might be in the 'home' region.[20]

The security and technological interests which have justified the existence of an independent European aerospace industry are still politically important.   Indeed, as the world moves away from military confrontation, the possession of high-value added industrial capabilities such as aerospace is perceived increasingly as a vital asset in maintaining national and regional economic competitiveness.   But as we have suggested in Chapter Seven, the traditional form of collaboration - the joint development and production programme conducted by autonomous national firms - may have reached a watershed.   If the logic of European collaboration remains valid, therefore, European aerospace should be looking for even closer, or at least different forms of industrial links.

There are still, of course, many alternative forms that the European industry, let alone global industrial development, could take.   As Trevor Taylor noted, there are many ways in which firms can manage aerospace and defence business across national boundaries.[21]   At one end of the spectrum there is still the traditional collaborative venture which can now draw upon the collective memory of over twenty years of organisational experience.   This type of collaboration is likely to remain an important option for companies and governments looking to protect key national assets through *juste retour* work-sharing and technology transfer agreements.   Some, such as Airbus Industrie, have the potential to evolve into more independent entities.   There would necessarily have to be some improvements in the organisation and management of *ad hoc* collaboration in order to capture much

needed efficiency gains.   But the advantage for both national firms
and governments in keeping to these type of collaborative strategies
is that they are usually able to retain greater control over decision-
making.

At the other end of the spectrum, there is activity in mergers and
acquisitions (M&A).   Transnationalism through cross-border
mergers and acquisitions has been particularly evident in the
electronics and equipment industries.   Thomson-CSF has been
especially positive, sweeping up firms in the US, Holland, Belgium
and the UK, where Thomson is now the third largest
defence/electronics contractor.   Siemens also has a share of Plessey
and GEC, of course, has a wider range of international links through
its other business interests.   As we will consider shortly, GEC and
Thomson have also emerged as important players in the creation of
European functionally-defined transnational aerospace groupings in
guided weapons and space technology. The extent of transnational
mergers and acquisitions should not be exaggerated.   Although, since
the mid 1980s, the rate of M&A activity in the aerospace industry
has increased globally by 38 per cent a year - involving 525
examples in Europe alone up to April 1990.   However, 42 per cent
of the European total represented national consolidations and a
further 35 per cent was accounted for by European investment in
the US industry, a move determined by the need to get inside the
world's largest defence market and facilitated by a weak dollar and
attractive tax regimes.   In the period covered by the data, only seven
per cent of the European M&A activity involved intra-European
deals and 16 per cent of European M&A comprised US firms taking
shares in the European industry.[22] The pattern of transnational
mergers in Europe was further skewed by the fact that the majority
was directed at one country, the UK, where procedures and attitudes
to mergers, and especially to foreign takeovers, were more liberal
than in France or Germany.   But changes in patterns of public
ownership in France and Italy, combined with the increasing impact
of EC competition policy, may help to encourage a more generalised
movement towards pan-European mergers.   The adoption by France
or by Italy of more free-market, profit-orientated attitudes to the
aerospace business could accelerate the rationalisation of the
European industry and erode barriers to the creation of
transnational subsidiaries.   It would, for example, answer British
objections to the 're-nationalisation' of the UK industry by foreign
publicly-owned enterprises.   The existence of such barriers has
slowed-down the re-structuring of the Europe aerospace industry -
a delay which is putting it at a disadvantage to the US, where the
industry can be rationalised, and costs cut, much more rapidly.

In between these two basic models of internationalisation,
however, there is a wide range of other links between firms across

national boundaries, which, although falling short of outright merger, nevertheless hint at something more advanced than *ad hoc* forms of cooperation. For example, there are strategic alliances which may focus on particular aerospace products or may reflect broader industrial and commercial considerations. A strategic alliance may, as in the case of the GEC-Matra-DASA space and satellite grouping, involve equity exchanges. Although the importance of equity swaps should not be overstated, as in the view of one senior German industrialist, their importance tends to be more psychological or symbolic than legal or organisational, implying a more comprehensive relationship than one based on *ad hoc* collaboration.[23] Less ambitiously, the relationship may revolve around generalised MoUs committing both sides simply to consider and to explore possible areas of cooperation. Examples of this kind are Daimler's wide ranging MoU with Mitsubishi and Aerospatiale's with Lockheed. In some case, Daimler's link with the Japanese for example, translation from outline agreement to concrete product development has proved more difficult to achieve, but there are signs of a growing chain of international links.[24]

More concretely, European firms are beginning to form product-based consortia, especially in the guided weapons sector. This has been something of a cascade, with the announcement of one grouping triggering other joint venture subsidiaries. The pace of trans-national European rationalisation was increased by the mergers in the US industry of Loral and LTV and Hughes and General Dynamics. In 1993, BAe and Matra formed a jointly-owned $1.5 billion turnover subsidiary to create one of the largest tactical missile groups in the world. Europe's other main missile producers, Thomson, GEC, Shorts and Aerospatiale have established similar links. In the case of Thomson, this has also entailed bringing work back to Europe from the US.[25] By the mid 1990s, the European missile industry will probably comprise just the two major groups. Other examples of internationally-owned subsidiaries can be found in the European satellite industry where two groupings have formed to compete for regional and world business. In this sector, both have ties with US manufacturers, reflecting the importance of the US market for commercial satellites.[26] The future of European defence avionics has also started to realign along trans-national lines. In 1992, Thomson and GEC forged an alliance to develop and build advanced airborne radars. The company, GEC Thomson Airborne Radar (GTAR), is trying to anticipated a likely global competition for phased array radars involving the US and Japan. The costs of developing this type of radar are such that neither firm could afford to go it alone. As a result, European governments are likely to be presented with a stark choice for the next generation of fighter radars - buy from the regional 'national champion' or look to the US or Japan.[27]

The emergence of comparable alliances in 'platforms' (civil and military) has been be slower. In the case of helicopters, there has been a move towards the full internationalisation of European production which might in the end come down to just the one main centre, perhaps based on Eurocopter.[28] But the importance of maintaining national design and development capabilities in core programmes such as advanced fighters is, perhaps, still too sensitive to allow control to pass into the hands of international consortia or subsidiaries. This may remain be the preserve of the nationally-owned company for some time yet.[29]

The civil sector remains in a fluid state. Airbus offers an existing focus for large airliner production, but as an organisation, it is still someway short of being a truly integrated and independent international company. There is also the prospect that European firms may individually or collectively work with US on High-Capacity airliners and advanced supersonics. Although Airbus Industrie has sought to enter the negotiations, there is a case for confining AI's work to conventional airliner production.[30] The prospects for consolidating the European regional airliner sector are more problematic. DASA's take-over of Fokker created one important pole, and the ATR grouping of Aerospatiale and Alenia represents another. BAe, on the other hand, has looked to the Far East with its deal with Taiwan. The Germans have suggested that the DASA-ATR groups could move closer together, possibly involving Saab. There are certainly too many projects and perhaps too many production centres and rationalisation is long over-due. However, building smaller airliners enables firms like BAe and Aerospatiale to retain an overall competence in civil aircraft design and production - a reminder that there may be life outside of Airbus.

Historically, the experience of broader-based European transnationals in the defence/aerospace sector has been problematic. The only example to date of a formal European aerospace cross-frontier merger, VFW-Fokker, broke up in the late 1970s due primarily to an inability to transfer military work from Holland to West Germany. US multinationals, such as Raytheon and Hughes, with existing European subsidiaries have had more success. However, the European aircraft industry is facing an increasingly uncertain future and pressures for change, evident for several years, are now increasing in their intensity. The macro effects of a European security system rapidly disengaging from Cold War confrontation are already evident in production cuts, cancellations and threatened programmes. There is still a need for a European military aerospace capability, but questions about its appropriate size and the direction of its efforts are far from easy to answer. Similarly, the gradual commitment to a more open market for defence products driven by budgetary concerns have become more pressing, potentially to be reinforced by the emergence of a common European security policy. All these factors may have helped to remove the barriers and political problems which undermined the VFW-Fokker union.

There is clear evidence that European transnationalism in all its forms is increasing and that several firms have deepened their relationship through equity sharing and cross-holdings. But the process is still fraught with difficulties. As we have noted above, the Airbus programme can still reveal sharp competitive instincts amongst its partners, and the collapse of EFA would have a very damaging effect on European aerospace. It is also instructive that Eurocopter has had to adopt a complex organisational structure in order to accommodate the industrial and technological interests of its two members.[31]

European transnationalism might also be helped by the evolution of a common approach to developing the region's aerospace technology base; especially as national budgetary allocations for defence-related R&D begin to fall. The bulk of European aerospace research is conducted on a national basis, though national research organisations cooperate on major projects, have a number of bilateral links and work together through formal but limited structures such as GARTEUR and AGARD. The British, German, French and Dutch governments have built a European Trans-sonic Wind Tunnel at Cologne which will be operated jointly by the four participating states. Other research initiatives, such as the Eureka programme and Euclid, its military equivalent, have addressed general R&D needs, including several aerospace-related projects, including the EUROFAR tilt-rotor feasibility study. The EC has also begun to explore means of encouraging the aerospace industry's competitive position. In 1987, it commissioned a study from the seven major European airframe companies which was used to form the basis of a modest extension of the European Brite/Euram Framework research programme to aerospace.[32] The EC is also being pressed to establish common industrial and airworthiness standards for the industry. But while some elements within the Commission have accepted the need for active measures to promote European aerospace technology, especially as the level of national defence R&D diminishes, there are others who do not agree with such a sectoral approach to R&D policy nor to the dual technology nature of aerospace activity.[33] The EC's role in aerospace is certainly complicated and constrained by the limitations on its competence in security-related issues. There are signs that the limitations of Article 223 of the Treaty of Rome might be relaxed, if not removed, as Europe moves towards a common foreign and security policy. Equally, the EC's procedures for bidding for R&D funds and the application of distributive policies has limited the real value of Community R&D programmes.[34]

If Europe is to match the US in terms of aerospace R&D, especially in the civil sector, improvements in the coordination of the various national efforts will be necessary. This means eliminating duplication and breaking down the reticence of companies to expose their core technologies to others. This 'crown jewels' syndrome must be diluted by the generation of a jointly owned and equally accessible body of basic research data, which necessarily includes the sponsorship of technology demonstrator programmes taking basic concepts much closer to a useful product.[35] It is debatable whether Europe needs a fully-fledged 'NASA' with its associated bureaucracy to co-ordinate R&D and other aeronautical policy issues. Nevertheless, without some form of focus for Europe's R&D activities, European aerospace will find it hard to match the investment being planned in the US. Even if the EC is not the most appropriate location, there is a strong case for a European structure to promote and to stimulate aerospace research.

A global industry?

Although we have so far been primarily concerned with European cooperation and the prospects for European industrial partnerships, internationalisation is a global phenomenon. All of the major US and European firms have commercial agreements with Far Eastern and other manufacturers in South and North America. As we have noted earlier, the politics of offset sales and teaming requirements led to many of these agreements. But the importance of access to low-cost production and dollar area suppliers, especially for European civil programmes, has become an even more important factor.

In Chapter Seven we also noted that there have been some signs that a number of American industrialists have realised that cooperation, especially with European firms trans-Atlantic, will have to be based on a more egalitarian partnership. Those firms with an established presence in the European defence and aerospace industries have increased their investment. Others have talked about the importance of acquiring equity shares and other forms of strategic alliances. Equally, several European firms have extended their links with the US. Finally, the scope of partnership activity at the level of suppliers and sub contractors has expanded, with several European firms involved in major US programmes such as the Boeing 777 and the F-22 whilst US industry remains a significant contributor to Airbus products. Indeed, the degree to which the US and European equipment and engine industries shared access to major civil aircraft on both sides of the Atlantic helped to defuse the tension over Airbus subsidies. In a sense, there are two tracks to trans-Atlantic aerospace relations: below the prime contractor level, there is a relatively high level of interdependence; at the narrow, but politically high profile pinnacle of the industry, collaboration is limited and declining in importance.

On a wider front, both the established aerospace regions have rapidly expanded their links with the Far East. The ambitious and work-hungry industries of Japan, Taiwan, Korea and Indonesia offer cost-savings and new sources of capital. There is, of course, the risk that this will serve to increase competition in the future, as the more adept and committed seek to develop indigenous products. To date, the challenge has been limited to co-produced, domestically enhanced design concepts such as the FSX. However, while some firms may fall by the wayside, some Asian companies will, sooner or later, join the ranks of the world industry as co-equal partners. Some, perhaps, rather sooner than may be comfortable for companies in Europe and the US.

By the same token, with the former Soviet aerospace industry looking for partners, another avenue for cooperation has opened up. In September 1993, there were over 56 agreements or MoUs linking the Russian aerospace industry with US, European and Asian firms.[36] Many of these are unlikely to go beyond initial contacts. But some, such as the agreement to link the US-led space-station with the Russian Mir, Boeing's contract with a leading Russian Research establishment and the Russian airliner re-engining programmes involving Rolls-Royce and P&W, were more substantial and high profile. Working with the ex-Soviet industry will not be easy. There are still major problems associated with capitalisation and the harmonisation of Russian legal practice and technical standards with those of the west.[37] However, access to Russian technical expertise and the region's potential market presents a major opportunity for western firms.[38] The danger, of course, is that Russia is better placed than most 'new entrants' to mount a genuine competitive threat to the established aerospace core industries of the US and Western Europe.

A more distant challenger could be China. The potential of the Chinese market has already attracted attention from western manufacturers, and several co-production agreements are in place. Although in the event much diluted, the 'Trunkliner' programme has signalled Chinese intent to supply much of that market from indigenous suppliers. China has also made something of a break-through in the satellite launcher market. More significant, given the usual trajectory of aerospace development, China is an established military power, with fewer inhibitions than, for example, Japan in projecting that power. The Chinese arms industry is already in the export business and its willingness to export missile technology has disturbed the US. China, more than Japan, has the ambition to become at least a regional Superpower and this would imply a strong, national defence industrial base. This again might be accomplished through cooperation with the west, but the former Soviet industry could offer an alternative set of partners. The development of a modern aerospace industry would still take time - although a closer *rapprochement* with Taiwan might help to speed the process. Nevertheless, looking forward to the next century, the full-flowering of Chinese economic and military potential may well provide a new force in the aerospace industry.

The Japanese, of course, have been identified as the most likely to challenge the existing core players. The 'threat' from Japan should not be exaggerated; while levels of R&D investment and commitment are currently impressive, Japan would have substantially to increase its defence budget in order to provide a solid base for the most advanced of aerospace activity. But a nightmare scenario for many western aerospace companies is that the Japanese aerospace industry successfully 'leap-frogs' into a prominent position by focusing on civil supersonic or even hyper sonic research. This outcome is not inconceivable, but more realistically, Japan should be able to reach a level comparable to current German capabilities early in the twenty-first century. Japanese industry is also likely to be linked to the US and Europe through a network of collaborative agreements with a few modest independent products based on Japanese-led joint ventures. However, a stronger domestic base would give Japanese firms a greater ability to influence the development of important international programmes and to lay claim to a share of higher value work. This would imply that any 'threat' from Japan could be most severely felt by western electronics-based aerospace suppliers.

In general, there is likely to be a leakage of aerospace work (and employment) to lower cost producers in the Far East, and a few other players in Taiwan and Korea may begin to approach Japanese levels of technological competence. In the short term, the competitive pressure from the Far East will hit structural sub contractors and equipment firms more than the systems integrators. However, an interesting development - and one which might pose a real competitive threat to US and European firms a decade or so into the next century, would be some form of pan-Asian programme either in the military, or more probably, in the civil aircraft sector. But, given adequate levels of national (or regional in the case of Europe) investment in R&D, the core technological capabilities of the established players should ensure a measure of protection against most competitive threats, at least as far as the most technologically advanced aspects of aerospace are concerned.

Whether by then aerospace will have become a genuinely trans-national industry, where national characteristics and concerns will have less significance for companies than the demands of global technology scanning, production and marketing, is a more debatable question. A key issue for the future is whether aerospace becomes a genuinely international industry operating in a largely free and open market, or whether circumstances force a continuation of nationally-orientated industrial development. There is evidence sufficient to suggest either route might be possible as we move into the next century. Even in the case of Europe, where there is already some movement in the direction of trans-national industrial structures, there is still a strong chance that core capabilities remain focussed on nationally-owned firms. The emergence of still broader-based international enterprises is certainly more problematic. Current trends suggest a widening and some deepening of global ties in the aerospace industry - especially in the equipment sector - but one senses that Europe and the US will wish to retain strong indigenous capabilities in order to satisfy both military and economic security interests. This would seem to offer a less than optimal solution, leading to more expensive defence products and, possibly, continuing international confrontation over state aid and other forms of assistance to civil programmes. Given the existing levels of interdependence between firms, as well as the willingness on the part of the US, the EU and others to resolve through negotiation disputes affecting aerospace trade, the prospect of a mutually damaging 'trade war' in aerospace is increasingly unlikely. But international competition in ever tighter markets will inevitably engender tension in relations between the two major producing centres. The aerospace industry has for several decades now been able to balance the conflicting demands of competition and collaboration, but the tightrope is not getting any less narrow and the safety-net very much stronger.

Notes

Chapter 1

1. See Section 1.2 for a discussion of the aircraft/aerospace distinction.

2. *Flight*, 2 August 1992, p.32; 2 September 1992, p.51.

3. See L.d'Andrea Tyson, *Who's Bashing Whom?: Trade Conflict in High Technology Industries*, (Washington D.C., 1992).

4. Office of Technology Assessment, *Competing Economies*, OTA-ITE-498, (Washington D.C., October 1991), p.342.

5. See K. Hayward, *Government and British Civil Aerospace*, (Manchester, 1983), pp.210-22.

6. Assemblée Nationale, *Rapport de la Commission d'enquête parlementaire sur l'utilisation des fonds publics alloués aux entreprises privées ou publiques de construction aéronautique*, 21 April 1977, Journal Official, No. 2815.

7. US AIA, *The US Aerospace Industry in the 1990s: a Global Perspective*, (Washington D.C., 1991), p.19.

8. US AIA *op cit*; SBAC, *Britain in Aerospace*, London 1990, p.9.

9. *Action Programme for the European Aeronautical Sector,* E E C Bulletin, November 1975, p.3.

10. European Commission, *A Competitive European Aeronautical Industry*, SEC 90/1456, p.3. Brussels, July 1990.

11. The links between civil and military aerospace technology are discussed in: US Congress Office of Technology Assessment, *Holding the Edge*, (Washington, D.C., April 1989), pp.168-171.

12. By fully capable, we mean having the ability to design and to develop advanced military aircraft, large commercial aircraft, missiles and space vehicles. There are many other aerospace firms able to design and to develop smaller, less complex aircraft.

13. More accurately, to be a prime contractor implies a more extensive management function; the ability to assume full and complete responsibility for the end product, or a number of related products and services.

14. AIAA, *op cit*, p.19.

15. An economy of scale follows from the repeated production of similar things; and an economy of scope reflects the flexible production of lots of different items.

16. OTA, *Holding the Edge, op cit*, pp.66-8.

17. During World War Two, many aircraft makers were surprised by the quality and effectiveness of automobile plants converted to build aeroplanes. Much of the sense of 'uniqueness' stems from the Cold War era and the demands of increasingly sophisticated military products.

18. The Boeing 747 may well have a life of over 70 years and several hundred DC-3s, built in the 1940s, are still in service.

19. See D. Todd and J Simpson, *The World Aircraft Industry*, (London, 1986) for a more detailed survey of the relationship between aerospace technology and the market.

Chapter 2

1. See Chapters 3 and 6.

2. *Aerospace: Facts and Figures, 1989-90,* AIAA, (Washington D.C., 1989), p. 10. Other data taken from AIAA, *The US Aerospace Industry in the 1990s: a Global Perspective,* (Washington, September 1991).

3. See, J Gansler *Affording Defense,* MIT, (Boston, 1989).

4. AIAA, *The US Aerospace Industry and the Trend Toward Internationalisation,* Washington DC, 1989, pp. 16-21; AIAA, *A Global Perspective,* (Washington D.C, 1991), p.19.

5. See Chapter 4.

6. Although US civil manufacturers were more willing to embrace collaboration, US determination to lead programmes may have cost the US several opportunities to head off the Airbus programme. See K. Hayward, *International Collaboration in Civil Aerospace,* (London 1986).

7. See Chapters, 4&7.

8. See Chapters 4&6.

9. J. Bright, *The Jet Makers,* (Kansas, 1978), Chapter 9.

10. Bright, *op cit,* pp.145-6; W. Franklyn, *The Defender,* (New York, 1986) pp.126-7.

11. Bright *op cit,* p.147; W. Biddle, *Barons of the Sky,* (New York, 1991). A similar problem affected the UK industry up to the mid 1960s.

12. B. Bluestone (*et al*), *Aircraft Industry Dynamics,* (Boston, 1981) pp.22-40 & Chapter 4.

13. Bright, *op cit,* p.146.

14. Bright, *op cit,* p.147 ; Bluestone, *op cit,* pp.12, 23-4.

15. Bill Anders, Chairman of General Dynamics, *Aviation Week,* 5 August 1991, p.39. Hughes' purchase of GD's missile division in May 1992 was the first major example of 'market-led' rationalisation.

16. *Aviation Week,* 5 August 1991, p.65.

17. *Interavia,* August 1990, pp. 627-9; *Flight,* 25 July 1990, p.16; *Business Week,* 30 July 1990, p. 31.

18. *The Financial Times,* 11 December 1989.

19. *Aviation Week,* 6 February 1989, p.65. See Chapter 6.

20. See *Flight* , 6 December 1989, p.3; *The Financial Times,* 23 May 1990.

21. The US Marine Corps is an honourable exception. The US Army also has a reasonable reputation; but the USAF is a particularly difficult customer for collaborative systems.

22. See *Defense News,* 22 July 1991, for comparison between US and European outlook.

23. All data taken from AECMA, *Panorama of EC Industry; Aerospace,* (Paris, December 1990).

24. See Commission of the European Communities, *The European Aircraft Industry,* (Brussels,May 1992).
25. AECMA, *op cit,* pp. 3-6 & 16.
26. See K. Hayward, *The West German Aerospace Industry,* Whitehall Papers No.2, Royal United Services Institute (London, 1990).
27. See table in *Interavia,* June 1991, p.15.
28. British Aerospace and Rolls-Royce have had periods of state-ownership and German provincial governments have had shares in German companies. The main exceptions in France were the privately-owned Dassault and Turbomeca.
29. See *Jane's Defence Weekly,* 23 November 1991, p.1017.
30. Chapters 7 & 8.
31. AECMA, *op cit,* p. 16.
32. See Chapters 7 & 8.
33. Again, this excludes the industries of the former Soviet Union.
34. To be more precise, we would have to define firms in terms of capability which would mean that Bombardier of Canada would rank well ahead of CASA in terms of contribution to the world industry.
35. See R. Samuels & B. C. Whipple, 'Defense Production and Industrial Development; the case of Japanese Aircraft' in C. Johnson *(et al) Politics and Productivity,* (New York, 1989).
36. Under South Korean law, for example, a proportion of all aerospace sales must be built or offset by other related work in Korea. *Interavia,* October 1988, p.995.
37. *Interavia,* July 1993, pp.32-4.
38. *Air et Cosmos,* 28 April 1991, pp.21-3; *Aviation Week,* 1 July 1991, 27 January 1992, p.42; *Flight,* 29 January 1992, p.5.
39. *Flight,* 3 June 1992, p.25.
40. *Jane's Defence Weekly,* 31 July 1993, pp.20-5.
41. *Far Eastern Economic Review,* 5 December 1991, pp.52-4; *Aerospace World,* February 1992, pp.21-3; *Interavia,* January, 1992, pp.38-9. See Chapter 7.
42. *Interavia,* February, 1992, pp.44-6.
43. *Flight,* 19 February 1992, pp.54-5.
44. *Flight,* 8 January 1992, pp.35-7; *Interavia,* April 1992, pp.44-9. At one point, the Trunkliner programme was valued at $10 billion and both MDC and Boeing fought hard to win the contract. In the event, Chinese investment has been much more modest.
45. *The Financial Times,* 2 July 1991; *Interavia,* March 1992, pp.29-32.
46. R. J. Samuels & B.C. Whipple, 'Defence Production and Industrial Development' *op cit* pp.275-81.
47. D. Mowery, 'The Japanese Commercial Aircraft Industry; déjà vu All Over Again?' paper presented at the ISA Conference, (London 1988), p.24.
48. *Aviation Week,* 29 July 1991.
49. Samuels and Whipple, *op cit,* p.290.
50. See Chapter 6; *Aviation Week,* 29 August 1991, pp.42-56.
51. Samuels and Whipple, *op cit,* p.283.
52. *The Economist,* 30 March 1991, pp.86-7.
53. Samuels and Whipple, *op cit,* pp.276 & 292.

54. *Ibid*, p.308.
55. *Flight*, 3 June 1992, pp.24-5.
56. *Aviation Week*, 29 July 1991, p.48.
57. *Aviation Week*, 25 November 1991, p.34; *Flight*, 8 January 1992, pp.35-7.

Chapter 3

1. See Henri Matre of Aerospatiale, *Armed Forces Journal*, June 1991.

2. Bluestone, *Aircraft Industry Dynamics, op cit,* p.170.

3. For example, the Brazilian government is endeavouring to sell shares in Embraer to raise new capital, to reduce serious debt problems and to improve the quality of decision-making. *Interavia*, March 1992, pp.44-9.

4. The Chinese aerospace industry is still structured in a similar way, but economic reform may also lead to some decentralisation and increased autonomy. See *Flight*, 28 August 1993, p.13.

5. There was an element of competition between design bureaux and persistent failure could lead to a loss of status and absorption by a stronger unit. In 1974, for example, the Korolev and Glushko rocket design teams were merged.

6. *Jane's Defence Weekly*, 28 September 1991, pp.566-7; *Aviation Week*, 23 September 1991, p.27; *Flight*, 9.10 91, p.10; *Aviation Week*, 30 September 1991, p.20.

7. *The Financial Times*, 19 February 1992.

8. See Chapter 6; *Aviation Week*, 26 August 1991, pp.24-5; 2 September 1991, pp.20-1.

9. See Chapter 6.

10. *Interavia*, October 1992, pp. 26-8; *Aviation Week*, 29 March 1993, p.20.

11. E. A. Kolodziej, *Making and Marketing Arms*, (Princeton, 1987), pp.275-6.

12. These links are reinforced by the interchange of personnel between government and the state aerospace firms. This system, known as *pantouflage*, does not prevent conflict between government and industry, but over time it helps to maintain a commonality of outlook.

13. Kolodziej, *op cit*, pp. 221-4. See also G. Jalabert, *Les Spatiale en France*, (Paris, 1974). During this period, the French government also resisted Snecma's ambitions to become a major player in civil aero-engines. In the event, the company pressed its case and eventually the French government became a staunch supporter of Snecma's shift to civil engines.

14. See, J. Gee, *Mirage*, (London, 1971) and C. Carlier, *Marcel Dassault, la Legende d'un Siecle*, (Paris, 1991).

15. Hayward, *International Collaboration, op cit*, p.37.

16. Assemblée Nationale, Session 1976-77, Rapport No. 2815, pp.97-103. See also Carlier, *op cit*; Chapters 6-8.

17. Hayward, *International Collaboration, op cit*, pp. 96-102.

18. See Rapport No. 2815, *op cit*.

19. *Air et Cosmos*, 16 June 1990, p.6; *Flight*, 20 June 1990, p.15.

20. *Military Technology*, February 1993, pp.77-8; *Jane's Defence Weekly*, 1 May 1993, pp.29-30.

21. For a history of relations between UK government and industry, see K. Hayward, *The British Aircraft Industry*, (Manchester, 1989).

22. *Ibid*, pp.50-2. The post-war government also shied away from taking on the powerful individuals, often the founders, who still ran 'their' firms.

23. *Ibid*, pp.73-82.

24. T. Taylor & K. Hayward, *The UK Defence Industrial Base*, (London 1989), pp.90-2.

25. *The The Economist*, 9 November 1991, p.112; *The Financial Times*, 22 October 1991.

26. 3rd Report from the Trade and Industry Committee, *The British Aerospace Industry*, HC 563, Session 1992-3, (HMSO, London, 1993). This report also carries details of the UK National Strategic Aerospace Technology Plan.

27. See K. Hayward, *The West German Aerospace Industry and its Contribution to Western Security, op cit.*

28. See Chapter 6.

29. K. Hayward, *The West German Aerospace Industry and its Contribution to Western Security, op cit*, pp.55-66.

30. A new Rolls-Royce BMW factory in the old DDR will be part funded by Bonn. *Interavia*, December, 1991, pp.38-42.

31. *Aerospace World*, January 1991, pp.11-13.

32. *Ibid*, July 1991, pp.18-19; *Aviation Week*, 29 April 1991, pp. 58-9.

33. See Chapter 8.

34. Samuels & Whipple, *Defence Production etc. op cit*, pp.282-3.

35. See *The The Economist*, 24 August 1991, p.54. The Japanese F-4 was reputedly so badly designed that Japanese pilots refused to fly it at night.

36. US pressure has now forced the Japanese to open up their commercial satellite market.

37. Samuels & Whipple, *op cit*, p.290.

38. *Aviation Week*, 23 March 1992, p.73, 3 August 1990, pp.38-87.

39. Hayward, *International Collaboration, op cit*, pp.46-7; *Flight*, 23 January 1988.

40. Samuels & Whipple, *op cit*, p.305.

41. Samuels & Whipple, *op cit*, p.290; *Interavia*, April 1991, p.45. Work on hypersonics has been in progress since 1987. The Japanese government has provided $48 million a year for 20 companies and universities. *Aviation Week*, 16 December 1991, pp.60-1.

42. Designated the YSX-75. *Flight*, 18 December 1991, pp.4-5.

43. See Bluestone & Bright, *Aircraft Industry Dynamics, op cit.*

44. *Aviation Week*, 29 July 1991, p.23, 30 March 1992, p.26; *Armed Forces Journal*, May 1991, p.14.

45. See *The Financial Times*, 14 March 1992.

46. See K. Hayward, *The United States Aerospace Industry*, Whitehall Paper No. 5, Royal United Services Institute, (London, 1991).

47. See Boeing evidence to the House of Commons Trade and Industry Committee, *British Aerospace Industry, op cit,* p.78.

48. *Ibid,* pp. 79-83.

49. Dr. George Milburn, Vice-President of the National Centre for Advanced Technologies, *Aviation Week,* 26 August 1991, p.63.

50. *Aviation Week,* 1 March 1993, pp.18-19. The aerospace infrastructure includes airport and air traffic control facilities.

51 *Commercial Aviation News,* 19 April 1993.

52. *The Financial Times,* 23 August 1993.

53. As recommended by Clinton's economic adviser, Laura d'Andrea Tyson. See Tyson, *Who's Bashing Whom? op cit.*

54. The UK Treasury believes this to be the only valid reason for supporting civil programmes such as Airbus.

55. Office of Technology Assessment, *Competing Economies,* OTA-ITE-498, (Washington D.C., October 1991), pp. 342-3.

56. K. Hayward, *International Collaboration, op cit* Chapter 5.

57. *An Economic and Financial Review of Airbus Industrie,* US Department of Commerce, (Washington D. C.), 1990. (The Gelman Report), Chapter 2; *Interavia,* July 1991, p.76.

58 See also, OTA, *Competing Economies, op cit,* pp.350-1.

59. OTA, *Competing Economies, op cit,* p.341.

60. See A. Philips, *Technology and Market Structure,* (Lexington, 1971). An exception was aid provided during the 1960s for the US SST. This amounted to over $1 billion.

61. For a detailed review of the role of public funding and the relationship between defence contracts and the early Boeing programmes, see C. Irving, *Wide-body: the story of the 747.* See also, Tyson, *Who's Bashing Whom? op cit,* pp.186-7.

62. Cited in *US Government Support of the US Commercial Aircraft Industry,* a report by Arnold & Porter Associates, (Washington D. C., November 1991), pp.103-6. This report was paid for the EC, and should be seen as a counter to the Gelman Report into Airbus financing. Despite its provenance, as Gelman does for European direct funding for civil, programmes, Arnold & Porter provide an exhaustive history and analysis of US indirect support.

63. *Ibid,* pp.7-6064.

64. OTA, *Competing Economies, op cit,* p.346.

65. See Chapter 4.

66. Arnold & Porter, *op cit,* pp. 345-6. See also Chapter 4.

67. Given European concern for NASA's support to the US aerospace industry, NASA officials have been increasingly concerned that European infrastructure has, in fact, crept ahead of the US. In the 1994 NASA budget proposal, $181 million was allocated to the revitalisation of NASA facilities, with an additional $200 million for a detailed design study of two new wind tunnels. According to NASA's new head of aeronautics, Kristin Hessenius, 'Our facilities are, on average, over 40 years old. Meanwhile, the Europeans have made tremendous investments in aeronautics facilities ... and they have superior capabilities in simulating flight conditions'. This has led US industry to use European, particularly British wind tunnels. In particular, research into hybrid laminar flow control (HLFC) was cited as an area where Europe was rapidly catching up with the US and the US lead would be lost in three to five years without new facilities. *Commercial Aviation News*, 19 April 1993.

68. OTA, *Competing Economies, op cit*, pp.346-7. Arnold & Porter, pp.60-96.

69. D. Mowery & N. Rosenberg, *Technology and the Pursuit of Economic Growth*, cited in Arnold & Porter, p.64.

70. Texas was reported willing to provide up to $1.5 billion in favourable loans to attract MD-12 production. *Aviation Week*, 5 July 1991, p.26. When Boeing bought de Havilland Canada, the Canadian government provided 35% of the cost of modernising the plant and 50% for development of a new variant of the Dash-8. J. Laux, 'Limits to Intervention', *International Journal*, Winter 1990-1, pp.132.

71. Though Boeing did raise some objections to MDC's proposed alliance with Taiwan. See Bob Shronz's views about facing 'another highly subsidized competitor'. *Aviation Week*, 25, November 1991, pp.155-6.

72. See Chapter Five for further discussion of the dollar pricing question.

73. See J. McDonnell, *Aviation Week*, 5 August 1991, p.62. The affect of this outburst was somewhat spoilt by a report in the same issue of MDC's demands for aid from US state governments as the price for locating new production facilities in their region.

74. An agreement under OECD auspices. See Hayward, *International Collaboration, op cit*, Chapter 5.

75. GATT, *Agreement on Trade in Civil Aircraft*, Article 6, cited by J Rallo 'The European Community Industry Policy Revisited', *Journal of Common Market Studies*, March 1984, pp.264-5.

76. *The Financial Times*, 24 May 1991.

77. US Dept. of Commerce, *An Economic and Financial Review of Airbus Industrie*, (Washington D.C, 4 September 1990) (The Gelman Report).

78. Arnold & Porter, *op cit*, pp.85-88.

79. *The Financial Times*, 5 December 1991; *Aviation Week*, 17 June 1991, pp. 155-6; *Flight*, 22 May 1991, pp.20-1.

80. *Business Week* , 8 October 1990, p.37; *Interavia*, March 1992, pp.12-17; *The Financial Times*, 13 March 1991.

81. *Aviation Week*, 10 June 1991, p.19; *Flight*, 22 May 1991, pp. 20-1.

82. EC SEC (90) p.13.

83. BAe and Fokker threatened legal action if DASA and others tried to launch an 80-120 seat airliner with launch aid to compete with their existing and planned developments. *The Financial Times*, 15 March 1991.

84. *The Financial Times*, 21 June 1991.

85. *The Financial Times*, 2 April 1992.

86. *Aviation Week*, 24 February 1992, p.42, 13 April 1992, p.32; *Air et Cosmos*, 13 April 1992, p.10; *The Financial Times*, 1 May 1992. The EC has refused to accept the GATT ruling on the German exchange rate guarantee scheme.

87. *Commercial Aviation News*, 8 March 1993, 15 March 1993.

88. See Chapter 8.

89. *Aviation Week*, 17 June 1991, p.155.

90. *Flight*, 11 December 1991, p.3.

91. See OTA, *Competing Economies, op cit*, p.358.

Chapter 4

1. See Chapter 5.
2. See, T. L. McNaugher, *New Weapons, Old Politics*, (Washington D.C., 1989).
3. T. L. McNaugher, *Defense Management Reform*, unpublished paper, Brookings Institute, (Washington D.C., January 1990), p.2.
4. T.L.McNaugher, *New Weapons, Old Politics, op cit*, pp.78-84.
5. *Armed Services Journal*, January 1989, p.32.
6. *Defense News*, 23 March 1990.
7. *International Herald Tribune*, 3 May 1988.
8. *Aviation Week*, 19 March 1990; *Defense News*, 30 October 1989; 21 May 1990.
9. *Armed Forces Journal*, January 1989; *Aviation Week*, 30 May 1989, pp.4-5.
10. *Defense News*, 4 September 1989.
11. *Defense News*, 23 March 1990.
12. *Armed Forces Journal*, February 1989, p.29; *Aviation Week*, 28 August 1989, p.23; *Defense News*, 11 December 1989.
13. *Defense News*, 29 April 1991.
14. *Defense News*, 9 April 1991.
15. *Defense News*, 5 August 1991.
16. Dr. William Perry, *Aerospace World*, November 1990, p.53.
17. *Aviation Week*, 4 February 1991, p.55, 5 April 1991, pp.18-24.
18. *Jane's Defence Weekly*, 9 February 1991, p.175.
19. *International Defense Review*, October 1990, pp.1157-9.
20. *Defense News*, 11 February 1991; *Aviation Week*, 14 January 1990, p.18-22.
21. *Business Week*, 21 January 1991, p.33; *Aviation Week*, 14 January 1991, p.23; *The The Economist*, 12 January 1991, p.39.
22 *Interavia*, June 1990, p.495.
23. *Interavia*, September 1990, pp.778-80.
24. T.L.McNaugher, *Defense Management Reform, op cit*, p.27.
25. *Business Week*, 6 May 1991, pp.28-9; *Flight*, 24 October 1990, p.14.
26. *Flight*, 1 May 1991, p.6.
27. See R. W. Drewes, *The Airforce and the Great Engine War*, (Washington D.C, 1987).
28. See a special report on management techniques in US industry, *Aviation Week*, 8 January 1990 and Chapter 6.
29. See D.L. Pilling, *Competition in Defense Procurement*, Brookings, (Washington D.C., 1989).
30. *Defense News*, 22 July 1991.
31. Cited in K. Hayward, *The US Aerospace Industry, op cit*, p.19.
32. *The Financial Times*, 3 August 1989; *Aviation Week*, 3 September 1990, p.183.
33. *Jane's Defence Weekly*, 27 January 1990, p.166.
34. *The Financial Times*, 26 March 1990.

35. *Janes' Defence Weekly*, 27 January 1990, p.166.

36. See Table in *Aviation Week*, 3 September 1990, p.179.

37. *Defense News*, 4 February 1991.

38. *Aviation Week*, 23 September 1991, p.45.

39. *Aviation Week*, 3 September 1990, pp.179-81; *Armed Service Journal*, November 1991, p.10.

40. *Defense News*, 16 September 1991.

41. *Aviation Week*, 18 March 1991, p.59.

42. *Defense News*, 30 October 1989.

43. See Chapter 8.

44. See Chapter 7.

45. *Flight* 31 March 1993, p.32; *Defense News*, 6 September, 1993.

46. See, for example, the BSE and Ferranti affair in the UK during the 1960s and in France, the Dassault scandal of the 1970s.

47. T. Taylor & K. Hayward, *The UK Defence Industrial Base, op cit*, p.106.

48. *Ibid*, p.74.

49. *Jane's Defence Weekly*, 13 April 1991, p.614.

50. *Jane's Defence Weekly*, 23 February 1991, p.275.

51. *Jane's Defence Weekly*, 21 October 1989, p.887; *Flight*, 15 July 1990, p.25.

52. Speech to the Royal United Services Institute, 20 June 1990.

53. *Jane's Defence Weekly*, 13 April 1991, p.613.

54. *The Financial Times*, 8 February 1991.

55. Cited in *Flight*, 5 July 1989, p.12.

56. *Aerospace World*, September 1990, p.27.

57. *Independent on Sunday*, 27 January 1991; *Flight*, 6 March 1991, p.18.

58. In the 1970s, a mistake on the Lynx contract had helped to undermine Westland finances which set the scene for the 1985/6 crisis. *Management Today*, April 1982, pp.71-2. For details of the EH-101 contract, see *Aviation Week*, 9 September 1991, pp.24-6.

59. *L'Expres*, 23 September 1988, pp.28-30.

60. *Interavia*, December 1989, p.1196.

61. *The Financial Times*, 11 June 1991.

62. See *Flight*, 3 January 1990, p.26.

63. *Interavia*, December 1989, p.1194.

64. House of Commons Defence Committee, *European Fighter Aircraft*, HC 299, Session 1991-2, Paras. 54-6.

65. *Jane's Defence Weekly*, 2 November 1991, pp.810-11.

66. *The Financial Times*, 15 October 1991.

67. *Aerospace World*, April 1991, pp.56-7.

68. See HC 563, *op cit*, Qs.891, 778 and evidence, p.192.

69. See remarks by John Weston, chief of BAe Military Aircraft Division, *Flight*, 7 December 1991, p.1094. See also, GEC answers to HC 563, *op cit*, Q. 273, BAe evidence, p.1 and Paras 106-116 of report.

70. *The Financial Times*, 10 March 1992.

71. *Jane's Defence Weekly*, 17 August 1991, p.283; *The Economist*, 24 August 1991, p.54.

72. Deutsche Bank, *The Peace Dividend - How to Pin it Down?* , (Frankfurt, 1991), p.7.

73. C.D. Volmer, 'The Future Defense Environment', *Washington Quarterly*, Spring 1990, p.100.

74. *Aviation Week*, 19 February 1990, pp.16-17; *Defense News*, 10 September 1990; 9 September 1993; *Jane's Defence Weekly*, 15 February 1992, pp.222-3.

75. *Aviation Week*, 17 June 1991, pp.62-3.

76. See, T. L. McNaugher, *New Weapons, Old Politics*, (Washington D.C., 1989); *Aviation Week*, 19 March 1990, pp.59-60. See also Chapter 8.

77. *Defense News*, 20 August 1990; *Aviation Week*, 4 March 1991, pp.52-5; 18 March 1991, pp.63-4; *Interavia*, September 1990, p.748.

78. *Defense News*, 18 March 1991; *Aerospace World*, May 1991, pp.50-1.

79. *Die Zeit*, 8 February 1991.

80. *Defense News*, 24 February 1992; *Jane's Defence Weekly*, 25 January 1992, p.110.

81. *The Financial Times*, 7 March 1990; 23 September 1990.

82. *Defense News*, 13 May 1990.

83. *The Financial Times*, 20 June 1990; 22 March 1991; *Jane's Defence Weekly*, 25 January 1992, pp.324-5.

84. *The Guardian*, 29 May 1991; *The Financial Times*, 29 May 1991.

85. *Flight*, 21 November 1990, p.14; *Defense News*, 17 September 1990.

86. *Defense News*, 17 September 1990; *Air et Cosmos*, 19 November 1990, pp.46-7; *The Financial Times*, 2 December 1989; 2 August 1991.

87. *Defense News*, 16 March 1992; 1 June 1992.

88. *Flight*, 31 March 1993, p.34.

89. Deutsche Bank, *op cit*, p.40; *Aviation Week*, 11 February 1991, pp.40-2; *Flight*, 31 March 1993, p.34.

90. See AIAA, *The US Aerospace Industry, op cit*, pp.67-8.

91. *The Financial Times*, 12 December 1990.

92. *Armed Forces Journal*, June 1989, pp.80-1; *Flight*, 20 November 1991, p.41.

93. See K. Hayward, *German Aerospace, op cit*, pp.33-40; *Armed Forces Journal*, May 1991, p.25; *The Financial Times*, 25 March 1991.

94. *Jane's Defence Weekly*, 23 October 1991, p.616.

95. K. Hayward, *The United States Aerospace Industry, op cit*, p.33.

96. K. Hayward, 'BAe Defence Business', *RUSI Journal*, June 1989, pp.39-45; *Independent on Sunday*, 3 March 1991; *Aviation Week*, 4 November 1991, p.59.

97. See B. Schemmer, *Armed Forces Journal*, January 1991, pp.44-8.

98. *Flight*, 21 July 1993, p.16.

99. *Defense News*, 11 March 1991, 3 June 1991, 16 June 1991.

100. *The Financial Times*, 17 September 1990; MDC was especially active trying to persuade Congress to allow its sale of F-15Cs to Saudi Arabia. *Defense News*, 13 January 1992.

101. *Defense News*, 21 October 1991. Some cynics have suggested that US concern for an arms transfer control regime in the Middle East is an attempt to level up the playing field for US competitors.

102. *Jane's Defence Weekly*, 13 February 1993, p.36.

103. An exception may be the Missile Technology Control Regime. The US's strong reaction in 1993 to the possibility that Chinese missile technology might be transferred to Pakistan gave some comfort to arms controllers. See *Defense News*, 13 September 1993.

104. *Business Week*, 20 September 1993, p.45.

105. *Aviation Week*, 16 March 1992, pp.43-4; *Janes' Defence Weekly*, 22 February 1992, pp. 324-5.

106. *The Financial Times*, 23 April 1990; *Defence News*, March 16, 1992.

107. *Jane's Defence Weekly*, 18 September 1993, pp.29-30.

Chapter 5

1. By comparing figures 4.1 & 5.1, the counter-cyclical effect can be seen. In 1965 and 1978 a high for civil orders matches a downturn in US military expenditure; the onset of the current downturn in defence spending in 1986 marks the beginnings of the massive increase in civil orders. From 1991/2, however, both are in decline.

2. At one point, toilet and galley units were being put into Boeing aircraft as they arrived in Seattle.

3. *Interavia*, June 1989, pp.520-23.

4. A large number of nationalised airlines have been privatised or are up for sale.

5. The Concorde was, perhaps, one major exception.

6. Hayward, *International Collaboration, op cit*, pp.25-6. For a more detailed analysis of airline procurement, see R. Doganis, *Flying Off Course* (2nd. Ed) (London, 1991).

7. Hayward, *International Collaboration, op cit*, pp.18-22.

8. *Ibid*, pp. 168-80.

9. Hayward, *International Collaboration, op cit*, pp.23-4; *The Guardian*, 15 October 1991.

10. Hayward, *Government and British Civil Aerospace, op cit*, pp.202-205.

11. Commission of the EC, *The European Aircraft Industry: First Assessment and Possible European Community Actions*, (Brussels, May 1992).

12. *Independent on Sunday*, 15 September 1991.

13. See J. Schaefffler, Chairman of DASA, *Aerospace World*, December 1990, p.16.

14. Opposition might also come from EC member states who would benefit little from such a scheme, but who would nevertheless have to pay for their share of its costs.

15. See Chapter 3.

16. See, V. Gollich, *The Political Economy of International Air Safety*, (London, 1989), pp.56-60.

17. *Aviation Week*, 27 May 1991, p.62.

18. Boeing Commercial Aircraft co. *Current Market Outlook, 1992,* (Seattle, February, 1992).

19. Boeing 1992, *op cit.*

20. *Flight,* 2 December 1991, p.22.

21. *Flight,* 11 December, 1991, p.11; 29 January 1992, p.11; 9 December 1992, p.27; 8 May 1993, p.5. *Aviation Week,* 3 January 1992, p.82.

22. *Flight,* 9 December 1992, p.27.

23. *Interavia,* February 1990, pp.133-6; *The Financial Times,* 27 January 1990.

24. Hayward, *International Collaboration, op cit,* pp. 181-84.

25. *Aerospace World,* February 1991, p.18; *The Financial Times,* 7 January 1991, 22 February 1991.

26. *Euromoney,* June 1989; *The Financial Times,* 1 June 1989.

27. *Interavia,* December 1991, p.22.

28. *Interavia,* December 1991, p.22.

29. *The Financial Times,* 7 January 1991; *Interavia,* January 1991, pp. 43-6; *The Economist* 1 December 1990, pp.127-8.

30. *Flight,* 6 March 1991, p.15; 3 February 1993, p.21; *The Financial Times,* 22 February 1991; 5 November 1991; 19 June 1992; 23 January 1993; 26 August 1993; *Interavia,* December 1991, pp.15-18.

31. *Flight,* 16 October 1991, pp.41-2.

32. *Flight,* 15 September 1993, p.26.

33. *The Financial Times,* 11 June 1991; *Interavia,* September 1991, p. 4; *Flight,* 11 September 1991, p.11.

34. Boeing 1991, pp. 44-6; *Flight,* 14 August 1991, pp.20-1.

35. For a wide review of civil aviation and the environment, see *Aviation Week,* 25 November 1991; *Interavia,* January 1992, pp.57-9.

36. See comments in *Interavia,* March 1992, pp.19-24 and *Flight,* 12 February 1992, p.4.

37. Boeing, *op cit.*

38. *Flight,* 20 January 1993, p.27.

39. *Interavia,* August 1991, pp.12-14; *Flight,* 18 March 1992, p.24.

40. *Flight,* 5 January 1993, p.35.

41. AIAA, *Global Prospects, op cit,* p.78.

42. *Aviation Week,* 16 August 1993, pp.24-5.

43. *Space Markets,* 2/1991, pp. 31-4; *Flight,* 21 August 1991, pp. 21-2;*The Financial Times,* 18 May 1992.

44. *Aviation Week,* 2 September 1991, p.71.

45. American law requires all publically-funded satellites to be launched by US rockets.

46. *Space Markets,* 4/1990; *Air et Cosmos,* 17 March 1991, pp.40-1; *The Financial Times,* 11 December 1990, 18 May 1992; *Interavia,* January 1993, p.60.

47. *Space Markets,* 4/1990; *Flight,* 2 December 1992, pp.25-6.

48. *Aerospace World,* September 1991, pp. 62-4; *Flight,* 13 January 1993, pp.34-5.

49. *The Financial Times,* 18 May 1992; *Flight,* 13 May 1992, pp.33-5.

50. *Air et Cosmos*, 20 May 1991, pp. 39-40; *Defense News*, 4 November 1991. The 1993 cuts in the French defence budget have called into question French commitment to Helios.

51. *Defence News*, 3 June 1991; *Flight*, 19 February 1992, p.32.

52. *Space Markets*, 4/1991, pp.4-13.

53. See W. Zegveld & C. Enzing, *SDI and Industrial and Technology Policy*, (London 1987).

54. *Defense News*, 2 September 1991.

55. Even in the case of the much praised Shuttle rescue of an ailing comsat in 1992, it would have been cheaper to have insured the satellite.

56. *Space Markets*, 3/1991, p.37.

57. AIAA, *Global Prospects, op cit*, p.77.

58. *Aviation Week*, 26 August 1991, p.24; 2 September 1991, pp.20-1; 9 September 1991, p.19; *Space Markets*, May 1991, p.12.

59. A possible link between Arianespace and the Proton organisation was announced in August 1993, and Lockheed reached an agreement to market Russian launches.

60. *Space Markets*, 4/1991, pp.21-5.

61. *Aerospace World,* June 1991, pp.72-3; *The Financial Times*, 24 September 1991; *Aviation Week*, 17 June 1991, pp.96-7; 25 November 1991, p.107. *Air et Cosmos*, 13 April 1992, pp.46-7.

62. *Aviation Week*, 16 November 1992, p.85.

63. See A.L Deckers, *Industry Policy in the European Space Sector*, unpublished MSc thesis for the University of Manchester, 1992; *Interavia*, February 1993, pp.58-60.

Chapter 6

1. Bright, *The Jet Makers, op cit*, p.134.

2. Conversion can also be used to describe changing the use of a defence product into a civilian application.

3. *Ibid*, Chapter 10.

4. Hayward, *The British Aircraft Industry, op cit*, pp.174-6.

5. *Aviation Week*, 29 May 1989, p.66.

6. *Defense News*, 26 March 1990.

7. See Taylor & Hayward, *The UK Defence Industrial Base, op cit*, Chapter 3.

8. *Armed Forces Journal*, May 1991, pp.42-4.

9. *Ibid*, pp.42-8.

10. See OTA, *Competing Economies, op cit*, pp.345-6.

11. *Ibid*, pp. 346 & 357.

12. Hayward, *International Collaboration, op cit*, pp.97-105; Carlier, *Dassault, op cit*, Chapter 6.

13. The Rolls-Royce auto marque was sold to Vickers.

14. To be fair, Saab has also found aerospace-auto synergies in areas such as cockpit/cabin ergonomics.

15. Bright, *The Jet Makers, op cit*, pp.144-5.

16. *Space Markets*, April 1990, p.203.

17. *Flight*, 24 June 1989, pp.49-51.

18. The European Commission later forced BAe to repay some of the 'subsidy' element. Hayward, *The British Aircraft Industry, op cit,* pp.176-7.

19. *The Financial Times,* 31 January 1990; 28 March 1990.

20. BAe also had a serious presentational problem with the City of London. Few brokers and analysts were really happy with BAe's hybrid characteristics.

21. Hayward, *The West German Aerospace Industry, op cit,* p.55.

22. *Ibid,* pp.55-6.

23. *Ibid.*

24. See *The Observer,* 29 September 1991; *The Financial Times,* 10 September 1991; 27 September 1991; 12 November 1991, 9 January 1992, 26 February 1992; *Defense News,* 21 October 1991. Under the terms of the original purchase agreement, BAe could not sell Rover before 1993 without incurring financial penalties.

25. *Flight,* 17 October 1990, p.30.

26. *The The Economist,* 27 April 1991, pp.87-8; *Die Zeit,* 13 March 1991; *The Financial Times,* 15 March 1991; 29 June 1990; *Aviation Week,* 21 October 1991.

27. *Independent on Sunday,* 15 September 1991; *The Observer,* 15 September 1991.

28. *Independent on Sunday,* 27 January 1991. BAe has certainly felt that it has not had a particular easy time from the UK government. See HoC 563, *op cit,* BAe evidence Qs. 38-48 & 74.

29. *Flight,* 24 June 1989, p.51.

30. See, for example, UN Disarmament Topical Papers No.5, *Conversion in an Age of Economic Adjustment,* (2 Vols.) (New York, 1991); G. Bischak, (ed) *Towards a Peace Economy in the United States,* (London, 1991)

31. *Defense News,* 26 March 1990.

32. *Flight,* 13 February 1991, p.14; *Aerospace World,* October 1991, pp.62-3.

33. *Aviation Week,* 2 June 1991, p.24; *Defense News,* 17 June 1991.

34. *The Financial Times,* 2 November 1991.

35. *Flight,* 24 April 1991, p.14.

36. *Aviation Week,* 6 April 1992, pp.44-54.

37. *The Guardian,* 10 September 1991; *Aerospace World,* May 1991; *Interavia,* September 1991, p.46. For example, despite having a group of 200 people exploring diversification and conversion possibilities, up to 1991, DASA had little to show for the exercise in terms of new business.

38. *Flight,* 25 September 1991, pp.36-7; *The Financial Times,* 22 November 1991; *Defense News* 25 November 1991.

39. *Times,* 15 October 1991.

40. See SBAC briefing, *Industrial Restructuring,* (London, 1992).

41. *Aviation Week,* 5 July 1991, p.31.

42. *Aviation Week,* 23 September 1991, p.44.

43. Significantly, those firms looking at the hazardous waste business want limits placed on their public liability rather than costing in the risks.

44. The author visited MDC Long Beach just after TQM was announced; the effect on morale was evident even to an outsider.

45. TQM, and other process technology/management systems concepts, have had considerable airing in the trade journals. A good review of the impact is to be found in *Aviation Week*, 9 December 1991, pp.56-69.

46. *Flight*, 26 February 1992, p.22.

47. See K Ballentine, 'Soviet Defence Industry Reform: the Problems of Conversion in an Unconverted Economy', *Canadian Institute for International Peace and Security*, Background Paper No. 36, July 1991; J. Cooper, *The Soviet Defence Industry: Conversion and Reform*, (London, 1991).

48. *The Guardian*, 5 September 1991; 6 September 1991; Ballentine, *op cit*; *Aviation Week*, 21 October 1991.

49. *Aviation Week*, 26 July 1991, pp.24-5; *The Financial Times*, 11 October 1991.

50. *Flight*, 2 October 1991, pp.43-5.

51. See K. Hornschild & G. Neckerman, *Die Deutsche Luft und Raumfahrt Industrie*, (Frankfurt, 1988).

52. Samuels and Whipple, *op cit*, p.190; *Aviation Week*, 29 July 1991, p.43.

53. *Aviation Week*, 29 July 1991, p.91.

54. Hayward, *British Aircraft Industry, op cit*, pp.59-82

55. See Chapter 4.

56. B. Sweetman, *Advanced Fighter Technology*, (Shrewsbury, 1987), pp.96-101.

57. *Flight*, 1 May 1991, p.6: *Jane's Defence Weekly*, 4 May 1981, pp.718-9; *Aviation Week* 29 April 1991, p.26.

58. *International Herald Tribune*, 5 September 1990; *Aviation Week*, 29 January 1990, pp.21-2.

59. *Aviation Week*, 16 September 1991, pp.22-3.

60. *Ibid*

61. *Defense News*, 29 April 1991.

62. *Defense News*, 22 July 1991.

63. *Defense News*, 22 January 1991; 2 October 1991, 13 January 1991; *Aviation Week* 5 July 1991; *Jane's Defence Weekly*, 1 April 1991, pp.477-9.

64. *Defense News*, 29 January 1990.

65. In 1993, GEC and BAe held tentative negotiations about a possible merger.

66. *The Financial Times*, 24 November 1992.

67. *Aviation Week*, 9 November 1992, p.23; 14 December 1992, pp.20-4.

68. Grumman has long been the most likely candidate for relegation, but in recent years, the spectre of MDC, the largest US defence contractor, going bust has been raised. Problems with projects such as the C-17 and cash flow difficulties with its civil programmes have led to speculation about its future. *Aviation Week*, 22 February 1993, pp.25-7; 19 April 1993, pp.43-8; *Defense News*, 7 December 1992.

69. One consequence of the Lockheed-GD take-over appears to have been the creation of three competing units within Lockheed. Bids for the US Navy's proposed Stealth fighter have included two from Lockheed. See *Defense News*, 13 September 1993.

70. *Jane's Defence Weekly*, 18 September 1993, pp.29-30.

Chapter 7

1. See Aerospace Industries Association of America, *The US Industry and the Trend Towards Internationalisation*, (Washington D.C., 1988).
2. See T. Taylor, 'Defence Industries in International Relations', *Review of International Studies*, January 1990, pp. 60-6.
3. K. Hartley, *NATO Arms Cooperation*, (London, 1983), p.124.
4. See M. Rich (*et al*), *Multinational Co-production of Military Aerospace Systems*, RAND, Santa Monica, 1981, R-2861.
5. IEPG, *Towards a Stronger Europe* (The Vredeling Report), (Brussels 1986), p.119.
6. The House of Commons Defence Committee, Session 1987-9, HC431, Qs. 76-8; The Comptroller and Auditor General, cited by M. Bittlestone, *Cooperation or Competition?*, Adelphi Paper No. 250, IISS, London Spring 1990, p.60.
7. HC 299 *op cit*, Para. 54.
8. *The Financial Times*, 16 December 1992.
9. There are again limits imposed by the realities of collaborative politics. Despite attempts to employ more stringent contracting procedures, EFA worksharing has led to some inefficiency, a problem 'inevitable in multinational projects'. HC 299, *op cit*, Para. 52
10. National Audit Office, *MoD Collaborative Projects*, House of Commons Paper No. 247, London 1991, paras. 4.24-4.27.
11. K. Hayward, *The West German Aerospace Industry, op cit*, pp.50-2.
12. See R Williams, *International Technological Collaboration*, (London, 1973).
13. K. Hayward, *International Collaboration, op cit*, Chapter 3.
14. *Ibid*, Chapter 4.
15. Dassault tended to get most of the blame for French intransigence, refusing to surrender programme leadership to a consortium. Dassault feel that the real stumbling bloc was the defence of the Snecma M-88 engine.
16. K. Hayward, *European Aerospace Collaboration, op cit*, pp.15-24.
17. *Interavia*, December 1989, pp.1193-4.
18. *Jane's Defence Weekly*, 22 July 1989, p.105; *Armed Forces Journal*, December 1989, p.82.
19. *Jane's Defence Weekly*, 16 December 1989, p.1318; 17 March 1990, p.487.
20. *The Financial Times*, 23 April 1990, 1 June 1992, 11 June 1992; *Defense News*, 12 March 1990, 18 May 1992, 8 June 1992; *Aviation Week*, 25 May 1992, pp.20-1; *Interavia*, September 1990, p.706; *Jane's Defence Weekly*, 3 February 1990, p.177.
21. *Interavia*, September 1990, p.706; *Defense News*, 21 May 1990; *The Financial Times*, 11 June 1992.
22. *Jane's Defence Weekly*, 26 October 1992, p.5.
23. *Flight*, 4 November 1992; *The Guardian*, 6 January 1993.
24. *Flight*, 17 March 1993, p.5; 7 April 1993, p.18.

25. *Flight*, 6 December 1991, p.6.

26. Cited in K. Hayward, *European Aerospace Collaboration, op cit,* p.44.

27. *The Financial Times*, 19 February 1992; *Defense News*, 18 February 1992.

28. K. Hayward, *European Aerospace Collaboration, op. cit.* pp.25-33.

29. *Ibid.*

30. *Ibid.*

31. *The Financial Times*, 7 March 1990; *Aviation Week*, 2 April 1990, pp.18-19; *Air et Cosmos* 8 July 1991, pp.10-11; *Aerospace World*, March 1992, pp.26-8.

32. The Spanish aircraft industry has a minor share of AI, and Dutch and Belgian firms are associate members.

33. M. Bangemann, *Can Europe Meet the Global Challenge*, (Bonn, 1992).

34. See K. Hayward, *International Collaboration in Civil Aerospace,* (London, 1986), Chapter 2.

35. Boeing, *Current Market Outlook, 1993,* Seattle, March 1993.

36. *Groupement d'Intérêts Economiques.*

37. Hayward, *European Aerospace Collaboration, op cit; The Financial Times,* 2 November 1989; 2 March 1990.

38. *Aerospace World*, October 1990, pp.29-31.

39. *Flight*, 23 May 1990, p.231; *The Financial Times*, 9 May 1990.

40. The creation of Eurocopter was delayed precisely because of such problems.

41. *Air et Cosmos*, 19 November 1990, p.18; *Flight*, 17 October 1990, pp.30-1.

42. *The Financial Times*, 14 October 1991.

43. The main exception to this rule has been the development of German expertise in composite materials and large composite structures.

44. See Hayward, *European Aerospace Collaboration, op cit*, pp.34-46.

45. *Ibid.*

46. *Flight*, 28 April 1993, p.12.

47. See HC 563, *op cit*, Q.33, Para 113.

48. See K Hayward, *The West German Aerospace Industry and its Contribution to Western Security*, RUSI, Whitehall Paper No.2, (London 1990).

49. *Aviation Week*, 11 January 1993, p.21.

50. The same could be said of the preliminary work between the US and Europe on an advanced supersonic airliner.

51. See Chapter 8.

52. The last EC Framework programme provided about 40MECU a year to aeronautics. Suggestions that this might be increased to 400MECU were shelved pending general decisions about the size and priorities of the 4th Framework programme. See Chapter 8.

53. This excludes the use of foreign equipment and engines in US aircraft.

54. A good example was the international F-16 programme involving Holland, Norway and Belgium.

55. *Defense News*, 17 September 1990. The CFM56 is something of an exception, but it was still a 'gap' filler for GE while vital to Snecma. More signifcant still, the US has taken the lead in the AV-8 programme and the UK is very much a junior partner in advanced Stol joint research activities.

56. K. Hayward, *International Collaboration, op cit*, Chapter 3.

57. *Interavia*, July 1991, pp.30-26.

58. Cited in K. Hayward, *The United States Aerospace Industry, op.cit*, p.55.

59. Cited in G. Haglund, *The Defense Industrial Base and the West*, (London 1989), pp.28-9.

60. K Hayward, *The United States Aerospace Industry, op cit*, pp.56-8.

61. K Hayward, *The United States Aerospace Industry, op cit*, p.57.

62. See, for example, the collapse of the Future International Military Airlifter programme. Five Europeans and Lockheed worked on a prelminary design, but the DoD would neither confirm Lockheed as the US contractor, or even give assurances that the US would buy the product. *Defense News*, 12 June 1989.

63. K Hayward, *The United States Aerospace Industry, op cit*, p.59.

64. *Aviation Week*, 5 February 1990, pp.38-9. The Europeans are themselves facing budgetary problems which call into question their commitment. ESA has also moved over to single year funding. See Chapter 5. For a more detailed analysis of the International Space Station see, K. Hayward, 'International Collaboration in Aerospace: the case of the International Space Station *Freedom*', *Science and Public Policy*, October 1993. The future of *Freedom* is far from assured. President Clinton has been lukewarm towards the programme and in 1993 NASA had to cut its scope yet again and to involve cooperation with the Russians. However, the implications of US decisions for ESA, Japan and Canada do appear to have been taken on board. See, *Aviation Week* 13. September 1993, pp.20-1. *Flight*, 3 March 1993, p.22.

65. See *Defense News*, 23 December 1991.

66. K Hayward, *The United States Aerospace Industry, op cit*, p.60.

67. See Haglund, *The Defense Industrial Base, op cit*, Chapters 6 & 7.

68. K Hayward, *The United States Aerospace Industry, op.cit*, p.72.

69. M. Currie, Hughes Aviation, *Defense News*, 26 June 1989.

70. *Jane's' Defence Weekly*, 17 October 1987, p.871.

71. K Hayward, *The United States Aerospace Industry, op cit*, p.65.

72. K. Hayward, *International Collaboration, op cit.*, pp.13-4; Samuels and Whipple, *op cit*, p.278. *Business Week*, 31 December 1991, pp.30-31.

73. Japanese views on the FSX were divided between those who feared the US reaction, and those who felt without such a programme Japan would never have a world class industry. Samuels and Whipple, *op cit*, pp. 295-6, 300-1.

74. K Hayward, *The United States Aerospace Industry, op cit*, p.71.

75. C. Prestowitz, *Trading Places*, (2nd ed.) (New York, 1989), pp.22-3.

76. K Hayward, *The United States Aerospace Industry, op cit*, pp.72-3; *Defense News*, 26 July 1991; *Aviation Week*, 4 November 1991, p.69. The exchanges over the FSX have continued, with the Japanese blaming GD for a substantial cost escalation.

77. K Hayward, *The United States Aerospace Industry, op cit,* pp.72-3.

78. K Hayward, *The United States Aerospace Industry, op cit,* pp.73-4.

79. *Jane's' Defence Weekly,* 27 July 1991, p.157.

80. Cited in K Hayward, *The United States Aerospace Industry, op cit,* p.74.

81. *Flight,* 24 July 1991, p.47.

82. *Ibid,*   p.249.

83. Cited in K Hayward, *The United States Aerospace Industry, op cit,* p.66.

84. *Ibid,* p.67.

85. See K Hayward, *The United States Aerospace Industry, op cit,* p.79.

86. Haglund, *Defense Industrial Base, op. cit,* p.270.

87. See L.d'Andrea Tyson, *Who's Bashing Whom? op cit,* pp.214-6.

88. US Congress; Office of Technology Assessment, *Arming our Allies,* (Washington, 1990), p.12.

89. See for example, the BAe-GEC opposition to the IBM-Westland EH-101 bid.

90. *Aviation Week,* 20 April 1992, pp.64-6, 25 May 1992, pp.22-3; *Defense News,* 8 June 1992.

91. See John Weston, Chairman of BAe Defence, *Jane's Defence Weekly,* 4 April 1992, p.554.

92. This was the strategy adopted by Snecma in the early 1970s; the link with GE was preferable to local dependence on Rolls. Talks in 1993 between Allied Signal and Sextant Avionique were also motivated by the US company to compete more effectively with Honeywell, and Rockwell Collins and the French to match GEC and Smiths in the UK.

93. *Aviation Week,* 25 January 1993, p.53; *The Guardian,* 28 August 1993. At the time of writing, the BAe-TAC deal had still to be finalised.

Chapter 8

1. *Business Week,* 24 February 1992, p.65.

2. *Flight,* 4 August 1993, pp.37-9.

3. Barclays-BZW Defence Conference, *EFA - the last transnational project?,* London, 27 February 1990.

4. *Interavia,*   August 1993,   pp.14-16. Some US analysts are suggesting that a $15-25 billion turnover is the minimum 'critical mass' for a prime contractor.

5. Barclays-BZW Defence Conference.

6. *The Financial Times,* 5 October 1989.

7. Speech to the Royal United Services Institute 21 November 1991. As, for example, in the on-off merger talks between BAe and GEC.

8. See, for example, President Clinton's plans for boosting US technology, *Commercial Aviation News,* 19 April 1993. In the UK, the DTI has sponsored a National Aerospace Strategic Technology Plan, the better to identify national R&D priorities. It remains moot, however, whether this will entail additional public expenditure for aerospace. See *Flight*, 28 July 1993, pp.26-7.

9. *Aviation Week*, 9 March 1992, p.21.

10. K Hayward, *The British Aircraft Industry, op cit*, Chapter 3.

11. *Flight*, 12 February 1992, p.20.

12. *Aviation Week*, 9 March 1992, p.21.

13. *Newsweek*, 15 July 1991, pp.39-40; *Defense News*, 2 December 1991.

14. K Hayward, *The British Aircraft Industry, op cit*, Chapter 2.

15. For a detailed examination of the changes in aerospace process technology, see; P.H Summerfield, 'Manufacturing Break-out 1941-91. Developments in aerospace manufacturing techniques'. *Aeronautical Journal*, February 1992, pp.35-46.

16. The main exception is in France, but the slow amalgamation of Aerospatiale and Dassault is underway. *Flight*, 3 June 1992, p.18.

17. K. Hayward, *The US Aerospace Industry, op cit*, p.45.

18. AIAA, *Global Prospects, op cit*, pp.26-7.

19. Dick Evans, BAe *The Financial Times*, 15 March 1990.

20. *The Financial Times*, 5 October 1989.

21. T. Taylor, 'Defence Industries in International Relations', *Review of International Studies*, January 1990, pp.60-6.

22. AIAA, *Global Perspectives, op cit*, pp.49-50.

23. See remarks made by Jurgen Schremp, Chairman of DASA, *International Defence Review*, July 1990, p.799.

24. To date, little substantive appears to have come of any of these MoUs.

25. *Defense News*, 9 September 1991; *Air et Cosmos*, 16 September 1991, pp.24-6.

26. The Matra-Marconi Space group links Matra with GEC and Fairchild Defence and Space. BAe is also involved on an individual project basis and given its financial problems may merge its space business to Matra-Espace. The second group comprises, Alcatel, Alenia and Aerospatiale and the US Space Systems/Loral group and DASA has links with both groups. *Space Markets*, No.2 1990, pp.73-6; *Aerospace World*, September 1991, pp.61-2.

27. *Aerospace World*, September 1991, pp.54-7.

28. There is scope for a second group centring on the Agusta and Westland partnership, but Eurocopter is trying to woo the Italians and the future of Westland-Agusta will depend on the success of the EH-101.

29. See A. Moravcsik, 'The European Arms Industry at the Crossroads', *Survival*, January/February 1990.

30. This would allow AI to compete with the likes of Boeing and MDC while its members worked with the Americans.

31. See *Interavia*, June 1991, pp.13-2; *Aerospace World*, March 1992, pp.26-8.

32. See Commission for the European Communities, *A Competitive European Aeronautics Industry* Brussels 23 July 1990, SEC(90) 1456.

33. See Commission of the European Communities, *The European Aircraft Industry: First Assessment and Possible European Community*

Actions, (Brussels, May 1992). A specific commitment to aerospace R&D was dropped from the 4th Framework programme.

34. For a brief review of the EC's aeronautics R&D programmes and their problems; see HC 563, *op cit,* Paras.103-105.

35. See EC Commission, DG12, *Focussing on the Future,* (Brussels, April 1992), for a detailed survey of European R&D efforts and proposals for consolidation. This report also explains the significance of demonstrator programmes in aerospace research.

36. See *Aviation Week,* 23 August 1993, pp.51-59.

37. One problem has been the tendency of the Russians to negotiate and apparently to confirm an agreement with one western company only to sign up with another.

38. This may include military projects. The US has expressed interest in Russian STOVL research. See *Defense News,* 19 July 1993.

Index